D1521839

GROWING IN WISDOM

Growing in Wisdom

Called to the Adventure of College

DALE GOLDSMITH

CASCADE *Books* • Eugene, Oregon

GROWING IN WISDOM
Called to the Adventure of College

Cascade Books
An Imprint of Wipf and Stock Publishers
199 W. 8th Ave., Suite 3
Eugene, OR 97401

www.wipfandstock.com

ISBN 13: 978-1-62564-587-6

Cataloguing-in-Publication data:

Goldsmith, Dale.

Growing in wisdom : called to the adventure of college /
Dale Goldsmith.

xviii + 240 pp. ; 23 cm. Includes bibliographical references and indices.

ISBN 13: 978-1-62564-587-6

1. College student orientation. 2. College students—conduct of life. I. Title.

LB2343.3 G57 2014

Manufactured in the U.S.A.

Scripture quotations are from the New Revised Standard Version of the Bible, copyright 1989, by the Division of Christian Education of the National Council of the Churches of Christ in the United States of America.

For

Amos

Aaron

Sutton

Ailee

Campbell

"You call me Teacher and Lord—
and you are right,
for that is what I am."

John 13:13

Contents

Part Three–The Co-Curriculum

Acknowledgments

Thanks to both the church and the academy for nurture, opportunities, challenges, and resources.

And to Father David J. Hassel, SJ, whose commitment to higher education for Christians was an early encouragement and whose ideas on Christology undergird the present book.

And to my fellow laborer in pursuit of actually doing higher education for Christians, Bob Green, with whom I was privileged to share time, space, teaching, and a wonderful collegiality on the second floor of Mohler Hall for nearly three decades; no one could have offered more helpful criticism and patient encouragement.

And to Mitch Williamson, director of the Navigators, and Rev. Daniel Dreher, director of the Catholic Student Center, both at West Texas State University, who revised and enlarged my understanding of today's college student.

And to Austin Thomas, Young Harris College student who offered better ways to communicate with contemporary readers.

And to the writers of previous "survival manuals" from whom I learned so much.

And to my editor Rodney Clapp who saw potential in this project and has shepherded it to fruition.

And to the staff of the Southwest Branch of the Amarillo (Texas) Public Library—my connection to so many resources.

And to Phil Rowe for calming technical assistance when I needed it most.

And to Joy Goldsmith for her innumerable contributions, from cheerleading to extensive technical support.

And to my lifetime collaborator and wife, Katy, for her insistence that these efforts be directed to support young people in their Christian vocation as students.

Introduction

You are going to college. What a great time in your life—whether you're eighteen, twenty-eight, thirty-eight, or sixty-eight! (This book is not just for "college agers" heading for school; the joys and challenges we will examine will face young, mature, full-time, part-time—*all* students in contemporary American higher education.)

College is exciting. It can put wings to your dreams. But you may also be feeling some uncertainty. A lot of Christians worry about going to college; and not without reason.

You are not the only one who may be worrying. Your parents are worried. The other students you will meet in college are worried. Even colleges are worrying because they know it costs a lot for you to attend and they are under pressure to do what it takes to make your college education worth the cost.

But there are definitely also some certainties. It is certain that you need not go to college alone and on your own. You can go to college with the full assurance of the Christian faith supporting you. (This will not be a time to take a vacation from that faith; in fact, instead of a faith-vacation, college should be a *faith-vocation*—the call from God for you to be a student and to love God with all your mind [Matt 22:37, Mark 12:30, Luke 10:27].) It is certain that colleges will be presenting a multitude of opportunities to make your experience more exciting and productive. You may be on the cutting edge of a new day in college education. It is almost certain that your college experience will be one of the greatest experiences of your life.

It is certain that college can challenge your Christian faith, but it is also certain that your faith's assets are strong enough and flexible enough to deal with any challenge the college experience offers. The problems that the church worries about you facing in college need not be scary or mysterious; with Jesus and Scripture as your main resources, that worry can be faced with confidence. In the face of these anxieties and possibilities—what you face and what colleges face—you will want to prepare in the best way you can.

Of course you will go off to college prepared with new clothes, a cell phone, up-to-date vaccinations, a checking account, and a lot of good advice. These preparations help you to be ready for the new life you anticipate. But preparations for what might happen to you *as a Christian* are seldom sufficient. Churches help Christians prepare for most of life's really big events: marriage, family life, illness, and death; so it is not unreasonable to expect some help for college. This preparation ought to go beyond presentation of a Bible (excellent idea) and the occasional scholarship (great!). Is that really enough preparation? Unless churches can make all colleges Christian (which has been tried and simply isn't going to happen), Christians going to college will face the challenges described in this book and reading it should be helpful whether you are alone, involved in a local church, or blessed with a campus minister who can be a great source of help. This manual can be a resource in all of these situations.

The church is rightly worried on your behalf. College is not a detour on the road of faith. Instead, these are crucial years. This may be when you meet your life partner. It is where you become equipped for your life's work. It will be absolutely central to making you who you will be in the future. It is well-known that each generation of young people that comes along is less affiliated with a church or religious faith tradition than preceding generations. Right now, that means that a third of college-age young people are not affiliated with a church.[1] The polling also suggests that as time passes and those young people achieve more education and the higher incomes that result from it, there is more possibility of deepening secularism and less religious commitment. There is not a set-in-stone destiny of the college impact on your faith, however. What is clear is that while each generation is revealing itself to be less committed to its religious tradition, those who love and support you don't want you to be one of those statistics.

So let's get prepared. (Let's include your parents and your church supporters and your pastor in reading this manual. That way, they will know better how to be of support to you.) This is a handbook of preparation for Christians who want to understand college and want to be equipped to experience college in the service of their Christian vocation as a student.

We all know there are hazards to face when you embark on the college voyage. Yes, college is a dangerous place. It isn't dangerous because of the increasing costs, exposure to new experiences, the perils of freedom, all the tempting "isms" that lie in wait, stress at leaving home, choosing a

---

1. See http://www.pewforum.org/2012/10/09/nones-on-the-rise.

major, the hazards of sex, alcohol, drugs, cheating, gambling, pornography, getting along with roommates, high rates of depression and suicide, writing research papers, terrorist attacks, confronting evolution, hazing, credit card debt, the inevitable weight gain, and a host of other possible problems. While these are real, they are not the greatest dangers to Christians. In fact, colleges often provide safety nets, counselors, and other help to deal with those problems.

For Christians, the greatest danger of the college experience will be found in a negative—in what is *not* Christian. It is not very academic to do this, but for the sake of simplicity, whatever we find in the college experience that is not Christian—not Christ-centered or based in Scripture—we will call "secular."

Secularism is any thinking or acting that is dissociated from Christian foundation, influence, or control. *"Secular"* is used to connote "non-Christian" (this could include any non-Christian religious faith also). Most colleges in America are secular and in them the Christian faith no longer dominates college life through mandatory chapel, dormitory regulations, required religion classes, or other means. These days even church-related colleges are more secular than you might think because most of the basic components of the college experience at any school are really secular.

But—and this is big—the *secular* environment is not as free from religious influences as you might think. If by religion we mean something that has to do with what is most important—what life is about, what the forces that control it are, what the good is and how you ought to live your life to achieve it—then you will find answers to all of those questions right there in the secular college experience. They may not be Christian answers but they are really religious answers asking you to replace your Christian faith with their counterfeit alternatives.

For example, it is appropriate in secularism to omit God from consideration. But if God is omitted, there will necessarily have to be some ultimate reality or fact to take God's place as the most important reality. What will that be? How will that alter your life?

Or if such Christian notions as sin or grace are dropped, some other explanation for war, murder, and hate needs to be introduced, and finding solutions to such problems will take a new direction. Or if Jesus Christ is dispensed with as your ultimate authority figure, who will take his place and what will that mean for getting the right answers to important questions? For almost every aspect of explicitly Christian faith that is abandoned, something will fill the space that the abandoned item occupied. Secularism *will* fill the religious vacuum it creates with new articles of faith. That is part of the danger. The other part of the danger is that secularism operates in such a way as to make you think this religious substitution is not happening!

The secular environment of college often marginalizes (dismisses) any religious faith with the argument that it is emotional, biased, irrelevant (or perhaps—conversely—dangerous!). Faith is often seen as simply a matter of personal preference better left at the classroom door. What happens in the classroom is asserted to be rational, objective, unbiased, and useful for life in the "real world." It is argued that religious faith is something people can take or leave; and if they take it, they should keep it to themselves. (Note: One big fear people have is that you might "lose" your faith in college. Sorry—you can't "lose" your faith; it is not a set of car keys you misplace. Real Christian faith can only be *replaced* by something else, by counterfeits. So one of your main tasks in college is to be on alert for those fakes; this manual will be helpful in that task.)

The notion that religious faith is optional and that anyone can live without beliefs is wrong and seldom critically examined. The truly religious substitutions secularism makes and that many have mistakenly accepted as Christian are rarely noticed. What is on offer in college—overtly and covertly, inside the classroom and outside of it—is a secular religion. What you *don't* see is what you get!

Here is a brief outline for navigating the sometimes rough waters of a college education. Part One (chapters 1–6) follows the format in the biblical letters of the Apostle Paul as he wrote to churches and individual Christians about the challenges they faced. The first thing he wrote about was the foundation that God had provided for them in Christ and his work. These first chapters lay out the essential groundwork of Christian faith as it might be experienced by the college student. Chapters 1 and 2 describe the centrality, simplicity, complexity, and *applicability* of Christian faith to *your* college experience. After all, faith is really what is at stake in the college experience; that's why it comes first.

Chapter 3 focuses on the purpose and nature of college; it is vocational in purpose but it is also a gift of God—but a gift flawed by human sin. Chapter 4 balances the need for students to get comfortable with the college environment, but—given its secular nature—not too comfortable. Chapters 5 and 6 commend the two primary resources that God has provided for you: the best Teacher, Jesus, and the best college textbook, Scripture. In important ways these chapters are the center of the book. They uniquely spell out how Jesus Christ is actually a player in the college experience and not just a heavenly, spiritual but distant onlooker who needs protection from insults and attacks. So too you will find Scripture speaking directly to problem situations in ways that are practical and that can serve as models for using Scripture to address future, unanticipated challenges to faith.

Part Two (chapters 7–11) takes you on a journey through the major academic aspects of the college experience (i.e., general education, the academic major, job training). Each chapter follows the same arrangement, beginning with an appropriate meditation on Scripture followed by an explanation of an important feature of the college experience, the identification of possible problems that that particular feature presents to faith, and a conclusion showing Jesus Christ's relevance in addressing that challenge.

Part Three (chapters 12–14) follows the same pattern but with a focus on the extra- or co-curricular, social aspects of the college experience.

All of this critical analysis is offered out of a love of Jesus, our Teacher, and a real enthusiasm for the college experience. It is written with the deepest appreciation of what the college experience can be. The author writes as one who has spent a lifetime in higher education and loves it dearly. What he knows about the college experience comes from being a student, teacher, parent (of college students), and "helper" (as a pastor and as a college administrator). *Some personal anecdotes appear in italics as illustrations but not directives.*

Once at a great American college I saw the following banner hung from high windows on either side of a main walkway. It proclaimed: "Jesus is Lord of the Universe!" While I completely agreed with the idea—don't we begin our confession in the creed saying that we believe in "God Almighty, maker of heaven and earth"?—I wondered if many people would agree with another more specific claim: that Jesus is Lord of the universe-ity.

While I have tried in various ways to make the schools with which I have been associated more "Christian," that project may be too big for any of us to complete in this secular time. So instead, this book is dedicated to a more modest goal which could have the following banner: Jesus is Lord and Teacher of this college student! (I mean you, reader.)

If college challenges you with faith substitutes, you should be prepared to recognize and reject them.

If a particular academic major seems uncomfortable to you, you can see it as God's gift to your growth as a servant of God should you choose to follow it.

If college offers you opportunities to move away from your faith, you will be able to see through the false promises and opt for the truth in Christ that will make you free.

If the secular world sees the Christian faith and community as irrelevant, you will know that they provide the most meaningful way to understand and deal with life.

If you see the polls and public opinion designating you—a Christian student—as an endangered species, you will know yourself as one who is known and loved by God, and is not just a statistic of popular opinion.

The purpose of this book is to challenge and engage you to approach every college experience with the "mind of Christ" (1 Cor 2:16), as a disciple on your faithful way to being more equipped for a life of loving service to others. The college experience can be an opportunity, in the words of the Apostle Paul, to "test everything [and to] hold fast to what is good" (1 Thess 5:21). The college experience, its awesome traditions, its divine vocation, and the marvelous things that can happen to you there—all this is going to be wonderful. As you prepare for it let's get you equipped for your vocation as a Christian student with "the whole armor of God" (Eph 6:11).

Dale Goldsmith
Amarillo, Texas
May 1, 2014

Abbreviations

Almanac	*Almanac of Higher Education.* An annual publication of the *Chronicle of Higher Education*
CHE	*Chronicle of Higher Education*
CR	*Chronicle Review* (A weekly supplement to the *Chronicle of Higher Education*)
NYT	*New York Times*
WCDict	*Webster's New World College Dictionary.* 4th edition, Cleveland, OH: Wiley Publishing, Inc., 2010.

part one

The Prerequisites

MATTHEW 28:18–20

*And Jesus came and said to them, "All authority in heaven
and on earth has been given to me . . . and remember,
I am with you always, to the end of the age."*

Jesus seems to have sent his disciples off on their own. But with this assertion and this promise. He had actually called each of them to a ministry. And so he has called you, and given you a calling, a *vocation*—to the ministry of study. He promises you that he is the one ultimately in charge of everything. That puts college into a precise context: college is there to serve God in teaching and nurturing you in your growth as a Christian.

And Jesus' promise to be with the disciples and you—available always and in every setting and every difficulty—is a promise no one else can make. How fortunate you are to receive such a promise from such a person.

Prayer: Thank you, God, for giving Jesus to call me and assure me with these powerful words. Amen.

We are summoned to acknowledge that we are God's; God offers us a *vocation* (Latin for "summons") or what we might label a "calling." Christians are "called" to all sorts of things: marriage (or celibacy), formal ministry (or not), one career or another. Going to college is a legitimate calling—as is *not* going but having a *vocation* to something else. One thing you'll have to deal with if you recognize your call to be that of a college student is something called a *prerequisite*. A prerequisite is the thing you

1

need to do before you can do the thing you want to do. Or, as the dictionary says, a prerequisite is "required beforehand . . . as a necessary condition for something following."[1] Some prerequisites you can dodge; others you can't. The contents of Part I are college prerequisites for the serious Christian so that she can begin to understand where she is Christian-faith-wise in the college experience.

First (chapters 1 and 2) you will be loved by God who wants you to live as God's creation, trusting and following Jesus Christ. That being the case, *faith* is a shorthand way of referring to being and living as a Christian, whatever path you take in life. It is your *faith* that many of us adults are concerned about when your Christian vocation is that of college student.

The popular fear is that you might "lose your faith" because (some people think) college just does that to Christians. So the first thing you ought to do is to examine just what faith is, how unlikely it is that you could "lose it" (as if it were a set of keys or a grocery receipt), how it might be challenged and, most importantly, how it might help you function positively in the college environment.

Second (chapter 3), just what *is* the "college environment"—its nature, its purpose? The answer to that question is crucial, because you—as a Christian—will need to be equipped to understand and deal with it. You will want at least a general map of where you are.

Third, we will take a look at when *faith* meets the *college experience* (chapter 4). By this time it will be clear that the two are not the same and so they will not mix smoothly together—regardless of what kind of a college you attend. This chapter will get you thinking of how you can be in two places at once: the Christian's kingdom of God and the secular college, and do your best in both.

Finally (chapters 5 and 6), it is important to know what resources you will have to support your Christian vocation in college. While we hope you will have a strong campus minister or chaplain, and Christian fellowship, you may not. Whether you do or don't have them, you will still have the best resources possible: Jesus Christ, the best Teacher available, and the Christian Scriptures, the best textbook available. You will not only be reminded *that* you have Jesus the Teacher and the holy Scriptures at the ready, but we will suggest specific ways that these two foundations for faithful living can be helpful on campus and in class.

College can be a terrific opportunity for the faithful Christian to mature in faith and in a vocation that will serve God and others. We hope that Part I will help you "put on the whole armor of God" (Eph 6:11a) and enter into the college experience with "the mind of Christ" (1 Cor 2:16).

---

1. *WCDict*, 1135.

1

Faith as Gift

"I know what I believe. I just can't put
it into words."—College Student

". . . for we walk by faith . . ." —2 Cor 5:7

Scripture Focus

MARK 9:24B

"I believe; help my unbelief!"

What a curious thing to say. "I believe; help my unbelief!" Did the
speaker believe? Or didn't he? To understand this confusion, we
need to know the situation that produced it.

A father has a problem: He has a child with a severe disorder that
throws the child into spasms that cause him to flail about, hurting, hitting,
and burning himself. What can the father do? There are no neurologists, no
anti-seizure drugs. So the father has brought the child to Jesus. But Jesus
isn't there and the disciples aren't able to do anything.

Probably the reason the father brought his child to Jesus was that he
had heard about Jesus' success in healing the sick. That would not have been
too hard to believe given the fame Jesus had already earned in his public
ministry. But the father was in a situation where the talk about Jesus was
no longer hearsay, rumor, or gossip. It was a matter of life and death for his

beloved son. We can almost hear his heart racing and his thoughts running: *Jesus may have healed others; but this is different. This is my child. This is the critical moment. This is my test; do I believe that he can help me since I have nowhere else to turn?*

Hearing that Jesus has solved others' problems is one thing. It is a different story when it is a matter of *your* problem and when the crucial issues are posed to *you*. That is what college will be like. While you probably will not be confronted with a life-or-death medical problem, your faith will be challenged in an almost infinite variety of ways. What will *faith* mean in those challenging moments?

So perhaps your cry will echo that of the father: "I believe; help my unbelief!" This is not an outlandish prayer. Affirming faith is good. Acknowledging the challenges to faith is good too. Fortunately Jesus is here to help.

Prayer: When I try to love you with my whole mind, please be patient with my unbelief. Amen.

What Is the Big Deal about Faith?

Faith is what the Christian faces the world with. So it is what you will need as you step out of the door to go to college. You might be wondering, "What is the big deal about faith? Can't a Christian just 'have faith' and move on?" Because *faith* refers to the substance of your whole relationship with God, it is complicated, just as your relationships with your mother or sister are complicated. As you grow and mature as a person, your relationship with God will change (grow and mature). It is helpful to pause to review that relationship with God and your understanding of faith now that you will be off to college.

You already know that genuine Christianity is not a matter of abstract propositions or confined to some past moment of public commitment in front of your church congregation. Instead, it is an ongoing relationship with God through Jesus Christ. It is easy to think: I've got it (faith) and I can move on to other things. But real faith is something so big and alive that instead of packing it along to college like a book or a pair of socks, it surrounds you and carries you along.

Because God made you, God's claim on you takes priority over everything else in your life. Accepting God's claim over your entire life is summarized in the term, in the act, in the relationship called *faith*. Because it is a claim over your entire life, it is not something that you "have" and then move on to other things. It is a total involvement that covers everything—including going to college.

Is there an official definition of Christian faith or can we each define it any way we please? Neither. There can be no single, official definition because there is so much involved. Nor is it "*whatever.*" You might have the impression that we could capture Christian faith in a simple picture, catching in one single moment all of whatever it takes to be a faithful Christian. Then you go on with the business of everyday life—your job, family, hobbies, friends—without a second thought as to how faith applies to all that you do in that everyday life.

As you prepare to start college, it may be time to clarify and expand your understanding of faith. One simple way to begin to organize the wonderful richness of faith is to notice that there is a kind of "grammar of faith."

Sometimes faith is a noun, sometimes it's a verb, and sometimes it takes on the form and function of an adjective or even an adverb. In the original Greek language of the New Testament, there is only one basic word translated into English as *faith* or *believe/belief*—it is the word *pistis* (faith) or *pisteuo* (believe). We can't define faith (a noun) by saying it is believing (a verb) or to clarify *believe* (a verb) by using *faith* (a noun). But we can start by stating the obvious: *faith* is a noun, and *believe* is a verb. In the minds of the writers of Scripture, these different words and different parts of speech are all expressions of the same core reality: a relationship between God and his children.

The Grammar of Faith: Nouns and Adjectives

Nouns are words that refer to things, places, people, and ideas. Faith is indeed *something*—a subject, an object, a relationship, an idea, an affirmation, a fact, a story, an understanding, a commitment. There is always content and substance to faith. Ultimately it may be a mystery, but in the short term, here and now, faith is about concrete specifics. The New Testament has an abundance of concrete assertions that we are invited to acknowledge as true or necessary: *God created us; God is love; Christ died for us; Jesus rose from the dead; Christ will come again.*

Another way to understand faith as concrete is to think of it as a story. In the Gospels we see Herod,

> ### Faith as a Noun
> *When Jesus saw some men carrying their paralyzed friend to him— going as far as to rip parts of the roof off of someone's house to lower the paralytic to where Jesus could be with him—it was their faith that he saw.*
> SEE MARK 2:1–12

the Pharisees, even the disciples, reject the story Jesus presents—the story that God loves and accepts everyone and that Jesus has come to make God's love a reality in peoples' lives. To live a faithful Christian life would be to live that story or at least to claim it as your own and aspire to live it.

This becomes clearer when you see other stories that compete for your approval and acceptance. These alternative narratives call you into other kinds of relationships and cast you as a participant in other stories. One such story is the story you see every day in American culture. You've heard it many times. You find versions of it in advertisements promising that the right beer or laundry soap will solve your problems. Politicians lure you with stories of racial or national superiority. Hollywood and computer games offer stories and games of escape and pleasure, power and popularity. The college experience will present you with many competing stories that will make claims for your approval and attempt to draw you away from the story of faith.

Are you able to recognize those misleading narratives and will you be faithful enough to reject them? God promises us that he and Jesus will be faithful in their love for you. It is in this relational sense that faith can be expressed as an adjective: faithful (as in: God is faithful) or as an adverb (Jesus lived faithfully). The loving God of whom we read in Scripture, celebrate in worship, pray to in our hearts, and acknowledge with our minds is the objective, "out there," aspect of faith—the part that is truly real and utterly independent from your existence and your belief. This is your faith—that you are not the final and ultimate reality but that God is and that God will behave faithfully toward you. This God who existed from before the beginning of anything, but who oversees everything and who will be there forever, is the solid content and object of your faith as a Christian. The extent to which you rely on this story and live it out determines if you have faith and are faithful.

The Grammar of Faith: Verbs

Verbs are words that convey action and show subjects doing things. When the New Testament uses the term *believe* it refers to an action. Sometimes it is found with the content or object of faith specifically mentioned: We believe *that* Jesus died and rose. Sometimes *believe* describes an action taken with the passion and desperation, like the father who hoped that Jesus would cure his child (Mark 9:24b). These are acts of commitment, of hope, of desperation. People *believe* God; they believe *in* God. They *hope* that God will respond to their needs.

Why is *believing* the primary form of our relationship with God? Why, for instance, couldn't your relationship with God be based on your behavior and how nice a person you are? (A lot of people think that is the case.)

Unfortunately, we have disappointed God too often for God to have a lot of confidence in us. But God created you, loves you, and continues to be faithful to you. God does not give up on you; God takes the initiative in approaching you. All you can really offer in response to God's

> **Believe as a Verb**
>
> *(Martha says to Jesus), "Yes, Lord, I believe that you are the Messiah, the Son of God, the one coming into the world."*
>
> JOHN 11:27

faithfulness is your acceptance of it and your dependence upon God. This is the subjective, "in here" side of faith. It is what makes the "out there" reality of God your own personal "in here" reality.

Faith in the College Experience: Getting Specific

This brief *grammar* of faith demonstrates the specific nature of this central mode of the Christian life. Faith is real in the sense that it always carries particular and definite content. (At the same time, of course, since faith is God's gift, its actual reality is much grander than we can understand.) Faith is real in the sense that it *is* something and it *does* something. It is relational and active. It is always about God's acts and our response. If you multiply all of the moments in your life when you are called to be faithful, and if your faith is to be tangible, you have a full-time thing going.

That challenge follows you to and meets you in the college experience. It isn't that being in college or being faithful in college is that much harder for a Christian than being faithful anywhere else, but it is different—a lot different.

The college experience will draw you into new and unexpected areas of thinking and into new and challenging relationships and opportunities. A healthy Christian faith can accompany you into new dimensions of faith, both in content (faith as noun) and style (faith as action). On the following pages you will find ways to think of faith and the ways in which it is experienced in college. Many will be familiar, some perhaps will be new. And not every dimension or facet of faith is described here; how could it be? But you will think of others that ought to be included.

Having in mind what your faith is when you get to college will put you in a position to gain enormous benefit from your college experience (more about that throughout the book) and to avoid the experience of this student who was in a class on Bible that I was teaching:

> *"Please describe faith," I asked her in what I hoped was a friendly and encouraging tone. She was obviously struggling with an answer, which she seemed unable to put into words. Finally, she burst into tears, blurting out, "I know what I believe, I just can't put it into words." I knew a lot of folks for whom that might be the answer, but for a Christian student in college? No way; that is not an adequate answer for a college student to give.*

First, the Bible has a lot of specific things to say about faith, so she would need something in the way of definition in order to do well in the class. Second, and more important, for a Christian, faith is really important; and if you are a Christian in college, you really are in a position to say a lot more about your faith. You will need to have a good grasp of what faith is and what it can do so that you will not only be protected from some of the dangers but also so that you can take fuller advantage of many of the opportunities. So here are several ways to think about faith and to begin to do so in ways that connect to some of the opportunities and challenges you will have in your college experience. The rest of this chapter offers descriptions of faith that express the primary characteristic of faith—that it is a gift from God.

Faith as Identity: Who Am I?

Personal identity is a concern for everyone—especially for those starting college. It drives your choices in everything from the clothes you wear to choosing a career. When you meet another person, one of the first questions usually asked is, "What do you do?" That seems to be our way of asking, "Who are you?" The implication is that you are what you do and that in some way you are the product of your own activity—that you have "made something" of yourself. Do we really think that we can create ourselves? When it comes to picking a college, this identity question intensifies. Since the school you attend will become part of your identity, you will have the joy or the stigma of having a particular institution as your *alma mater*.[1] Do

---

1. *Alma*—the soul; *mater*—mother. This Latin expression is often used about colleges to express the idea that the college will "mother" or nurture the inner, spiritual center of the student.

you really want to be identified that closely with *that* school? Your choice of school could enhance or hinder your self-concept.

Then there is the choice of a career—a choice that will most likely be affected by the college you choose. (The impact may be in terms of which career but probably more importantly in the particular way your college prepares you for that specific career.) What if you choose the wrong career? Will you be locked forever into something you don't want? Do you run the risk of making yourself into someone you don't want to be? So, what answer does faith give for the identity question?

Scripture provides a rich description of human identity. Beginning with the creation account in the book of Genesis 1–3, humans are depicted as God's special and beloved creation, made just right, with the freedom to love and cooperate with each other. According to that Genesis account, God made you in his own image—a social being, intended to live in harmony and cooperation with others, and entrusted with the responsible management of the earth.

When the report of creation is given in Genesis 1, each act is pronounced "good." When God made people he made them "*very* good" (Gen 1:31). As you read on through Scripture, ethical models appear, directing you to think and act on behalf of others and assuring you that your own fulfillment will be found in living in harmony with God's other creatures. Finally, you are given the possibility that you can have the "mind of Christ" (1 Cor 2:16)—a promise tantalizing and perhaps mystifying or even terrifying. In any case, the faithful Christian can find an identity model in Scripture and need not rely on the failed models offered by Hollywood, advertising, athletics, politics, and other secular sources.

God made a good world for us. But we have tried to remake it after our own ideas and it hasn't worked out very well. The Christian has choices to make in terms of identity: Whose picture of yourself shall you accept? Which portrait of who you ought to be shall you adopt? Whose version of the good life shall you pursue?

A Christian understands that he is who God made him to be. That may not "sell" well in America. If you are satisfied with the job God did in creating you, there will be no need for a makeover. Americans spend billions of dollars every year on operations to change (improve?) their appearance. That sort of "self-improvement" was precisely what Eve and Adam were up to when they committed what is called "original sin." That first sin was just like every sin committed since. It happens when you set off on your own plan. Face it: you can't make things better than God made them.

The Christian view was well stated by a sixteen-year-old who wrote, "Simply put, I am what God wants me to be. I'm not sure yet what that will be, but I trust in God to guide me." Approaching the college experience with that attitude provides a good starting point for your identity concerns.

Faith as Connectedness: God Keeps in Touch so We Can Be in Touch

Popular culture, in its music, frames us as solitary individuals, unable to form lasting and meaningful relationships, moving through life looking for fulfillment that we are unable to find in other people. Going to college can reinforce that feeling of lonely independence because it disrupts the life you have known before, tearing you from the comforting fabric of home and family. The experience can be unsettling. It pits you in competition with others new and strange to you. You are distanced from family and friends who find themselves out of touch simply because their student is involved in something foreign to them.

American culture and economy prefer that we remain as individualistic and separated as possible. This is so much the case that we almost forget that we always belong to some group or other. Instead of being a lone wolf, or the Lone Ranger, or just plain lonely, at the core of the Christian faith is a powerful force pulling us together. The faithful Christian is planted firmly in that great congregation that stretches backward and forward, east and west, into all corners of the world and to all moments in time. Faith immediately thrusts you into connection with all others of faith. This is voiced in a variety of expressions used by Christians, from Paul's notion of the church as "the body of Christ" (1 Cor 12:27) through Peter's description of the church as "God's people" (1 Pet 2:10) to a more contemporary notion of the "communion of saints" or "fellowship of believers." Faith automatically connects the believer with all of God's other creatures. It connects you just as God intended you to be connected when you were created.

Of course, we also—despite our individualistic tendencies—belong to many other groups. Some are tightly organized and clearly recognizable: our family, the United States of America. Others are less clearly delineated, but nonetheless very influential: your peer group, school, or region of the country. None of these groups—except the church—are faith groups. There is a great deal of difference between the kingdom of God and the other groups—even your family. The kingdom of God group—let's call it the church universal—is one that is based on the most solid foundation there could be: the eternal God. And it is a group that spans the globe. It is much broader than any other group you could imagine. And it is a group that reaches backward in time and will draw you into and beyond the future.

If you go to college, you will become a member of at least two more groups—the "student body," and later, the alumni association (students—past, present, and future) of that college. Here is hoping that membership in those groups will be great experiences. But be warned: the college is not the body of Christ. Neither is America. There is no group that belongs to God except the one God has called together.

Faith as Life in the Spirit

Spirituality is "in"—at least in popular, secular culture. Popular spirituality is about the search for meaning *inside* of us or for meaning we each seek in our own individual ways. Spirituality is popular because external resources—from popular culture and consumerism to traditional religion—have failed to provide people with the meaningful experiences that they seek.

But life in the spirit can't be lived on resources you seek within yourself. The plain truth is that like so many false hopes available in our secular environment, this kind of popular, non-religious spirituality turns out to be a do-it-yourself project for which you just don't have the resources.

True spirituality is real; it is not an escape from reality. It is a penetration into the deep and incomprehensible heart of God, whose Spirit moved over the face of the primordial waters at the moment of creation (Gen 1:2). All that you need is to be found in the God who created you, not in an isolating focus on your own inner self and personal resources. True faith always encompasses more than can be thought, said, or done. This spiritual dimension of faith invites you into a spirituality rich in possibilities beyond what culture offers and beyond what you are able to imagine if you confine yourself to your own human powers.

Christian faith is the true life in the spiritual. It is the only real spirituality because it relies on *the* Spirit that is God. College is not the place to go to escape from God's Spirit nor is it where you can finally build your own spirituality. God is there and quite accessible to help you with the real thing. Jesus' promise that the Spirit will guide us into all truth is one that is especially important to you in college (John 16:13).

Faith as Salvation

Have you been saved?" was one of the common questions asked in the circles where I grew up. Once an aunt told me she had been asked, "Have you been saved"? and her response had been, "No, thank you." Before that I had never thought about the question seriously and realized that the question implied a being saved from something. What was that something from which Christ the Savior saves us?

Salvation is not just about going to heaven (or being saved from hell). In the New Testament stories, salvation is defined on a case-by-case basis: people are saved from deafness, blindness, leprosy, and death—all pretty bad things. They are saved from whatever it is that is keeping them from living a full life in the here and now. Today, if you have those problems, you go to the doctor and usually get fixed. But there aren't "fixes" for everything. You still need to be saved from those things that keep you from living the full life God intends for you.

But Jesus also "saved" people from sin. What is sin? Sin is something you get yourself into. *Sin is a problem or condition out of which you are unable to get yourself.* How strange: we get ourselves into sin but can't get ourselves out. Sin is always something that separates you from others—God, other people, and even the true self you were created to be.

You need salvation from your own self-centeredness, whether it is expressed in materialism, in religion, in work—in anything that separates you from the *you* God created you to be. You need salvation from the superpatriotism and racism that shuts you off from God's creations who you think are different. You need salvation from your warped self-understanding in which you attempt to improve on God's creation. You need to be saved from every apparently good and reasonable effort of your own that diverts you from God's community. You need to be saved from the whole *condition* called sin, not just from one bad habit or another. You need to be saved *for* the full life lived in faith and open to the enjoyment of God's creation and fellowship with God's creatures.

Sorry, but the college experience cannot save you. If education produced goodness, America—with its abundance of great colleges and millions of well-educated college graduates—would be the nicest place in the world, with the most exemplary history of public and private morality and packed full of the most kind, honest, and charitable folks imaginable. But there are dark sides to the story of America and education does not save anyone. It might be able to provide some raw material that the Savior can use, but unless he saves you, you are not saved (Acts 4:12).

Faith as Knowledge: Knowing and Being Known

The theme of Paul's Letter to the Galatians is faith. He writes that, as a result of faith, his readers have come to *know* God. He then immediately seems to correct himself: "or rather *to be known by God*" (Gal 4:9). Faith is a relationship and when a relationship is really close and deep, mutual knowledge develops. Instead of living as an agnostic (from the Greek *a* [not] + *gnostic* [knowing]), the Christian comes to know God or at least to know something about God. This happens because Jesus is the image of God (Col 1:15); if you want to see God you look to Jesus (John 1:18). Even better than you knowing God is the fact that God knows *you*. And even better still is the fact that God loves you—in spite of knowing you so well!

In discussing faith as a "higher knowledge," the theologian John Calvin (1509–1564) makes it clear that such knowledge is not about the subject matter you will study. What you do know is that you are God's child. Calvin concludes, "The knowledge of faith consists in assurance rather than in comprehension."[2] In facing the rigors of the college experience, faith does not give you an edge on learning. (Each Christian must participate on the basis of the rules established by the college and must be evaluated by those standards.) What the knowledge of faith provides, however, is stability, assurance, and a frame of reference within which whatever you come up against can begin to make sense.

Faith as Meaning

You grew up in a community (family, neighborhood, school, club, nation) that provided you with an understanding of what life is about. It was there, in that community, that you learned how to behave, what to say and wear, who your friends should be, and all of those techniques you need to get along in life. Since our popular American culture is so individualistic, you may not always be aware of the powerful influences that your surroundings exert in making you who you are.

When you get into college, your childhood notions begin to get tested. You may begin to wonder if that original version of what's what is reliable. *My home neighborhood was basically Protestant, so I had some ideas about Catholics that were negative. My neighborhood was also ethnically divided; naturally I thought our group was better than the other one. Once in college,*

2. Calvin, *Institutes*, 560.

I was challenged on these beliefs—other students pointed out that they were prejudices!—and I had to rethink them.

As you grow, you become more aware of life's limitations and contradictions, and are confronted with the possibility that there may be no meaning to life—that even the most convincing story is one that finally makes no sense at all. (That would come from a worldview called existentialism that you might study in college.) The realization that you will eventually die can contribute to the depressing possibility that the story that explains things for you may be unworkable, and the concern for meaning that is truly reliable can become more urgent.

What can make sense of a world in which so many unjust things happen? Is there some meaning-making story or power, something that can maintain the world as a reasonable place in which to live? Is there a worldview or a frame of reference that explains stuff? That makes for a positive outlook? Is there at least a story or power that can maintain you in a world that refuses to be reasonable and reliable? The college experience offers many possibilities to consider. It may come via philosophical systems, other religious traditions, political ideologies, scientific paradigms, or even literary constructs. Best of all is when it comes in God's faithfulness.

The Christian faith is a source of meaning that has claimed many and holds out the promise of reliable and significant meaning. The Christian faith promises to make life understandable, or, when not understandable, at least acceptable, or, when not acceptable, at least possible, because it affirms that the God who loves you is ultimately in charge. More precisely, it is God who offers meaning in Jesus Christ. Faith is the acceptance of that offer of meaning. One writer put it this way: "faith is . . . *the activity of seeking and discovering meaning in the most comprehensive dimensions of our experience.*"[3] When you start with your faith in Christ, "seeking and discovering" is a search that can be enhanced in the college experience.

Jesus lays the foundation for you to "get it"—to find an understanding or worldview or frame of reference in which you begin to understand that God is the ultimate reality, power, and hope. College lays out a virtual buffet of learning opportunities, among which will be things that you can use to build on that foundation and find that faith leads to more meaning and understanding.

---

3. Parks, *Big Questions*, 7.

Faith as Freedom: Set Free for Freedom

"For freedom Christ has set us free," wrote Paul (Gal 5:1a), in what seems a totally redundant expression. Freedom is one of the watchwords of your generation. In going to college you will find an astonishing variety of freedoms at your disposal—going to bed when you want, getting up when you feel like it, eating whatever, studying (or not) on your own schedule, using your new credit card for anything you desire . . . You believe that you are free, but will often find yourself enslaved by a wide variety of masters—popularity, power, money, drugs, sex, work, fear, habits, prestige, gambling, anxiety, security, addictions, family expectations, peer pressure, pornography.

Every freedom is guaranteed and limited by the authority that offers it. Whoever gives it can take it back. The Christian faith promises a freedom beyond those granted by law or discovered in the absence of parental eyes. The freedom promised by faith in Christ is exceptional because it is rooted in God to whom you can pray: "Set me free from a past that I cannot change; open to me a future in which I can be changed." God is the one to ask for freedom because freedom is only as good as its giver and guarantor.

Freedom in Christ is not only freedom *from* the narrow constraints of cultural and peer expectations, *from* sin and guilt and *from* selfishness; it is a freedom *for* the enjoyment of your true mission in life as God's own creature, a freedom to be *for* others. So if freedom is what you want, the Christian faith is where to find it. And it is a gift!

Faith: No Fear

President Franklin Roosevelt, in leading the United States out of the Great Depression back when your grandparents were probably getting married, proclaimed, "The only thing we have to fear is fear itself." Since Roosevelt's day, many people believe that a number of new things have come upon the scene that Roosevelt hadn't heard of and that could be an exception to his hopeful proclamation. Perhaps there are things that we should fear: Nuclear weapons? Overpopulation? Global warming? Terrorists? Racism? AIDS?

A popular brand of clothing claims "No Fear." Do the manufacturers believe that fear has been banished? Do the people who wear clothing with that brand want to announce that they are not afraid of anything? The college environment seems to be a great place to banish fear. American universities do research that produces knowledge and reduces ignorance. When we finally know everything perhaps there will really be nothing to fear. A famous scientist, whose life work has been to probe the ultimate secrets of the universe, said that once we discover the answers to our fundamental questions about the universe we will know the mind of God.[4] Will fear then be banished from the human experience and from our vocabulary?

Long ago, Jesus already proclaimed that faith banished fear. On any number of occasions, Jesus' call to faith and his promise of comfort came in the form of a reassuring admonition: "Do not be afraid" (Matt 14:27; Rev 1:17) or "Do not fear" (Mark 5:36; Luke 8:50). For Jesus, the opposite of fear was faith; to believe was to banish fear. If you truly want to deal with fear, then faith is the way to go. Belief in the God who ultimately controls everything is the only thing that can do away with fear—just one more gift of faith.

You might think of "faith" as a file folder; in it go all those things that are scary.

Faith Does NOT Need Proof

Don't think that you will have to believe absolutely and unshakably in everything Christian in order to be a Christian, a person of faith. Don't forget that the first disciples misunderstood Jesus, doubted him, and even denied him. So don't think that you will have to come to college prepared with a complete set of irrefutable arguments to earn God's favor. In fact, you may encounter doubts in stuff you read, from the taunts of classmates, or by the sophistication of professors. But you don't need to have killer arguments that prove that faith is logical, or intellectually unassailable. You don't have time for that. God is not counting on you to defend him or to be a successful evangelist, just a student who depends on him and studies hard.

> *Faith is a gift of God; do not believe that we said it was a gift of reasoning.*
>
> —Pascal (1623–1662)

Faith as Safety Net

When something does knock you off of your feet and you stumble, faith— God's loving care—is there to pick you up. If you don't get picked up, at least faith is the net in which you can hold that problem until it is time for you and God to sort it out. Faith simply means that doubt can be handled. Finally, faith cannot be lost. You could try to replace it with something else,

4. Hawking, *A Brief History of Time*, 175.

some poor substitute that has been advertised as "the real thing." College is dangerous because there are a lot of those imitations floating around. This manual is designed to help you recognize and reject the fakes on your way to becoming that mature adult Christian believer that God intends you to become.

Faith as Vocation (not Vacation)

God made all of us, but in the big story of the whole world, we each have gone our own way, instead of God's. (In other words, we have sinned [Rom 3:23].) But most of Scripture is about God calling us back to our originally intended life. It does this through the Law, the prophets, and most especially, through Jesus Christ. This "calling" business is also known as "vocation" from the Latin *vocatio* ("call"). Every person in the world has a *vocation* because God is calling each of us back to be what we were created to be. God doesn't call us because we are so great, but because he loves us and wants the best for us. And God's *vocation* doesn't end when you happen to answer that call and come to faith.

At that point the *vocation* becomes more specific. God may be calling you to be a wife and mother, or a brain surgeon, or a policewoman; God may be calling you to be a farmer, or a politician, or a computer programmer. Or maybe God is just calling you to be a college student—someone called to the *vocation* of study, of learning, and becoming an expert in doing something that God has already prepared for you to do with that learning (Eph 2:10).

So "going to college" can be pretty much identical with God's call, your current *vocation* as a Christian. When you think of college you might automatically be thinking about preparing for a job; or, more elegantly, a career. Christian faith elevates that "job, work, career" topic into *vocation*, or a "calling." Since faith is already your entire relationship with God, it is not a big step to see that what you do as a job is going to be included in your thinking about faith. Since God has called you to faith, God is also calling you to a particular way of expressing that faith that can earn you a living and make you more helpful to others of God's creatures.

So *vocation* is a word that has the huge meaning of being called by God in general, *and* has the more mundane meaning of God's call to a certain kind of work—a work that uses your specific talents, a work that gives you joy, and a work that enriches your faith, and serves others who need what it is that you have to offer.

College can be the place where you learn the needed skills and can develop the talents that your *vocation* can use to the glory of God and your own fulfillment. Despite what anyone says, college can be a great place for faith to strengthen, deepen, and grow. Your college experience can be God's further gift to guide you to a fuller and more productive life. God speed!

Faith Is NOT a Value

Oh—one more thing. This many-sided gift of faith God gives is not what is popularly referred to as "Christian values." The reason we will avoid using the term "value" in describing the Christian faith is that neither Scripture nor even Jesus himself ever spoke of "values." Faith is concrete—facts and acts, commitments and relationships. Faith is something that actually happens. Values are something else. They are abstract ideas like "cleanliness" or "punctuality," "patriotism" or "quickness." People can affirm values without ever having to do anything about them. Everyone is *for* values and your college will probably make claims about values. The real question for the Christian is faith, not values (whatever they might be).

Do you remember the father who brought his desperately ill child to Jesus? The father didn't call out, "I value health, fatherhood, youth, and family; help me to value them more!" As you face the exciting prospect of college, it will be the faithfulness of God in Christ that you will find most reliable and helpful. Maybe your best prayer would be the same as that father's: "Lord, I believe, help my unbelief."

Thought and Discussion Questions

1. What do you think might threaten your faith in college? What steps could you take to prevent that?

2. Can you add some "Faith is . . ." sections to this chapter?

3. What is your biggest fear about your faith?

2

Faith . . . With Works

"Faith is not a thing which one 'loses,'
We merely cease to shape our lives by it."

—GEORGES BERNANOS

"So faith by itself, if it has no works, is dead."

—JAMES 2:17

Scripture Focus

HEBREWS 11:32–34

And what more should I say? For time would fail me to tell of Gideon, Barak, Samson, Jephthah, of David and Samuel and the prophets— who through faith conquered kingdoms, administered justice, obtained promises, shut the mouths of lions, quenched raging fire, escaped the edge of the sword, won strength out of weakness . . .

Usually "faith" is found in an absolute form in the New Testament; the writers and readers are all in the Christian movement and share the central experience and convictions of that group; that center is "faith" and that word stands for their connection with God, for what Jesus has done, for what shapes and establishes the cohesiveness of their movement. But occasionally, the things that faith causes to happen are mentioned—like here in the middle of the Letter to the Hebrews.

The writer gives a definition of faith—*the assurance of things hoped for, the conviction of things not seen* (11:1)—and then lays down an impressive lineup of the biblical ancestors, from Abel to David, who are remembered for their stalwart deeds of leadership and reliability over the course of centuries. It is like faith is the fuel in the tank of the ancestors and predecessors of the Christian movement. It was against that background that Jesus and his perseverance in faithfully enduring the cross is described in the very next chapter (Heb 12:2–3). And it will be faith that carries believers like you on through difficulties and even persecution to fulfillment.

Prayer: Let me experience the liveliness of faith in my life. Amen.

You may be wondering why we need *two* chapters on faith? First, faith is what is at stake during your college experience so it needs to be treated seriously—and fully; second, faith is so big, or so multi-faceted, that there are many different ways that faith makes a difference for us; and third, faith is a gift (as we saw in chapter 1) but it is a gift that prompts responses—so in this chapter we look at some of the responses that faith inspires in us.

Faith as Hard Work

I hope it has become absolutely clear by this time that faith is about what God does for us through Jesus Christ. But it is also about your response to that divine initiative. The Apostle Paul tells his readers to "work out your own salvation with fear and trembling" (Phil 2:12b). The salvation is a free gift; but the "working out" part—actually the living it out—can be hard work.

The college environment is characterized by several features that make living faith out difficult. Sometimes there is opposition to the content of faith or to the relationships it calls for. You wind up bucking the authority of very smart and well-educated people. More often—and equally challenging—is the popular notion that so much in the college environment creates a kind of "whatever" attitude in which anything is compatible with the Christian faith. In such an environment, there is *no* challenge to faith; it won't matter what you do or say or think because it can all be considered "Christian" or at least compatible with Christianity. Or you may be assured that religious belief is private and personal and has nothing to do with the business of college. You may be told that college deals with fact, with this world, with reasoning and empirical proof; and besides, so many questions are still unanswered that it would be premature to insist on any conclusions or commitment. You are not exempt from faith while in college. Keeping the faith and growing as a Christian will not be easy in college. But you have God's promise of help.

Faith Is Something to Be Worked Out

James wants his readers to know that they are transformed by Christ into new creations who think first about the needs of others and—perhaps even more striking—aren't constrained by the accepted social norms. That is, they aren't to suck up to the rich or think that the poor are of less worth (Jas 2:1–9).

The point is that being faithful can be a pretty precarious position to be in. Unless there is some concrete, explicit, visible, tangible result and some action on your part, who is going to know that there is anything there in the "faith" place?

So James gets explicit. He offers a whole list of things that happen as a result of faith, including care for widows and orphans (1:27). Sometimes it means *not* doing what everyone else is doing, like: not catering to the rich when the poor are also there (2:4); not just wishing good luck to the needy while offering no help (2:16); not saying something nasty (3:10). Sometimes it just means *knowing* something important: that the rich are the ones who oppress (2:6); that mercy is more powerful than judgment (2:13).

It is clear from James (and Jesus, and Paul, and the prophets, and . . .) that faith—if you have it—doesn't just lie there. It is having Jesus Christ *in* you, responding to the world as you experience it.

Let's look at some ways faith can be understood as active, productive, supportive—*doing* something in your life in college.

Faith as Obedience: Just Do It

Do you remember when you were a small child and you were trying things like sticking your finger in an electrical outlet? Your dad or mom would freak out and shout something like, "Don't"—except at 120 decibels. If you asked, "Why not?" the answer might well have been the short one—"Because I said so," rather than the longer one explaining the physics of an invisible power that might kill you. So you obeyed (and survived!).

But now you will be in college, where *obedience* is not a popular word. No one wants to be subservient. Independence, not obedience, is the watchword for Americans—and especially for college students. You want to decide for yourself, be in charge, call no one master, do your own thing. Americans are obsessed with individualism and independence. The college experience is a great place to pursue individualism and independence. Despite the fact that students must follow at least some of the rules, the basic mode on campus is one of independence in thinking and behavior. Freedom—academic and otherwise—is the motto of students and teachers. Disobedience is sometimes even admired.

However, a deeply correct insight of faith is that we all are ultimately obedient to something or someone. Will it be to ourselves and our own desires? To popular culture? To some other sad imitation of the true God? None of those options can ultimately pay off; they are impermanent and unreliable. Let's not kid ourselves about this obedience business. Christians at least know to whom they are obedient: first to God and then to God's children—specifically in their need. Don't be fooled; don't accept substitutes: pick the right master. Sometimes that master will call for you to do (or not do) something for reasons that aren't immediately apparent. But remember—that master loves you even more than that shouting parent who was freaking out to protect you from yourself.

> *Obedience is the "virtue-making virtue."*
> —GEORGE HAYES

Faith as the Best Option (Pascal's Wager)

One question always comes up: Is Christianity *true* or not? For Christian believers, there are often good reasons for their faith. In a tradition that goes back to the very beginnings of Christianity, *reasons* for belief play a central role in Christians' thinking. God made us with excellent minds. We are rational creatures who have the capacity for reasoned thought. The Christian faith has been around for a long time and has weathered many intellectual storms. It continues to offer good, reasoned answers to life's questions and solutions to life's dilemmas. The college experience increases the likelihood of confrontations with arguments for (and against) the Christian faith.

This does not mean that Christianity can be *proven* to be correct and that other, competing faiths can be *proven* false. Many believers have made arguments that are supposed to prove the truth of the Christian faith and prove the absolute veracity of Scripture. Many Christians depend on a variety of arguments to prove that what they believe is certain and true. The problem with that is that such an approach makes faith depend on some particular argument or proof and not on the ultimate guarantor of faith, God.

Probably just as many smart non-Christians have argued that Christianity is false; and many have believed those contradicting arguments. But since faith is not simply a matter of engaging our minds but rather our whole lives—including our feelings—the conviction that the Christian faith is what you want (or don't want) is going to be a matter that is more than simply an argument, though not a matter that ignores your mind either.

The twenty-first century is not the first time in human history that people are cynical and claim that they do not believe in much of anything. Several hundred years ago, a French philosopher/mathematician named Blaise Pascal (1623–1662) was thinking through his own Christian faith and did not find a lot of irrefutable logical or scientific support for it. But he concluded that it would be better to believe than not to believe. He figured that if Christianity ultimately turned out to be true, he would be in a better position if he believed in it than he would as a non-believer. If it turned out not to be true, it wouldn't have mattered whether he had had faith or not. Now, *Pascal's wager* (or bet) may appear kind of strange, but it is the way one serious and very smart believer—who knew that there were convincing arguments on both sides—worked through the intellectual issues connected with faith.

Of course, the way Pascal "solved" the proof issues does not really solve it at all. You will be faced with tough intellectual challenges to your faith, but you should not fear that there might be an argument out there that trumps your argument supporting God's care for you. Most of us probably want to believe in something that seems pretty good, positive, and hopeful, something that makes sense, something that might "get us through" or give meaning to life.

Christian faithfulness in this sense is the choosing—out of all possibilities—that the Christian answer is the best one. We believe that the Christian life is the fullest one, that the Christian hope is the most promising one, and that the Christian diagnosis of the human condition is the most authentic one. We trust that the Christian faith is the option best suited to the college experience—even for those of a cynical makeup. And we know that all of this is God's gracious (free!) gift.

All that's left is for us to accept it; that acceptance is the first active step in faith.

Faith as "In But Not Of"

Faith recognizes that this life is God's awe-filled gift, full of wonder, joy, love, relationships, sunrises, and sunsets. Faith also knows that this life is not complete in and of itself. It is a finite experience set in God's infinite creation. It lacks the ultimate in justice and perfection. No person, experience, organization, or idea can satisfy all of your deepest needs.

Faith offers a "place" that encompasses both the passing satisfactions of this life and the promised fulfillment in the next. On the one hand, without faith, you might feel contented with this earthly life and all of its ultimate shortcomings and you might fall for any goofy escapism that denies the goodness of this life, the richness of human communion, and the beauties of nature.

The college experience will increase your knowledge of the wonders of the world and the proposals made by both the wise and the weird down through the ages as to how to deal with life. The Psalmist (Ps 8:5) describes us as a little lower than the angels. We are humans, neither gods nor animals, but uniquely in between. Faith enables us to dwell in the "in between" and to find the joy in each (Ps 8:5; Heb 2:7). It can be hard work.

Faith as Bragging Rights

We all want something to feel good about—even occasionally to brag about: perhaps your family, a personal accomplishment, or your hometown. College will provide new opportunities to brag: about your professor, your team, your school. These are all things that you could use to bolster your own sense of worth. If your professor is the most popular, you may enjoy the envy of others. If you team wins, you can claim bragging rights over the losing team and its students and supporters. To the extent that your college enjoys a good reputation, your association with it raises you to another level. Since what you brag on also makes you in some ways liable for that on which you brag, be careful what it is that you choose to brag about (and believe in).

The Apostle Paul has an interesting take on bragging. He writes to one church that they should brag about one thing and one thing only: the cross of Christ (Gal 6:14). The cross could never have been seen by Jesus's contemporaries as anything but hateful, fearful, and disgusting. This was so because of the role the cross played in the Roman government's humiliating execution of people, including Jesus. Boasting in the cross was a dramatic way for Christians to affirm the centrality of Jesus as the object of their faith. Christians have no reason to boast of our own gifts or performance or goodness. All of those thing some from God as gifts. In college you will be tempted to boast in (believe in) many things. The choice is clear: Jesus Christ or something else. Boasting in (believing in) Jesus Christ *is* everything. Nothing else is worth bragging on or hoping in.

Faith as Apology

Why would a Christian need to apologize? In one way, she wouldn't. There is nothing to be ashamed of or sorry for in being a Christian. The original (Greek) meaning of *apology* is "to speak in defense of"—to explain, to vindicate, or present evidence in support of something. While going to college will not require you to proselytize, evangelize, buttonhole or confront others with your Christian witness or personal testimony, or to pursue philosophical, logical, linguistic, geological, or biological arguments to prove the truth of faith, there may be occasions on which others may need to hear your own explanation of why you believe what you believe.

It is (sadly) true that many college survival handbooks place making personal testimonies and witnessing at or near the top of the Christian college student's "to do" list. When Jesus sent his disciples to cast out demons and preach, He promised them that when they found themselves forced to "bear testimony (i.e., defend their faith) before authorities, they were not to worry about it. They need not prepare arguments to their challengers. Instead, Jesus promised this gift: "What you are to say will be given to you at that time" (Matt 10:19b). In other words, their defense was not up to them, but instead it would be given to them when they needed it. So? So as a student, focus on being a student. If you need to tell anyone why you are a Christian, you will be empowered by Jesus to say what you need to say when the time comes.

It is (sadly) true that many college survival manuals place making personal testimonies and witnessing at or near the top of the Christian student's "to do" list. Don't take that attitude with you.

Let's face it—you will be with a lot of smart people and with a lot of well-educated people. (Smart and well-educated are not necessarily the same.) If you go in with a chip on your shoulder for Jesus and the attitude that only you have the truth and want everyone to know it, that chip will soon be knocked off.

A realistic attitude is found in 1 Pet 3:15b–16a: "Always be ready to make your defense [*apologia*] to anyone who demands from you an accounting for the hope that is in you; yet do it with gentleness and reverence"—and humility. Your reasons ("arguments" if you insist) must be your own—and they can range from A to Z. This isn't about converting others as much as it is about laying out whatever is most important and convincing to you that makes you embrace faith. That is one of the fun things about knowing that God loves you—personally and particularly. You can have your own special and personal and particular reasons for accepting and being confident in the faith God has given you.

Faith as Urgency: Help!

Everyone can count on having one or more crises. That is when you really need help. Even a quick reading of the Gospels shows that most of the people who called on Jesus for help were in crisis. Remember the father with the ill child? For some, their whole life was a disaster: there were the mentally deranged, the demon-possessed, the socially outcast, and those with irreversible health conditions. For others, the crisis was more momentary—hunger, danger of drowning, facing a hard decision. They came to Jesus and he fixed their problem. On several occasions, Jesus commended their faith and attributed their cures to that faith; faith overcame crisis. Any number of desperate people (the leper in Matthew 8:2–4, the Centurion with the sick servant in Matthew 8:5–13; the friends with the paralytic in Matthew 9:2–7) found help at this moment of faith.

But wait a bit! What is that faith to which Jesus referred? If it was something that these petitioners already had that cured their problems, why did they need Jesus? Why didn't that faith itself take care of the problem earlier?

What those folks showed Jesus was simply and only their desperation and willingness to let him know how bad it was and that they were entrusting themselves to him. They thrust their problems at him and virtually said, "Look at this awful thing that has happened to me and about which I am totally unable to do anything. I've tried everything. You're my last hope. Help!"

That kind of desperation is usually unnecessary in our culture. Cell phones, insurance, air bags, welfare, lawyers, lifeguards, social security, and hospital emergency rooms have pretty well protected us from the effects of most of the problems that drove people in desperation to Jesus. In our culture, that kind of desperation is generally viewed as inappropriate behavior; it reveals a lack of self-confidence, an embarrassing weakness of character, or simply ignorance about where to go for help. Such an attitude is even less appropriate for those in the college experience because you are the people who are the achievers and the overachievers in our society. You are the people who—as one advertisement proclaimed—will succeed on your own terms. It may be hard for you as a faithful college student to admit that you still are dependent on God through Christ.

In the long run, of course, the major moments in your life are all moments of utter dependence on others. Birth and death are the obvious ones, but marriage, school graduations, illnesses, car breakdowns, and even getting your next meal all reveal the need you have for considerable contributions from others. Only the naive believe that they will never need help.

Faith is asking for help when you need it (and when you don't). Remember (Mark 2:4–5) when Jesus saw the faith of the friends of the paralyzed man? They couldn't cure the cripple, but they were there, carrying him, even up onto somebody else's roof, trying to get to help. Jesus saw that.

Faith as Fight: Where Do I Throw My Inkwell?

Christians are expected to get along and be nice. All the time.

Maybe that is not as it ought to be. There is a famous story about Martin Luther (1483–1546), the Protestant reformer of the sixteenth century who, while working in his study, suddenly saw the Devil across his desk. Luther was fully convinced that the Devil was real and he knew that the Devil was his enemy. Recognizing that his enemy was so close and the moment was opportune, he picked up the inkwell from the desk and hurled it at his adversary.

Whether or not the missile struck its target we do not know. The point of the story is that Luther not only knew the source of his salvation, which was God in Christ, but he also could identify the enemy—anything that diverted his reliance upon God.[1]

During a lecture, a prominent theologian of recent years was asked what he saw as the greatest need for the church in America. His answer was startling: "The church," he said, "needs to learn how to say 'God damn it!'" He went on to explain that the church is so uncritical, so "sweet," so

---

1. One of Luther's most important contributions was to translate Scripture into the language of the people (German) and he is supposed to have said that he had "driven the devil away with ink"—referring to the impact of his own translation. That historical fact may be the truth behind this anecdote, which may be an "urban legend."

anxious to avoid offending, that Christians no longer have a sense of right and wrong. We have difficulty identifying the enemy.

The Christian faith is not only the positive commitment to God in Christ and the joyous gospel of Jesus. It is also the recognition of and resistance to that which denies the gospel. Whatever denies God or harms any of God's creatures is the enemy of faith. Faith is not a license to fight, but it recognizes its opponents and is prepared to *name* and *oppose* whatever might oppose God's will and God's grace.

The opportunities that college offers to examine and evaluate the world in the light of faith ought to be embraced as gifts from God for your journey of faith. College is a place to identify the enemy (and it's *not* the college) and call it by name. In our creedal confessions (like the Apostles' Creed) we say who we are and what we stand for. There is also a time to say what we stand against. We are against *sin*. Call it out! Expose it. Point to it wherever it is. Accuse it. Ridicule it. Help others recognize it. Remember, you are already armed with the "shield of faith" (Eph 6:16).

Faith as a Journey: What a Trip!

Some things change and some don't. Some things change *and* don't change. God's love for you does not change, but the *way* in which God's love is expressed can vary since *you* change, have different needs, and can receive love in new ways. Just as life can be seen as a journey from infancy to maturity, from childhood to grandparenting, or from innocence to knowledge, faith can change, grow and deepen in response. "When I was a child, I spoke like a child . . . when I became an adult, I put an end to childish ways," wrote Paul (1 Cor 13:11) as he considered his own changing journey through life in relationship to the constants of faith, hope, and love.

As you live out your life, moving from relationship to relationship, school to school, place to place, job to job, God's love surrounds you. But you are changing and you can draw on God's presence in a variety of ways, old and new.

Much of your life may seem stable or even stagnant and you get impatient while you await changes. But there are times when you are suddenly thrust into rapid changes. Your parents' divorce, an unexpected pregnancy, the loss of a job, a broken relationship, the death of a loved one, an accident, or even going to college—these events can suddenly change your life and reorient your relationships. They also affect your relationship with God, drawing you closer because you like the change or causing anger because you dislike the change. Although *your* relationship to God in your life's journey may change, God's promise of faithfulness to you does not. So as you travel this road, you are assured that you do not travel alone.

The college experience is one part of your journey that will accelerate the changes. Faith connects you to that unchanging but adapting center for your life—God in Christ. With that place of centeredness and stability you can deal with new relationships and experiences and ideas and challenges. God can handle the changes of direction and speed of your life's journey. God can help you deal with the changes, but he will need you to take responsibility for accelerating, braking, turning, and gassing up.

Faith as Thankfulness, Hospitality, etc., etc. . . .

"Faith by itself, if it has no works, is dead" (Jas 2:17). Unfortunately, too often the deeds expected of people of faith are framed in the negative: Don't do this! Don't do that!

Scripture paints a different picture and the reason it doesn't come across very well these days is that what Scripture offers in terms of "faith in action" is so different from American (and even American college) culture.

For example: giving thanks rather than complaining and criticizing; welcoming strangers rather than maintaining cliques; loving rather than hating enemies; risking for, rather than protecting selves from, others; co-operating with, rather than competing against, others; forgiving rather than getting even. For another detailed list, read Paul's breakdown of various aspects of the "fruit of the Spirit" in Galatians 5:22–23a: "love, joy, peace, patience, kindness, generosity, faithfulness, gentleness and self-control." The list could go on and on, but you get the point.

Note: Everything thing on Paul's list of "fruit of the Spirit" has these two characteristics: (1) each is about your relationships with other people; and (2) each is your choice to do.

Faith as Far Out: Becoming Truly Radical

Are you looking for something really radical, cool, far out, and different? The term *radical* comes from a Latin term meaning "root." Living by the Christian faith is utterly radical when compared with how Americans typically live and think. Living in radical faith means going back to faith's roots—to Jesus Christ. To know that we are all essentially the same, that is, creatures of God and made in God's image—despite our age, haircut, clothes, profession—now *that* is amazingly radical! To rely on God rather than on ourselves—now *that* is even more radical! To be related to others in love rather than on a competitive basis—*that* is totally radical! If you are looking to be radical, your search is over when you opt for Christian faith.

This is the faith of Paul, who saw himself as one called to complete the work of Christ. Imagine that—that the work of Christ is not complete? Look at what Paul says: "I am now rejoicing in my sufferings for your sake, and in my flesh I am completing what is lacking in Christ's afflictions for the sake of his body, that is, the church" (Col 1:24). Does that mean that you also are needed to "complete what is lacking"? And what exactly is lacking in Christ's afflictions for the church? That's a radical challenge.

Faith as the Good Old Days: Becoming Truly Conservative

If, however, something more conservative is your desire, if the world is already too liberal and too messed up and you don't feel like contributing to an already wacky situation, then the life of faith might be just your calming and quieting ideal. There is nothing as "back to basics" as the Christian faith, nothing as reassuring in uncertain times, nothing that puts you in touch with your roots and your past, nothing as solidly founded on ultimate truth and certainty. Here is tradition that goes back 2,000 years. Here are eternal truths: "Jesus Christ is the same yesterday and today and forever" (Heb 13:8). Here is solid footing to keep you from being swept away by the next crazy notion that turns everyone else on but is way off base (Eph 4:14; Jude 11).

Faith as a Minority Position

Isn't everyone a Christian? That may be how it looks sometimes (like on Easter Sunday), but your local church or America's president concluding his speeches with "God Bless America" or even your money talking to you ("In God We Trust") should not be taken as proof that everyone is committed to the life of faith that God would love everyone to follow. The proportion of Americans who profess to be Christians is dropping; the level of commitment of those still on church rolls seems weaker as secularism penetrates every dimension of life. Real commitment becomes rarer.

And then there are "the issues" and the question of whether faith commits us to be on the right side of important questions. There were moments when the courageous and truly Christian thing to do was to oppose slavery; to invite women to share positions of leadership; to oppose segregation; to accept the divorced brother; to oppose misuse of the world God had created. When Christians began to take these new and unpopular positions, they were only following Jesus Christ, who had opposed abuse of the poor, exclusion of the adulteress, and condemnation of the sinner.

"Christian" can be a tight spot to be in sometimes; but it's the best one. Some day you might be called to step up and be "an army of one" on behalf of the faith.

Fides Quarens Intellectum

Say what? That's Latin for "faith seeks understanding." It was written a millennium ago by another Christian student named Anselm (1033–1109). He knew that faith was a rich and deep mystery with many aspects to it. In many ways, he was like you—he took God on faith. But he also realized that his faith was urging him to ask, ponder, inquire, investigate, study—in short, to become a student. College is the perfect place for a person of faith

> *The first key to wisdom is assiduous and frequent questioning . . . For by doubting we come to inquiry, and by inquiry we arrive at truth.*
> —Peter Abelard (1079–1142)

to be and to let faith do its own thing—seek to understand. Understand what? Anything! Everything! If you are equipped with faith, you have the best asset a college student could have. You are ready to inquire, to ask all kinds of questions, to look around with interest at everything. You are propelled by inquisitiveness or divinely inspired nosiness! Just follow your faith and you will be a successful college student in the bargain.

Thought and Discussion Questions

1. What is your favorite (most useful, current) way of describing faith?

2. In what way(s) is faith the same for all Christians? In what way(s) might it be different?

3. In rapid succession, list a number of life situations—developing a personal budget, going on a date, deciding for whom to vote, selecting a research topic, buying a car. How could faith relate to each situation and help to determine your response?

3

College 101—Introduction

Alma mater—(Latin for "fostering mother")

—Webster's New World College Dictionary

"My mother and my brothers are those
who hear the word of God and do it."

—Jesus in Luke 8:21

Scripture Focus

Matthew 22:37

*He said to him: "You shall love the Lord your God with all your
heart, and with all your soul, and with all your mind."*

This was the first half of Jesus' answer to the question, "Which is the
great commandment?" The second half was that we are also to love
our neighbor as we love ourselves.

The Pharisee lawyer who asked Jesus about the greatest commandment thought he was asking a simple question. He was asking which was *the*
(as in one, only, top, first) greatest commandment. To an apparently simple
question Jesus gives an answer that has at least two parts, each with qualifications. We also note that Jesus added no criteria for accurately measuring
to see if one has fulfilled the command.

There is something in this exchange between Jesus and the Pharisee lawyer that sounds a lot like what you will encounter in your college experience: ask a simple question and you'll get a complicated answer. Be ready for it. Or don't ask. But it sounds as if Jesus really encourages us to ask questions, since part of the most important command of all is to use our minds to love God.

When we really want answers to our questions we go to authorities, the people who are supposed to know. Colleges have people who know (professors) and books with information and many opportunities to illuminate the path to good answers through formal and informal conversation. College could be the very place to carry out Jesus' command to love God with your mind. While Jesus will be your best teacher, he cannot be expected to answer all of the detailed questions you have. So the combination of Jesus and college can provide the means to help you increase your ability to fulfill this commandment; you will be learning new skills that you can apply to loving your neighbor.

Oh—and one more thing. It is remarkable that even though the Pharisee's question is about commandments, Jesus' answer is not about obeying but about loving. That makes his answer sort of impossible—impossible to measure peoples' performance and impossible to complete. How do you accurately measure love? And how do you know when you are done or have loved enough? (Have you ever been loved enough?) His answer leaves you hanging—like a lot of answers you might hear in college. But it is an answer that does give you a definite direction, and should prompt you to want to know more.

Prayer: Lord God, help me to love you with everything I have. Amen.

What Is College?

What is college? What is it like to attend college? What happens to you at college? What is college for? Would God want you to go?

College—By the Numbers: College—let's use the term *college* to cover everything from junior colleges to universities—is huge! Currently there are 5,454 colleges employing 3,763,592 people, and spending $393,790,985,593 to educate the 21,592,738 students enrolled (18,644,298 of whom are undergraduates).[1] Despite all of the big numbers, the big question for you is whether college is worth the cost and the effort.

---

1. *Almanac 2013–14*, 19, 52–53, 105.

Purpose: The best way to answer the *what-is-college* question and the *is-it-worth-it* question is to find out what college is for; what is its purpose. These days, college is primarily about preparing *you* for employment, a job, a profession, a career. While some folks (some students and some professors) hold that college should be for developing your mind, liberally educating you out of the restrictive thinking of the past, or building your character so you will be a good citizen, the majority (most parents, students, politicians, businesses) are thoroughly agreed that if college is going to be worth anything—did we mention that it is expensive, and getting more expensive all the time?—it needs to focus on preparing students for the jobs and the careers that our country (and the world) needs. Studies show that students increasingly see college as primarily for their job preparation. College makes you more employable and you will earn more money with a college degree. Colleges seem happy enough to go along with that idea even though they will claim that they can do all sorts of additional good things for you. (Just read the catalogues and other brochures from the schools that interest you or want you.) There is nothing new about the idea that colleges exist to prepare students for jobs.

A quick history of colleges will show that they were born out of the Christian church's need for educated leaders—priests, teachers, lawyers, statesmen. About 800 years ago, the first of these colleges appeared in Paris and was soon followed by others in Spain, Italy, and England.

Later, and closer to home, with the establishment of Harvard College in 1636, American colleges were founded for much the same reason: to provide training for ministers. Getting preparation on the American side of the Atlantic was preferable to sending young men (sorry, no women in college yet!) across the Atlantic Ocean for ministerial training in Europe.

The growth from the early small colleges into the large campuses of today has come about largely because of the changes in our world—from colonial beginnings to an independent nation, from an agrarian to a fully industrial economy. These enormous changes created pressures for more and different kinds of college education. From the early focus on religious and classical training, new emphases in math, science, technology, and business drove new research, necessitated new courses, and remade the face of American colleges.

As a nation was built, it needed skilled political leaders; as industries developed, they needed skilled engineers and builders; as the economy grew, it needed business experts; and now the appetite of a continually expanding global economy for graduates with sophisticated training is insatiable.

Economic Advantages of Education[2]

Unemployment rate	Educational Level Completed	Income for Men	Income for Women	Women's earnings as a percentage of men's
12.4%	Less than a high-school diploma	$24,808	$15,508	63%
8.3%	High-school diploma	$34,005	$22,484	66%
7.7%	Some college, no degree	$40,426	$26,742	66%
6.2%	Associate degree	$45,300	$31,397	69%
4.5%	Bachelor's degree	$60,242	$41,013	68%
3.5%	Master's degree	$76,215	$51,187	67%
2.1%	Professional degree	$101,399	$70,373	69%

Another change was in the demographic makeup of the college. At first everyone was white and male. By the mid-nineteenth century, women began to arrive on campus, both as students and as teachers. (Today there are more women enrolled in American colleges than ever before: just over 57 percent of *all* students are women,[3] and they earn the majority [57.1 percent] of Bachelor's degrees.[4]) Then, slowly, other previously excluded groups gained access. The increasing presence of diverse populations compounded the changes resulting from differences in new curricula driven by demands of the job market. It meant that colleges were not simply and totally Protestant. With the matriculation of Roman Catholics, Jews, Muslims, other faiths, and non-believers, the domination of Protestant Christians' thinking, behavior, and faith weakened. But no matter how big, complex, and diverse the college became, the basic purpose remained: job preparation.

2. *Almanac 2013–14*, 35, 43.

3. *Almanac 2013–14*, 105.

4. *Almanac 2012–13*, 28.

Value Added? There is something else that goes with the college experience that has persisted through all the other changes. Sometimes it is called the "value added" factor.

The experience in college is objectively described by what will be noted on your transcript—the courses taken and the grades received. But there will be more, much more that you will receive simply by being a part of a particular college experience. That added value consists of the habits, feelings, attitudes, memories, ideas, friends, experiences, and all of the other things that come into your life along with the preparation for a job or career. Sometimes that added "something" is obvious; sometimes it is not so obvious. When it is in the "not so obvious" category, it is still instruction but instruction in the *hidden* curriculum or *implicit* curriculum.[5] You could call it the stuff that you pick up unconsciously simply by being in a particular place for a while.

Let's go back to those early days when American colleges were focused on teaching young men how to be ministers. That student needed to know how to read the Bible in the original Hebrew and Greek languages and how to preach; but he also needed to know how to *behave* as a clergyman and what would be expected of him as a member of that profession. That was the "value added" piece of an early American college education. (Today we might call this "character formation.") Some of it was done explicitly through the rules of the school, and some was done implicitly, in a "seat of the pants" way, absorbed by the student simply by living in the college community and following the example of teachers. It is important to note that the earliest goal of American colleges incorporated both the academic content as well as the moral and social behavior desired for the future ministers of the colonies' churches. The goal was to achieve a marriage of professional training *and* a lifestyle which, in that setting, was considered "Christian."

Until about one hundred years ago, schools were focused on ensuring that graduates received this same Christian religious content as well as the professional training expected of the educated leadership, even if they were studying to be something other than a minister—say, a teacher, or lawyer, or doctor. To that end, the final course for college students was usually a capstone course emphasizing the morals the graduates were expected to carry with them beyond college and into their careers. This course was so important that it was usually taught by none other than the college president.

---

5. "The unwritten norms, values, and expectations that unofficially govern the interactions among students, faculty, professional staff, and administrators (xiv) . . . [the] unwritten rules (17) . . . [the] embedded cultural capital (58)." Smith, *Hidden Curriculum.*

Secular vs. Christian "Values." As more and more students opted for non-religious courses of study, it became more difficult to pass on Christian virtues and character traits to them. But the general expectation was that every student, regardless of major, would be educated in a Christian environment. This continued to be the case even as public, tax-supported schools came on the scene in the late nineteenth century and the vocational options expanded and diversified to include training for secular professions. Americans saw themselves then (as now) as generally Christian, or at least religious in a Christian sort of way.

The modern college, as you know it today, began to emerge in the late nineteenth century as several characteristics of today's college were developed: undergraduate "majors" were established to devote more study to prepare the student for a specific employment; the broad, classical education of the past was reduced to a general education program required of all students; and graduate level programs were introduced. All of this helped colleges offer a more vocationally relevant education. But despite the diversification in vocational training, the passing on of Christian morals remained a part of the college experience.

In the twentieth century, most colleges had become less explicitly Christian but still remained generally religious in the sense of emphasizing values that could pass for some sort of religiousness. That which specifically defined Christianity—faith in Jesus Christ, conversion, salvation from sin, specific denominational practices, the centrality of Scripture—lessened in importance and was replaced with moral and religious generalities such as belief in God and living a (vaguely defined) good moral life. College was becoming less explicitly religious and more secular.

The question became: How to ensure that higher education would continue to provide students with popularly approved spiritual and moral development at the same time that it turned its attention to the more practical demands of undergraduate job preparation? School officials sought a variety of means to ensure that some sort of religious and moral values were communicated to students in other ways.[6]

In some cases, schools relied on the teaching of religion as a subject. Another strategy was to make sure that the instructors lived up to the desired moral standards and conveyed them to students by means of personal example. But by the start of the twentieth century, ensuring that the common Christian precepts were conveyed via the curriculum, subject matter, or through teacher example was no longer working.

6. Reuben, *Making the Modern University*, 88, 160, 211, 245–48, 255–59.

Then the position or office of *dean of student services* was invented. This allowed for the explicitly religious part of education to be moved into the realm of the extra- or co-curricular—such as literary, musical, and theatrical activities, concerts, outside speakers, and athletic activities. (Amos Alonzo Stagg, one of the most famous of the early college football coaches, claimed that coaching football gave him the best opportunity to communicate Christianity to his students.) Student social life did not keep pace and, finally, churches stepped in again and the colleges "outsourced [the religious care of students] to denominational chaplains."[7] Finally, in the early twenty-first century, even support for that approach is weakening. The secular was winning the battle of values, and it was winning with its own secular values.

Secularization and Secular Values: Was this secularization to be the end of religion, morality, and character formation in college?

Not at all. In fact, growing invisibly right under the nose of higher education was a new set of secular values, which became a substitute for religion. This secularism claims independence from all religious faith and in fact incorporates a lot of what must be called religion. This competitor to the Christian faith was the unintended consequence of a system of education that tried to provide an acceptable but inoffensive set of values for students preparing for life in an increasingly secular America. The shift to secular values as a replacement for Christian belief and virtues was well under way.

So colleges are still about skill-, job-, career-training *and* still interested in students getting the right values. But wait. If you talk with most college teachers, they will insist that their teaching is not biased by any values; instead, the best professor will teach in a value-free manner.

So what is really going on when it comes to values—that other half of vocational education—that "value-added" dimension of the education that American colleges have sought to provide for so long and in so many ways? The short answer is: college will assault you with values, some you notice, many of which you don't. The long answer is: read chapters 7–14 that follow to see an inventory of the ways in which college will continue to offer you values—not the old Christian character formation training of centuries past, but new, non-Christian, secular values that will substitute something secular and non-Christian in the place of your Christian faith. The value part of college is confusing; in fact, it is a mess. In subsequent chapters you will not only see what the secular threats you will face are, but, more importantly, what the positive alternatives are that faith can draw out of that college experience.

7. Summerfield, *Decline of the Secular University*, 17.

It is a mess and you will become a part of it simply by being in college. You will be an alumnus (graduate) of a college; that will be a part of your identity for life. You will also become a member of smaller groups within the college—perhaps a sorority or fraternity, the choir, an athletic team, an academic honor society, and, of course, that special group of lifelong friends and companions with which the college experience is likely to bless you. As a part of each group, you will be influenced and some of those influences will challenge the most important group to which you belong: the body of Christ. So how is a Christian to come to an understanding in terms of his relationship with all of these groups?

What Should Christians Think About College?

Second (you'll find "first" is in the next paragraph), know that your college *wants to be your mama!* Yes, your *mater,* your "mother." Or more precisely—to distinguish college from your biological mother—the mother of your *alma*—your "soul." The "soul" or *alma* in this *alma mater* thing is not just your "soul" in the Christian, religious sense, but that aspect of yourself that is the thinking, committing, valuing, and understanding part. While you go to college to learn, the *alma* includes the learning and intellectual part of your life. So, in short, the college and the professors there want you to take them so seriously that you are transformed into someone like them in their thinking, valuing, believing, and living. And if you think about it, by the time you graduate, you will have been with that would-be *alma mater* for almost a quarter of the time you have been out of diapers.

First, know that *God already* is *your Father!* And God is already Jesus' Father. And Jesus has already made it clear that his mother is only that one who hears the word of God and does it (Luke 8:21).

So if you need to combine these ideas to help make sense of your college experience you could do it this way:

> *God is my Father; college is my alma mater . . . but only to the extent that my college hears the word of God and does it—in the regular curriculum, the co-curriculum, and the secret, hidden, implicit curriculum.*

Some Christians don't think very seriously about college. They just go and don't worry too much about their faith and how college might relate to their life as a Christian. And they certainly aren't focused on Christian virtues.

Some Christians do think about what might happen to them as Christians in college, and they get worried. They should. But they often worry overly much about a few things but not about other, more important ones.

This book invites you to be a Christian who thinks very seriously about college and who wants to have as complete a picture as possible of the college experience—the good news and the bad news.

Okay: so far we have seen that college is mainly about preparing you to be a skilled professional in a field that (hopefully) excites you. That is good news, because as a Christian you will want to be as well prepared as possible for your *vocation* serving God and others through your chosen work. It is more and more likely these days that you will need the kind of training that higher education offers in order to qualify for that work.

The other not-so-good news is that the college experience is going to open you to a lot of added stuff—that's the "value added" extras that you simply can't get away from no matter what college you pick. That is where the bad news needs to be noticed: the values to which you are exposed need to be carefully evaluated.

But there is more good news: it is that God provides you with the college experience. As our creator, he made us with good minds. As the creator of all powers in the universe, he is ultimately the creator of the college experience where his invitation that we "love him with all of our mind" can take place (Matt 22:37; Mark 12:30; Luke 10:27).

But, you are wondering, how does this make sense? If God is the creator of something good, why are we being warned that college can be dangerous to our faith?

Excellent question.

This is how it makes sense: God, the creator, has created all things and all powers; God has allowed humans to create their own institutions for the proper management of human life (for example: government, marriage, family, business). One of those cultural institutions or powers is education. Education is found in every culture, but is organized differently from one place to another. One form of education is the college system. Because God is ultimately responsible for creating—or allowing the existence of—these institutions that are intended for our benefit, we can confidently conclude that they are intended to be good, divinely ordained and purposeful. They are institutions and they, like us individuals, have a *vocation*. The vocation of a college is to educate, enrich, and enable God's creatures; they are intended as an expression of God's love for us.[8] The college is "born from the heart of

---

8. This idea that colleges are intended (not created) by God for our benefit and therefore have a divinely established *vocation*, and the following ideas about how colleges—like every other human institution—have had their divine *vocations* compromised

the church"[9] so that we may have a great resource with which to love God with all of our hearts.

Nonetheless, sin can infect and compromise a whole institution—even a college. Remember sin? Sin is the misuse of God's intention in creation. When the college deviates from its God-intended vocation of enabling God's creatures to love him by learning how to care for one another, you can know that sin has taken over. No one can escape sin; we have all sinned—even colleges—and fallen short of God's will (Rom 3:23).

You may be thinking: *That is the weirdest idea I've heard about college yet.* How can a college be sinful? It is true that most of the "college survival manuals" have been written with the idea that college is antagonistic to Christian faith. The problem with that is that most manuals seem to find the evils of college concentrated in only a few places—especially in parts of the social life, in other students (diversity), in alcohol and sex; and in a few classes: biology, sociology, and philosophy.

You might ask—in fact, you must ask: What about other parts of college? What about other classes? Isn't sin found elsewhere? That is a very good question; and the answer is, "Yes, of course it is." Sin isn't just somebody else's fault. It isn't just in one place and not another. As a Christian, you have to be ready to deal with sin every place; that is why faith takes so many forms and is such a big deal. And that is why you should consider college a divinely ordained institution that has sinned.

Values: One more time: So let's go back to the value thing. Schools claim to teach values—just look at your college's promotional materials. Or your college might claim that its particular version of the college experience offers you a value-packed experience. A fairly harmless example of this kind of claim to teach values argues that the values of truth, freedom, equality, individuation, justice, and community are in fact taught or communicated by colleges.[10] (It is interesting, however, that colleges never offer proof that the values that they want students to acquire are ever actually delivered.

---

by sin—are inspired by the writings of Walter Wink, a New Testament scholar who argued that the *powers* and *principalities* mentioned in Scripture should be understood as real forces in the world, created by God but inevitably affected and compromised by sin. See Wink, *Naming the Powers*, especially 85, 129. In a second book, *Unmasking the Powers,* Wink "unmasks" human institutions (military, Hollywood, politics, Madison Avenue, etc.) and suggests ways in which they must be understood as challenges to the kingdom of God.

9. Compare the recent official Roman Catholic statement on Catholic Universities by Pope John Paul II, *ex corde ecclesiae,* which opens with a statement about the nature of college: "Born from the heart of the Church (*ex corde ecclesiae*)," 3.

10. See Young, *No Neutral Ground.*

We'll see more about whether colleges can prove that they actually teach any values successfully in chapter 12.)

Colleges have not always done well even on values. For example, it has been painfully clear that the value of freedom—touted so highly in higher education—has not always been enjoyed equally by everyone. History shows that women, African-Americans, Jews, Catholics, homosexuals, foreigners, liberals, and conservatives have all at one time or other been refused freedoms granted to others by America's colleges.

On the other hand, the most up-to-date professors will deny that values play any role in their teaching. (*And they really mean it. Having been a professor, I know how hard it is to keep values out of the classroom.*)

Then there are the values that nobody notices—some of which you will find exposed in this book. They can be subtle, even hidden. They can be "taught" by just about any feature of any college by means of its history, its mission, the makeup of the student body or faculty, the nature of campus social life, its location, architecture, mascot, alumni activity (or passivity), athletics, extra-curricular activities, what is made known or hidden by administrators or campus publications; this list goes on and on. As we have noted, sometimes the sum total of these and other aspects of a college is called its *hidden* or *implicit* (as compared to its *explicit*) curriculum. It is the stuff that's just there and even though you don't notice it, it influences you.

So college is a great thing, but deeply enmeshed, as we all are, in human sin. That may sound harsh, but Christians need to be aware of the reality of sin. So there is a tension between the values that the college boasts—all presumably well-intentioned—and what could be seen as Christian values—if Christians actually had values. Which we don't. (Remember page 18 in chapter 1?) This is because values are abstract while Christians want to focus on the concrete and specific—especially the specific actions of God in Christ and our specific reactions in the living of our lives. But in order to be able to contrast the secular values that lie at the heart of the college experience with what lies at the heart of the Christian faith, we will—for the sake of discussion and clarity, but only temporarily and only for the sake of discussion—"translate" the concrete actions of God in Christ into "values." While this takes all the powerful edge off of what Christian faith is all about, the exercise can still be instructive. Here is a quick comparison of the secular college experience and the Christian faith:

Values of the College Experience	Christian *Commitments*
career	vocation
community	kingdom of God
competition	cooperation, peace
confidence	humility
consumption	sharing
control	submission
efficiency	care-less-ness
elitism	brother/sisterhood
enjoyment	hope
equality	mutuality
fragmentation	coherence
freedom from	freedom for
haste	patience
hierarchy	family/brother-sisterhood, servant hood
how?	why?
I	you (Thou)
independence of individual	social interdependence
information	wisdom
inquiry	belief
isolation (ivory tower)	incarnation
job preparation	all of life
justice	righteousness
knowing	being known
objectivity	commitment
observation/examination	wonder
pleasure	sympathy
positivism	flesh & spirit
power	love
pragmatism	helping
proof	faith
retaliation	forgiveness
self-development	Christ-, other-centeredness

Values of the College Experience	Christian *Commitments*
specialization	inclusion
standards	compassion
success	service
tolerance	engagement/hospitality
truth	Jesus Christ
winning	peace
work for personal success	work that serves others

This is an astonishing list both for its length as well as for the dramatic clarity of the differences between Christian faith and those secular values typically favored in the college experience. The college experience's challenge to faith is not from one or two isolated features of college life such as confronting the theory of evolution or deciding whether or not to experiment with drugs. The challenge is deeper and more widespread and more complex. Its roots are in the very structure of the college experience itself and the contrast can be seen as demonstrated above.

In this time of great interest in spirituality, with individuals looking inward for meaning, it should not be difficult to imagine that institutions might also be seen to have their own inwardness, their character or personality. Christians might call it the colleges' own unique (secular) spirituality.

The college is not only a community; it is also a spiritual reality. It is a spirituality because it exists within the reality of God's creation. But it may not be a Christian spiritual reality because its vocation is most likely bent to serve the pressing current needs of secular American culture—particularly its economic needs. That means that American culture and the values of America as a society are central to what you will get in college.

But God always promises hope, and that is good news. Just as our/your sin is taken seriously by God, God does not abandon us; neither does he abandon any of his creatures. So even though college must be approached as a sinful reality, your hope—as a Christian—is not in the college itself but in the promise that God will eventually redeem that college, or at least redeem your college experience, by his grace.

That is how a Christian might think about college.

What Could a Christian DO About College?

First, fear not; you have important things going for you. You know that the college is within God's embrace because it is one of God's creations—no matter if it is messed up in some ways—and that God can redeem the college experience for you and make it a positive time in your life. You will have the best resources for understanding and dealing with each particular or individual challenge to your faith in Jesus, the Savior and Teacher, and in Scripture (chapters 5 and 6).

Jesus Christ offers his gospel—the "good news"—which is a different story than the one most American colleges tell and want you to absorb. Go back to the list of college values; there you will find the story that the college lives and sells: compete to improve yourself so that you can succeed socially and economically. But Christian faith has a different story: depend upon God to lead you into paths of service where you will find the richest of rewards. It is a more helpful story to explain life's questions and resolve life's difficulties. Can Christ help you get the good out of college and protect you from the dangers? Can he help you understand the secular values that the college as *alma mater*—your would-be spiritual mother—wants you to have? Yes, he can help you understand and offer pathways to success.

The college works at mothering and influencing students through her curriculum, faculty, history, lore, mission, athletic, and other social activities; through the school song, clothing, seal, motto, and mascot. After graduation, the alumni magazine, alumni association, homecoming, fund drives and continuous athletic activities reinforce the ever present secular values of the institution.

None of these components of the college experience necessarily convey or embody the things important for Christians. So it is time for you to prepare to be a part of two families—the church (the body of Christ) is your primary family; the college will be your temporary "worldly" location. Remember, throughout Scripture, God's children were always God's children even though they simultaneously lived in Palestine, or Rome, or Corinth, or Colossae. It will be hard to be in two communities with different natures. But not impossible. Each can nurture you.

You have not been abandoned. Now that you know what college is, you can put on the full armor of God (Eph 6:13) and move ahead, into college, where you can continue to love God with all your mind and follow God's call—your Christian vocation—in the most faithful way. College should never be confused or identified with the Christian community.[11] The

11. That churches and religious contributors do not seem very interested in

commitment to unmask the difficulties of college and point toward more faithful ways to learn calls for you, the student, to participate in the work of unmasking, and discerning, and engaging[12] the college experience in ways that are based in faith and aimed in hope at a positive and joyous academic career. You are called to that discernment and "unmasking," not to save the world (that is Jesus' task) but first of all so that you can be an informed and critical student.

Second (we're still on what a Christian could do about college), if you feel you need to attend college in order to prepare for a particular vocation, do it. If you are not sure about your vocational interest(s), college is a great place to look at many options and to have stimulating, broadening, and deepening experiences.

Third, begin to think seriously about it now so that you will be equipped to understand and be ready for what will be coming at you in big, fast, powerful waves. After all, college is about ideas—old ones, new ones, good ones, and even bad ones—and the fact is that ideas have consequences in actions and in the way people live. This book invites you to be a Christian who thinks very seriously about college and is not afraid to face both the good news as well as the bad news.

Let's get back to the matter of loving God with our minds. Perhaps the Christian answer to the question, "What is college about?" should be: college is the best place to love God with your mind. It looks as though there are two purposes for college: one is to love God with your mind; the other is to prepare for a job. As a Christian you can see that those are two wonderful purposes. You might even agree with Pope John Paul II that college—at least the general idea of college—is something that has its very origin in the "heart of the church."

---

supporting (and in the process influencing) colleges is suggested by the fact that their financial support of American colleges amounts to no more than .05 percent or about one half of one percent of all contributions from all sources that support American higher education. My own unpublished research; and *Almanac 2010–11,* 16.

12. See Wink, *Engaging the Powers.*

Thought and Discussion Questions

1. What do you think a college is? What should its purpose be?

2. Are the positive and negative things we have said about the college experience correct as far as you know?

3. Are there other problems you anticipate in college?

4. What do you foresee as the best things about college?

4

Getting Settled—
But Not Too Settled

"The devil is in the details."

—ENGLISH PROVERB

"Beloved, I urge you as aliens and exiles . . ."

—1 PETER 2:11a

Scripture Focus

JOHN 17:6–19

*. . . they are **in** the world . . .[but]. . .*
*they do not belong **to** the world*

We all know about living in the world: bills to pay, deadlines and expectations to meet, a job (or more than one) to attend to, relationships to cultivate, people to see, places to go, things to do, and on and on. Then try to put going to college on top of all that—more details, forms to complete, packing the right clothes, getting required inoculations, saying goodbye to the neighbors, getting a new cell phone, and on and on. It just never stops.

We might wonder what Jesus knew about living "*in* the world." Don't we usually think of him as "otherworldly"? We also remember that he lived ages ago when the world was much less complicated. (Was it really?) We remember that he got in total trouble with all of the authorities and was executed; that might suggest he really did not have much effective knowledge about living *in* the world. Before we rush to conclusions, however, let's see how he spoke to his disciples about living *in* but not *of* this world.

"*In?*" "*Of?*" What's the difference? And what would it matter? There is a saying: "The devil is in the details." And in understanding the saying of Jesus about living *in* but not *of* the world, that proverb could not be more correct. There is a huge difference between "*in*" and "*of.*" And it does matter. But let's back up for a second. What was Jesus talking about in this Johannine passage? And why does he seem to be ambivalent about the "world?"

By the seventeenth chapter of John, the writer was beginning to wrap up the story of Jesus and bring it to a close. As Jesus was about to be crucified and leave this world and his disciples, John records Jesus' long, final prayer. He prayed that God would protect his disciples who were about to be left leaderless in the world. In his prayer he reminds God that he is leaving these disciples in the world while he, Jesus, will be leaving this world and returning to God, his father. The disciples saw Jesus as their Teacher and Lord (John 13:13) and Jesus rightly sees them as his disciples (students). He wants them to focus on him as he goes to that "other world." He doesn't want them to focus on this world, the one that is rejecting him.

Of course Jesus knew that God had created the world and that it was good; but he also knew that the people who ran the world—kings, governors, soldiers, priests—were conspiring to kill him, even though all he ever wanted to do was to help. What Scripture speaks of as "principalities" and "powers" are not some winged devils floating around up in the air or in dark places in the bad part of town; they are the forces at work messing things up for the powerless people in the world. No wonder Jesus had a good news/ bad news attitude toward the world and those in charge who made the important decisions. He knew that his disciples would be in a tight spot—*in* the world that had rejected and killed him. No wonder he wanted them as far away from this world as they could get while they were still *in* it.

But can you really be two places at once? *In* but not *of?* Sure you can. Haven't you ever been someplace (*in*) but desperately felt that you needed to be somewhere else (*of*)? That somewhere else is an "*of*" because that somewhere else is where you really belong.

Well, here you are at college, settling down, trying to get comfortable—trying to fit *in*. Since this will be your new home, you want to feel at ease. But Jesus' caution is that you not get too comfortable. College is a wonderful place to be (that is the *in* part). But you already have been alerted to some of the pitfalls and you will see more in the following pages. You have heard that the values and goals of college are so different from those of the Christian faith that college is not the place to be *of*—at least for a Christian. From the beginning, Scripture pictures God's people as not *of* this world.

As early as the Old Testament Book of Deuteronomy (26:5), Abraham is described as a "wandering Aramean" who began the saga of God's people by leaving his home in response to God's call. Throughout the Old Testament, God's people spent less time dwelling in their own land than they did "wandering" about, in exile, or worse yet, enslaved. Scripture makes it abundantly clear that God's people do not fundamentally belong to any place or institution of this world. We are here—*in* this world made so good by God—but we are really God's so we are *of* another world.

Jesus made it clear that he also had no permanent place *in* this world: "The Son of Man has nowhere to lay his head" (Matt 8:20b; Luke 9:58b); and think also of his admission that "I was a stranger" (Matt 25:35b). The Apostle Paul puts it starkly: "our citizenship is in heaven" (Phil 3:20). We have been called by Jesus into that other world; he introduces it, he prays for it to come, and illustrates it with his parables and his behavior—it is the kingdom of God. Another way to put it would be to think of ourselves as pilgrims or like the early Christian monastics who separated themselves from "the world." In other words, our real home, the place we truly belong, the source of our entire orientation, is not this world but heaven. This world calls you with its vocational options—to be both *in* it and *of* it. The Christian's vocation is to be *of* God, while you are still *in* the world.

So . . . get on with getting settled *in*, but don't get too comfortable. Your prayer might be: "*Sustain me* in *this world and keep me in the knowledge that I am of your world, O Lord God of all the worlds that are. Amen.*"

Welcome to College; It Can Be Dangerous

As affirmed in chapter 3, college is a gift of God, ultimately existing—like all human institutions (e.g., government, marriage, industry)—with the primary vocation of enriching the lives of his creatures. As a Christian, you can view the original vocation of college (to serve God) coming together with your own personal vocation of serving God and others. Unfortunately, colleges have often ignored their true vocation and have opted for something different. In that sense they deserve to be seen as demonic. College is—like every human institution—infected and affected by human sin. The divine vocation to be a source of good to all of God's children is not always fulfilled.

The reasons for that failure are two: the obvious one is that these institutions are run by humans, like you and me, who are imperfect (or sinful) but try to do what they think is best, and often settle for second best.

The second reason is less obvious: institutions—like the church, the government, the military, the whole of any given culture—take on a life of their own and have their own spirit or personality or character. So when people work in such an environment, they take on the character of the group; it is difficult if not impossible to change the group.

Take, for example, your family. You were born into it and you have probably taken on the thinking and behaviors of the family; your parents are unlikely to have adopted many of your characteristics. So it is with the college. It is a result of what it has been and is not likely to have changed because one or another really good (or really bad) person has been the president, dean, professor, or student there. The college is an institution composed of buildings and classes and sports teams, but these are only the external representation of the inward spirit of the college. That inner spirit or spirituality is not a Christian spirituality but a secular one, as we described in the previous chapter.

> *The Clery Act—School Safety and Crime Statistics: All schools receiving federal financial aid must make their campus security policies and crime statistics available. Encouraging reports from many campuses show that students, faculty, and college administrators are working to eliminate sexual harassment and sex offenses.*
>
> —CHE

If this sounds critical, you're right. The problem with college is not so simple as saying either "college is evil" or "college is good"; rather, it is correct to see college as God's gift to people who—because sin is universal—have turned it from its essential vocation to serve God toward another goal. That goal could be to be the best academic institution, or to be a national sports champion, or to build the most famous faculty, or simply to make money. It is strange that Christians have not understood this. Only recently are colleges themselves beginning to reflect on how they're doing, so you may be getting to college just in time to help with that important task of critical self-analysis.

I have attended sixty or seventy college graduation ceremonies. They have all been pretty much the same—especially when the (usually famous or important) speaker gets up to deliver the commencement address. They have all been forgettable. I have forgotten sixty or seventy. Except for one back in 1985. One of my daughters was graduating and the speaker was not famous but he was important: he was one of my daughter's professors. His address was memorable because in it, instead of reminding the graduates what they had learned and encouraging them to "go forth, etc. . . ," he criticized their own college for not teaching them enough and reminded them they still had a lot to learn. Wow!

While the college experience ought to provide the opportunity for real growth as a Christian, we have suggested that college can also be hazardous to your faith. It can also be dangerous in many other ways. For instance, here is a quick and dirty list of some of the most obvious hazards, many of which you already know about: homesickness, gaining weight, overusing a credit card, gambling, cheating, ID theft, hazing, drinking, drugs, sex, depression, suicide, guns. Fortunately, the statistical likelihood of your getting victimized in any one of these areas is low. And your college will likely provide help for you to face many of these threats. But you do need to be aware of the possibilities.

The most obvious thing about your arrival will be the fact that you are with other people and in the midst of a new world, the world of college, with its seen and unseen pressures, lures, enticements, opportunities, and experiences. We will try to expose at least some of this inner working in later chapters. For starters, however, let's walk through the getting started process.

Getting Started

You had to be admitted to college; so you had to apply. Once accepted you had to pay (or arrange to pay) tuition; so you probably needed to see the financial aid office. Then you needed to register for classes; so you needed to see the registrar or your academic counselor. Then there is housing; so you needed to visit the housing office. Do you ever get hungry? You had to see student services for a meal ticket.

So you will begin to become a part of a complex (and sometimes complicated and confusing) community. These are some of the relationships in that community that you will need to maintain. You need to engage these relationships even if you don't agree with them or don't like the way they function. As a student, you will definitely be in those relationships.

Bureaucracy

First thing you meet is the institution itself—in the person of the people who work there. But you don't meet them as people, you meet them as registrar, or dean, or clerk, or janitor—sure, they're real people, but you meet them as employees of the college who are interested in a part of you—new student, with money to pay (or to borrow), or the new kid in room 222. Welcome to the bureaucracy.

There is the registration process that will involve filling out papers. This is about selecting particular classes. In some cases, you will have to qualify for specific classes—either because you have advanced abilities or because there is limited space. You will be assigned an advisor. This will be a person who primarily is responsible to see that you register for the classes that best suit your needs and work out a schedule that fits you. It may be that you have an advisor who is interested not just in your classes but also in your well-being, someone who cares for you. That would be a blessing.

One of my daughters went off to college wanting to study pre-med. She was assigned an advisor. He liked to talk. She was very good at listening. He liked to talk about himself. She listened. He was very sensitive—especially to his own problems—of which there were many. He was so busy talking that he didn't listen very much to her. Her plans to be a doctor fell on deaf ears. He enrolled her in courses that would not lead in the right direction for medicine. He was not a blessing. If your advisor is not a blessing, you can usually change and get another advisor.

Since most students are on some sort of financial aid, that needs to be attended to—again with the filling out of papers. The folks in financial aid should be of some help. They work for the college but the rules and guidelines they follow are set by the government and other aid providers. So there are forces at work behind the scenes. That may take time and be complicated; patience may be required. Did we mention that there are deadlines for all of these procedures?

You are in the world. It is complicated, full of rules and regulations, requirements and deadlines. You are in a world where the regulations are set by the college and even by other institutions, each of which has its own interests. Being in this world is complex and high maintenance. Success—in college, in your career, indeed, in any venture—requires vigilance. Skills developed here will help all through life.

Students

Then there are the people. This is where it gets interesting and fun. It is likely that you will encounter people that you have never seen before. Of course there will be a lot who are like you, but there will also be some who are really different: students from other parts of the country; students from other countries; students from your part of the country but totally different anyway. And lots of women.

"Race" and Ethnicity of Entering Freshmen[1]

Group	% in 2007	% in 2012
American Indian, Alaska Native	2.1%	2.6%
Asian-American, Asian	8.0%	10.7%
Native Hawaiian, Pacific Islander	1.1%	1.2%
African-American, Black	10.7%	11.5%
Mexican-American, Chicano	4.0%	7.7%
Puerto Rican	1.3%	1.6%
Other Latino	3.5%	5.2%
White/Caucasian	75.1%	69.7%
Other	3.4%	3.5%

Lots of Women![2]

Students	2011	2015 (est.)
All	19,712,690	21,081,610
Male	8,512,761	8,849,941
Female	11,199,927	12,231,672

If you live on campus, it is likely that your school will assign roommates; hope for the best. Sometimes that works out; sometimes it doesn't. If you and your assigned roommates do not hit it off right away, it may be a sign that you were not meant to be. Or not; don't necessarily rush to rash conclusions, like quitting school or demanding to move to another room. It may be that it will take awhile.

1. *CHE*, February 1, 2008, A23; *Almanac 2013–14*, 36. Note: "race" is not a biological fact; it is an idea people made up to distinguish themselves from people they considered "other." Check out what Scripture says in Galatians 3:28. (Also note that nearly 4 percent of all college students last year were from foreign countries: Institute of International Education, "Open Doors 2013.")

2. *Almanac 2011–12*, 32.

Are you an only child? You aren't any more—not with hundreds of other students in the same boat. Have you had your own room at home? Not anymore; college is about learning—in this case, learning how to get along with somebody else. Did your mother clean your room at home? Sorry, she isn't available any more. College may be your *alma mater* but that doesn't mean that the college will clean your dorm room. College means assuming all kinds of responsibilities you never had before.

If your roommate situation doesn't work out, you may just have to make changes. But it may surprise you. *Lots of stories are like mine: I and my college-assigned roommate Mike seemed an unlikely match on paper. He was an academically-focused Episcopalian from an elite Eastern prep school while I was a Baptist (would-be) jock from a public school in Chicago. But we have subsequently been lifelong friends, including serving as best man at each other's weddings. College promises many good surprises.*

Many of these new people will become close to you: roommates, suite mates, classmates, study mates, team mates, boyfriends, girlfriends, fiancés, even spouses. There is a good possibility that you are in the vicinity of your future life partner. *While researching to write this book, I tried to find out how many college students marry someone they meet in their own college. Astonishingly, there seem to be no statistics available on this question. Personal experience suggests, however, that this happens quite frequently. I once conducted a "quick and dirty" survey at the college where I worked. It turned out that 31 percent of the employees at the university who responded to my questionnaire had married someone who was also a student at the college they had attended.*

Example of *Value Added*—Better Marriages[3]

Level Educational Achievement	% of Married Who Divorce	% Still with First Spouse
Less than High School	58.8%	37.6%
High School Diploma	49.1%	48.6%
Bachelor's Degree	**29.8%**	**69.0%**

You will be in the same dorm, in the same class, in the same activity with many students with whom you may never be of the same mind or attitude—ever. You will wind up with friends who hold ideas radically different from your own. That is fully consistent with the Christian faith, which not only

3. See http://stats.bls.gov/opub/mir/2013/article/marriage-and-divorce-patterns-by gender-race-and-educational-attainment.

encourages us to test all things but also to truly engage hospitably with all others. Remember: God made all sorts of different beings. Remember Noah's ark? Remember boys and girls (big differences there). Diversity is not dangerous. Many colleges have gone out of their way to attract a diverse student body on the premise that differences will help everyone learn more and better. Soon you will meet your teachers—another set of different folks.

Political Views of 2012 Freshmen[4]

Far Left	2.8%
Liberal	26.8%
Middle-of-the-road	47.5%
Conservative	21.1%
Far Right	1.8%

Teachers

Since it is likely that the percentage of Christians working in American colleges is lower than the percentage of believers in the general population, it is unlikely that there will be overwhelming support for your Christian faith among the most influential people you meet—the professors. But they are not out to get you as some think. You don't have to feel that you need to argue with them and try to convert them to the Christian faith. Most of them won't even care whether you are a Christian, atheist, or whatever. As college faculty they have too much to do to spend any effort attacking your religious beliefs. But as a Christian you are free to share the hospitality God has shown you with others who may not fully appreciate you.

> *College faculty confess less belief in God and see religion as less important in their lives than the average American. Ironically, the percentage of college teachers who want their children to have religious training is almost identical with other Americans.*
>
> —TOBIN AND WEINBERG, *PROFILES*

But you might be surprised. There is a small but strong upsurge of college teachers across American colleges—church-related and public—who are committed to "Christian scholarship." That means that they—like you—take their Christian faith seriously, do their research and teaching in ways that take Christian faith as

4. *Almanac 2013–14, 36.*

true and important (without letting faith influence or change the content of their teaching), and are concerned about relating positively and helpfully to Christian students.

So although there might be only a few students like you and a few like those Christian teachers, you need not feel abandoned because Christ is with you always. You are not in college to be missionaries and witnesses to everyone there; your vocation—your call from God—is to be the best student you can be.

Blasts from the Past

The next important group of people you will meet are those you meet through your classes. They are the thinkers and writers who will offer you new ideas to consider. They will come to you with the invitation to hear, understand and accept their ideas in art, economics, politics, religion, science—every realm of human activity.

It is astonishing that these intellectual giants and thoughtful disturbers of the *status quo* from the past are almost never mentioned in many survival manuals designed to protect you as you sneak through college speedily without being touched by anything that happens in the classroom, lab, or library.[5] Don't be a stealth student—so invisible that your teachers don't suspect you are there. Make yourself known by doing good work and by engaging with the material your teachers and reading present you. Especially ask questions.

Along with new people come new experiences and ideas. And with them comes the responsibility of evaluating them to see if they can enrich

---

5. The primary names most often mentioned in many survival manuals are those whom the manual authors want you to fear or avoid: Karl Marx and Charles Darwin are the most mentioned. Among those almost never mentioned: Aristotle, Boccaccio, Cervantes, Dante, Einstein, Frost, Goethe, Hegel, Ibsen, James, Kierkegaard, Luther, Milton, Newton, Orwell, Pushkin, Quintilian, Rousseau, Shakespeare, Tolstoy, Unamuno, Voltaire, Wesley, Xenophon, Yeats, or Zeno. You would get the impression that authors of survival manuals hadn't heard or retained many good ideas in college.

While most survival manuals never mention the positive, constructive, or helpful things that students might learn in college, I was struck by one unique and notable exception. Quoting Christian students' struggles in college, one manual includes the following from a student named "Heather": "The more time I spent with thinkers and writers like St. Augustine, St. Thomas Aquinas, Dante, the Inklings, and Flannery O'Connor, the more my thought life was guided and deepened by faithful professors, the more my questions and (often petty) discontents were contextualized and judged by comparison." Gibson and Thomas, *Game Plan*, 90.

and deepen your faith or enable you to mature in your Christian vocation. This means that you will need to do more than simply tolerate new ideas.

To tolerate is to "live and let live." To tolerate is to "put up with" something by not taking it seriously. But Christians are called to hospitality—to engage deeply and consider seriously—not just "blow off" the ideas of others with whom they disagree. To do that responsibly, you need criteria that are good. Popular culture tells you what is "in." Political leaders and religious leaders point out what is "in." Business constantly reminds us what products and services are "in." The Christian is not "in" unless Jesus approves; and Jesus is not of this world.

Worldly Furniture

When I entered my assigned room for the first time as a freshman it had a light bulb; that was all. Mike and I had to go out and find furniture. The rest of the college was already there with all of the other stuff—library, classrooms, student union, etc. But we had to get our own furniture.

There is a lot of other "stuff" at college that you need to be aware of. You don't need to get comfortable with it or even get used to it. These are things that the college does not sponsor or endorse but nonetheless happen at college. They are things that have the potential to influence you and they offer opportunities for you to make good use of your freedom and your ability to make good choices—or to make really bad mistakes. Just as the college experience mirrors much of American culture, but at higher speed and with greater intensity, an amazing variety of activities beckon for the use of your free, out of class, non-structured time. These are opportunities to experiment with service activities, alcohol, drugs, a job, gambling, sex, church fellowship, and other activities. Choose with care. Some of these options are officially frowned upon but the general college environment provides plenty of opportunity and often silent encouragement to pursue them.

Preparation for these is important. "Just say 'No'" is not a particularly effective antidote to bad stuff since it is a response that lacks any grounding in reasons that are deeply persuasive to new college students.

I met Bob when he was a college junior. He had been in a large state university for two years. While there, instead of studying and attending class, he had played cards. He played cards for two years, every day, all day. When the news of his total academic catastrophe reached his parents, they made him change his school and his habits. In his case, it worked.

Liz did not fare so well. She was vivacious, popular, bright, a cheerleader, and was the best student in my ethics class. We were astonished to awake one

Sunday to news that she had died of alcohol poisoning earlier that morning. This tragedy was compounded by the fact that the campus treated this death as "one of those things" that happens in college. And life went on—except, of course, for her family.[6]

These promising students (both from church backgrounds) were *in* the world and into the world's offering. They were unprepared to be *not of* the world.

Living *in* a world in which these "temptation" activities are valued—considered cool, worth doing—means living surrounded by people who are also *of* a world in which concern for others is not as high a priority as concern for self. This is *in and of*—not a good combination.

The world is not just an idea. It is the good creation of God. It becomes bad only when we decide to remake it according to our own plans. (When Adam and Even tried to reorder the world in the Genesis story, it turned out to be a mess; we call their decision and actions sin.) This has not been a good idea; it has not worked; the world is in a lot of trouble precisely because we have tried to run it our way. When we are *in* the world and prefer our version of it to God's, then Jesus calls us to be *not of* the world we have distorted. Jesus understood that there are profound and major demarcations between *in* and *of*. He knows that we are *in* the world and he knows from his own tough experience what the world is like—its values, its commitments, its activities, its results. He knows that those are not what God intended for God's children. But Jesus lived *in* the world because God had sent him to this world in order to alert us to what it was that God really had intended for us. So Jesus lived—and encouraged us to live—*in* a complex combination of *in* but *not of* the world. We know about the *in* from human institutions, groups, traditions and individuals; we know about the *not of* the world from Jesus himself.

There are plenty of positive opportunities that you will find in college that are not stuck in that negativity of the secular college world. And it is not that hard to distinguish between the bad stuff and the good stuff.

---

6. Of course death is not "just one of those things." But I have noticed that campuses don't know what to do when a student dies. Once at each of the two schools I served as dean there was a student death—once from a car accident, the other from an alcohol overdose. In neither case did those in positions to address the causes in an effort to avoid future tragedies do anything about it.

Jesus Your Companion

It sometimes seems that Christians in college have been abandoned. Sometimes it looks like the church only cares for small children, adults who can make sizeable cash donations, and old people. Sometimes it looks like the church is willing for you to go off to college and just hopes you might return later—after you graduate, get married, establish a career, and have children to bring to church and money to put into the offering plate. In the words of two concerned authors, you may well feel like a member of an "abandoned generation"—benignly ignored by a church that isn't aware how entry into the college experience places Christians in jeopardy.[7] Or maybe churches just don't know what to do about it.

It is tragic that such a high percentage of Christian students do not hold on to the gift of faith.

Are you on your own? Is it up to you individually to sink or swim? Christians claim that their strength is in God and in Jesus Christ. Will Jesus be able to be the one to come to your aid in college? Can he get you through? Can the Lord of the universe indeed be the Lord of the universe-ity? Can the first-century teacher be your teacher in the college of the twenty-first century? Can Jesus Christ and all he is and all he does apply to the college experience? Is college on the faith journey, or is it a detour along which there is no protection and no help? Is college exempt from the Lordship of Jesus Christ? All these questions and more can be addressed to Jesus Christ, who is with you wherever you are, however alone you might feel.

> **Student Faith—Nuns or Nones?**
>
> *Are college students religious? Polls show that a quarter of eighteen to twenty-four year-olds are not religiously affiliated. When asked about their beliefs, many check the "none" option.*

By the grace of God, Jesus has promised to be with us always (Matt 28:20) and nothing is going to separate us from Christ (Rom 8:38–39). So how does that work—in practical terms—for you, the college student? Christ will be available in some way or another—in Scripture (more about that in chapter 6) and, yes, in the church. There will be a church near your school. It may not be quite sure what manner of person a "college student" is, but it is likely that, since it is in a college area, there will be a sensitivity for ministry to you. And if you are fortunate, there will be a campus ministry or a campus pastor whose main job is to provide support and fellowship on behalf of the whole of the church—which is, after all, Christ's body.

---

7. Willimon and Naylor, *Abandoned Generation.*

So here you are *in* the world, but trying to be *not of* it. And at least near the body of Christ, a church, a campus ministry, a supportive fellowship of fellow Christians. Most important, Jesus is your best bet because he himself is both *in* the world and *of* God's kingdom. He is *in* the world by the fact that he is totally and utterly human—flesh, bone, blood, hunger, tears, friends—you name it. But he is from God and therefore *of* another world, God's reality. So he has all bases covered, understanding who you are and what you are going through as you deal with your difficult walk.

What advice might you hear from Jesus of Nazareth, who "settled in" to his earthly life in ancient Palestine and who obeyed all human authority? Can he tell you about getting settled into the college experience but not be transformed (for the worse) by it? For starters, he might suggest that you would do well to submit to authority. This means obeying the rules, meeting deadlines. This can be done without embracing the values of the host community. This doesn't mean that you give in to whatever spirit and rules from your college environment press in powerfully upon you. It means that you get started slowly, thoughtfully, with an open mind and heart to what God might have in store for you in your college experience.

As a teen, I wanted to be special, to stand out and be noticed. So I did a lot of silly things. Finally, my mother sagely advised me that if I really wanted to be noticed, I would do well to seek other avenues than those of dressing or behaving outrageously. Pick something important, she urged; make your stand on something that will really have an impact. Her advice was certainly right on the mark. If you choose to ignore or deny authority, you will definitely be noticed—and definitely not taken seriously. And you will always lose. Remember, the establishment always wins. You can't beat city hall. Even Jesus was executed.

But, of course, that wasn't the end of the story, so . . .

Second, whether your college is hospitable to you or not, practice hospitality to others. Remember, all whom you meet are God's beloved; they are—each one—created in the very image of God. We all may just be passing by one another but God loves others as much as he loves you.

Third, focus on others; not on yourself. That can be pretty hard given the fact that you are the new one and the school has been there for decades if not hundreds of years. But as soon as you focus on yourself you are not only *in* but also *of* this world. You've already collapsed into a one-dimensional person and are not the rich person God made you to be.

Fourth, be ready to ask for help. Just because your focus is on others doesn't mean you can't ask for help for yourself. In fact, asking for help acknowledges that you aren't the focus, the center, the know-it-all. Asking for help means you will get things done more quickly than if you had to find them out for yourself. It will bring others who might not be in touch closer to you. Particularly ask questions in class. Asking questions will result in your learning better. It will blow your professor away. Especially if your questions are good ones. (Good questions are those that result from really wanting to learn but coming up against some difficulties; as you struggle with those obstacles and express what you *do* know and what is keeping you from knowing more your professor will enthusiastically come to your aid and you will be able to move ahead.)

Fifth and by no means least in importance, look for the Christian resources that are available. This can always be found in the study and application to your life of Scripture. In some cases that will be a campus minister or local church. Finding such good help will jump start your college career. Such a ministry can help you focus on the *of* to which you want to be attentive.

Writing to the Christians in Rome 2000 years ago, Paul guessed that his readers were both *in* and *of* this world. His exhortation to them (Rom 12:1–2) was that they not be conformed to the world but be transformed in their minds. In another passage, Paul tells his readers—including you—that you can have the "mind of Christ" (1 Cor 2:16). This, too, is a promise to you as a college student.

So, get settled *in*—but not too settled, because even though college is God's gift, it, like everything else in this world, has been compromised and has become *of* the world. But you are only *in* the world; you are finally and most truly *of* God. Now we need to see how to walk that fence between *in* and *of*.

Thought and Discussion Questions

1. What is the best thing about living *in* the world? What is the worst?

2. How would living *not of* the world help you?

3. How do we tell the difference between *in* and *not of* when it comes to the life of faith?

4. What do you foresee as the most unsettling thing in college?

5

Jesus, Your Best Teacher

"Man's most human characteristic is not his ability to learn, which he shares with many other species, but his ability to teach and store what others have developed and taught him."

—MARGARET MEAD, ANTHROPOLOGIST

"Jesus as educator has laid out for us the true life and has affected the education of the one who abides in Christ."

—CLEMENT OF ALEXANDRIA

Scripture Focus

JOHN 13:13

You call me Teacher and Lord—
and you are right, for that is what I am.

The popular view of Jesus today is that he was primarily a teacher. *After teaching introductory courses on the New Testament to college students for years I learned that the one thing that every student—Christian or not, churchgoer or not—is convinced that he or she knows about Jesus is that Jesus is a teacher. Sometimes even after a semester of study that is all that students know. If the only question on the final exam were "Who* was Jesus?" the only answer many students would give would be, "Jesus was a teacher who taught us what we need to do in order to get to heaven."

The view of Jesus as a teacher and only as a teacher is one of our most deeply entrenched (and inadequate) notions. If that were all Jesus was, we would be in big trouble because it would be crazy to think we could do enough of what he teaches to get a passing grade.

Yes, everybody knows that Jesus is a teacher. But a lot of folks don't take him seriously as teacher. So there is frequently a backup position where they figure that Jesus—in some secondary role as Savior or Lamb of God— has done everything for us (i.e., redeemed us from sin) so that we are now free to roam about the world and do as we please.

Whoa! While it is true that Jesus, as Savior, "saves" us from sin, that is nowhere near the end of things. The one act of accepting Jesus or receiving baptism to join the church does not license us to go off on our own to whatever it is we want to do. Rather it is simply the beginning of a lifelong relationship in which we find Jesus encountering us over and over again in many new ways. That is where Jesus fits into our lives as a teacher—as the Teacher. As we seek to live out our faith relationship with God through Jesus, it is Jesus who provides the best directions. Think of *Jesus the Teacher* as the operations manual for your life as a Christian. You commit to that new life, and *then* look to the instructions for putting the pieces of that new life in the right places. So Jesus the Teacher must be taken seriously.

But don't make the mistake of some who take Jesus only as a teacher. They think that Jesus is *only* a teacher and they see their faith as something that is only definable in terms of following Jesus' orders. They base their hopes on their own success in obeying the Teacher's teaching.

Is there a middle ground—some way to take Jesus the Teacher seriously but not only as the giver of orders we follow on our own? Seeing him as Teacher and Lord seems to be just the right combination. He is a teacher with real authority.

Can we pray: "*Lord Jesus, be my Teacher*"? Can we be more explicit? "*Lord Jesus, be my Teacher in college. Amen.*"

Introduction: College Teachers

Being a teacher is a wonderful life. Most teachers love what they do. Most teachers respond to the call to teach out of love. They love students or they love the subject matter that they study and they work hard to pass on that information and their enthusiasm for the subject to students. They must love it because it certainly doesn't pay very well! Still, there are terrific benefits to being a teacher that are not found in other professions. On the light side, one colleague used to say there were three great reasons to be a teacher: June, July, and August. On the serious side, there is the constantly renewed opportunity to interact with students and learn with them.

You might have been thinking that students are the heart of college and that your social life with your peers was what it would be all about. You can have peers anywhere—grade school, high school, the military, just about any job. But in college—when you truly take it seriously—your important peer relationships are developed in the context of a larger community, the leaders of which are faculty.

Teachers are really the heart of any college. What teachers do with students—in and out of the classroom—is the heart of the college experience. Teachers gather, organize, and transmit information. Good teachers create an environment in which students get excited about a topic and truly learn something.

Colleges try to select the best teachers that they can. Colleges also work at trying to make sure that the teachers stay up-to-date in their subject and are effective in teaching students. Usually colleges have systems in place to monitor teacher performance. Students are even asked to evaluate instructors—something you probably never did in K-12.

You will spend forty to fifty hours with a teacher during a typical one-semester class. During that time surprising things can happen. Since these teachers are specialists in their subject areas they can help you see what you never had seen before. *The student interested only in the sport that brought him to college discovered a whole new world in his Shakespeare class and committed himself to a career in teaching.* That is not an unusual story.

Teachers do more than teach. If you are fortunate, you may find a teacher who truly cares for you as more than just a student in a class. *The final exam in my college freshman biology class was scheduled for the very last slot in the two-week exam period; it was on Saturday night! In January! It was snowing! About an hour into the exam, the professor came into the room with a crate of refreshments for us; what a welcome act of hospitality on an otherwise gloomy Saturday night.*

A student whose schooling had been interrupted by the death of her sister returned to school still grieving and with anxiety over having missed so many classes. She was greeted at her room by a bouquet of roses from her major professor.

Teachers aren't just teachers. In their spare time, when they are not teaching, they are often actually real human beings—just regular folks, with

families and hobbies, political opinions or surprising tastes. The other parts
of their lives can be interesting and mysterious.

*One applicant I interviewed for a teaching position claimed that he held
the* Guinness Book of World Records *mark for doing the highest number of
consecutive pushups. Another, a zoologist, revealed that he liked to make beer
in his apartment. One of my own Bible teachers was an expert on the history
of submarines in World War I. I learned a lot about these teachers as human
beings from these glimpses into their personal lives.*

In the end, however, the commitment of teachers is to impart their information and then issue their judgment on your performance in the form
of a grade. But teachers' commitment to students is only part of their commitment. They have additional commitments to the college that employs
them, and finally and perhaps most energetically to their subject matter or
professional field of study. In this era of competition, their commitment
to their profession can be intense. At times the audience that they work
hardest to impress consists of other teachers in their discipline. They have
this commitment in order to ensure salary increases, promotions, and even
securing better jobs at other schools. So if a teacher seems preoccupied and
not as sensitive to your needs as you might wish, it may be that his "teacher
side" is overwhelmed by one of his other "non-teacher sides."

With all these things going on, most teachers are not going to harass
you for your Christian faith. If your professor has to get lectures ready, teach
classes, grade papers, serve on college committees, advise students, do research so she can write and publish papers and books and still have time
to go on a date with a spouse, attend a child's soccer game, and mow the
lawn—there will be little energy left to "harass or humiliate students."[1]

The most important thing you want to know about your teachers has
to do with how they will treat you. Will they tell the truth? Will they teach
the *whole* truth? Do they *live* according to what and how they teach? Will
they have time for *you*? How will they deal with you if you *don't learn*?[2]

---

1. Most college survival manuals have little to say about professors. Some vilify
them: David Wheaton, in *University of Destruction,* says that professors "want to dis-
mantle your Christian faith [89]. . . [are] proud . . . liars [90–91] . . . their very nature is
to teach what is contrary to God and His Word [94] . . . You may be mocked, shamed,
ridiculed, persecuted, and embarrassed by your professor . . . even given a lower grade
[101]." Abby Nye, in *Fish Out of Water,* tells her readers to prepare for "open hostility
and ridicule [10] . . .[and] to face the intimidation of the professor [51] . . . and far-left
academia nuts [77]." In most manuals, faculty get virtually no positive consideration.

2. Information in the insets about the religious beliefs of faculty is available on the
Internet: www.jewishresearch.org/PDFs2/FacultyReligion07.pdf. See also Tobin and
Weinberg, *Profiles of the American University.*

Teachers give information, tell you what to do, then evaluate you to see if you can do it. One aspect of your commitment to learning is that you believe you are actually capable of doing what a teacher teaches you to do. But you also know from practical experience that that is not always possible. If you don't learn the material, even the most caring teacher will have to issue a failing grade. That is what college teachers do.

If you want a teacher who cares for *you,* enables *you,* and gives *you* a whole, integrated, and coherent instruction on life, human teachers are generally not up to the job. You are unlikely to find one who is both professionally qualified for college teaching and personally disposed to serve the individual needs of all of his students. Is there anything you can do about this?

Don't think you are going to change your teacher. Not only is that not likely; it is not your job. A lot of the survival manuals written for Christians make a couple of mistakes on this particular topic. First, they scare you into believing that most of your teachers are out to destroy your faith by attacking the Christian religion and publicly embarrassing you. Second, they lay a burden on Christian students to change (witness to, evangelize, and even convert) these same professors. The truth is that statistics show there is less religiosity among college faculty than among the population in general. But as we indicated, those college teachers have a lot more important things on their minds than de-Christianizing college kids. And while the truth is that Christians are to "let their light shine" before others, you are first and foremost called to be a student and have as your number one responsibility to love God with all your mind—that means to focus on your studies.

In college you do get to pick your teachers. This is an old idea. Centuries ago, in the infancy of the modern college, teachers had to prove their worth to students, not to school boards or accrediting agencies. If—in the mind of the students—the teacher failed to do his job, students might refuse to pay their fees and abandon the teacher for another instructor. Students voted with their feet.

Then times changed and teachers came to be evaluated by school boards, regents, state regulations, professional standards instead of by students. *I recall my years as a student in elementary school—good old Irving Park Elementary. I would have known—had I thought of it while in kindergarten—who my teacher would be in every grade. Some were good and some were not so good. It didn't matter. Since none of them ever moved, retired, or even died, I was foreordained to sit at the feet of whoever was there. I had no choice. Ever.*

Of course in college, the bigger the school, the more possibility of choice in picking a professor. When you go to college, you finally will have some real options and can usually choose the teachers you want. At some large schools, the students even publish evaluations of teachers to help in your selection process. This possibility of choosing enables you to look for the easiest teacher, the most entertaining one, the smartest one, the most respected one. It also reminds you that you are now free to choose with regard to larger issues. The most important free choice is: What will be the authority to which you will submit your life?

Jesus, the Teacher for the College Experience

One of the most important things you do in college is to choose your authorities. This is probably the first time in your life that you can freely choose who or what it is that you will acknowledge as the authority. This is a free choice and a profoundly important one. If you have chosen Christ, you have chosen the best authority figure and the best Teacher. Someone might object that the college experience, with its claim to supply teachers for multiple subjects, is simply too big and complex to allow you to acknowledge only one teacher.

Others might argue that Jesus has no business at college in the first place. After all, he didn't even graduate from high school! Jesus would be unqualified by any current standard used in hiring college teachers. He lacks any degree; he has no specialty—unless it is religion and that is not a subject of great importance in most college curricula. How less qualified could anyone be? So what does he have going?

Let's look at it the way college folks might look at a topic—as something to think about in a serious and organized way—as a discipline like English or history. For many topics that we study, the Greek language has provided the descriptive terminology. The names of many disciplines studied in the college curriculum are formed from the Greek name of the subject plus the addition of the word *logy*, from the Greek word for *word*.

So, for example, the study of humanity (or man) is given a label constructed of the Greek term for man (*anthropos*) and the Greek for "the word about" (*logy*), hence the "word" about humans: anthropo+logy. So biology, from the word for life (*bios*); cardiology, from the word for heart (*kardia*); dermatology, from the word for skin (*dermis*); pharmacology, from the word for drug (*pharmacon*); geology, from the word for earth (*geo*); herpetology, from the word for snake (*herpetos*); ichtheology, from the word for fish (*ichthyus*) . . . You get the idea.

And how about theology, from the word for God (*theos*)? Such a study would involve systematic thinking about what you know and/or what you believe about God. Finally, you come to Christology, the "word about (Jesus) Christ." When you do Christology you are organizing your thoughts around the topic of the very special nature of Jesus. This involves using the special vocabulary the church uses to describe Jesus.

The following is a list of many of the Christological titles found for Jesus in the New Testament. You could pause at each title and "unpack" it to meditate on how that particular title either expresses what you already experience in Jesus or what it opens up to you about his particular relevance for your life in college. For now, just run your eyes over the partial list and be amazed at the audacity of the claims and the number of possibilities. (In the chapters that follow, we will examine in detail a number of these Christologies, or ways to think about Jesus, that are particularly applicable to the college situation.)

> ### Word For The Chapter
>
> Christology (n.)—a title, name, or "nickname" given to Jesus to help us understand better the richness of who he was.

Almighty (Rev 1:8)
Alpha and Omega (Rev 1:8; 21:6; 22:13)
Apostle (Heb 3:1)
Author of Life (Acts 3:15)
Bread of Life (John 6:35, 41, 48)
Bright Morning Star (Rev 22:16)
Christ (Matt 1:1 and 613 more times)
Cornerstone (Eph 2:20)
Counselor (Isa 9:6)
Faithful Witness (Rev 1:5)
First born of the Dead (Rev 1:4)
Gate (John 10:7)
God (John 20:28)
Good Shepherd (John 10:11, 14)
High Priest (Hebrews 8 times)
Is, Was, and Is to Come (Rev 1:8)
Lamb of God (John 1:29)
Life (John 11:25)
Living Bread (John 6:51)
Lord (Luke 22:49 and [about] 600 more times)
King of the Jews (Matt 2:2; 27:37)
Master (Luke 17:13 and others)
Messiah (John 1:41; 4:25)
Passover (1 Cor 5:7)

Peace (Eph 2:14); Prince of Peace (Isa 9:6)
Pioneer and Perfecter of the Faith (Heb 12:2)
Prophet (Matt 21:11)
Rabbi (John 1:49)
Resurrection (John 11:25)
Rock (1 Cor 10:4)
Root and Offspring of David (Rev 22:16)
Ruler of the Kings of the Earth (Rev 1:5)
Son of David (Matt 1:1 and numerous)
Son of God (Matt 14:33 and numerous)
Son of Man (Matt 8:20 and numerous)
Truth (John 14:6)
Vine (John 15:1, 5)
Way (John 14:6)

And you need not confine your Christology just to the language explicit in the New Testament. Faithful Christians continue to address Jesus with ever new titles as they find new ways to appreciate him, for example, in hymns ("Lord of the Dance" or "Lover of My Soul"), pop music ("Bridge Over Troubled Water"[3]), poetry ("Hound of Heaven"[4]), or modern theology ("Man for Others"[5]). Not every title suggested has stuck,[6] but the time-honored importance of Christology encourages you to be free to experiment and seek titles that express Jesus' significance for you. The point is that Jesus is such a powerful and multifaceted being that his significance can't be captured in only one title or label. In fact, we find it impossible to fully describe him even using many labels. So whenever you think of Jesus as Teacher, you do two things: you remind yourself of the instructions and the words he utters as Teacher for your benefit, and you also keep in mind all of the other Christological functions he continues to fulfill. In other words, just because you are taking Jesus Christ with utmost seriousness as the Teacher in this book does not mean that you don't take him with utmost seriousness at the same time as you remember he is Savior, Lord, Shepherd, Lamb of God, etc.

The first word Jesus is reported as saying publicly in the Gospels is, "Repent." Actually, "Repent, and believe in the good news" is the whole

3. This Simon and Garfunkel song topped the charts in early 1970. Though not written about Jesus, the title lends itself as an apt description of who/what Jesus is.

4. The title of a poem by British writer Francis Thompson, written before his death in 1907. It also became the title of several Christian rock songs in recent years.

5. A specifically Christological title used by Dietrich Bonhoeffer, the German theologian condemned and hanged for his complicity in the plot to kill Hitler near the end of World War II. *Letters and Papers*, 381.

6. For instance: "The World's Greatest Salesman."

sentence in his first public utterance (Mark 1:15). He gave a call to believe, a call to faith. But remember that faith has substance and content. Despite the fact that Jesus' very first public word was, "Repent," don't let such a religious sounding word conjure up some wild-eyed, pulpit-pounding weirdo. The word *repent* is a translation of the original Greek word which means "change of mind." Jesus' first word was a call to a change of mind to an entirely new worldview.

It is a way of saying it is necessary to "unlearn" a lot of stuff you learned from school, TV, movies, family, friends, and American culture in general.

For instance:

- the world teaches people to be obedient to the rules; Jesus dispensed with the rules in favor of being merciful and kind and helpful—and got killed by a coalition of Romans and Jews.

- the world teaches people to be exclusive and to ignore or reject those who fail to fit our criteria for acceptance; Jesus practiced inclusivity—and was condemned by the Jewish leaders keen to protect their group.

- the world teaches prudence and care for oneself; Jesus taught love, actively loved others—and was hated by the "good" people who ran the country.

- the world teaches that power comes from the muzzle of a gun; Jesus taught the kingdom of God—and was killed on the duly approved instrument of capital punishment employed by those in power (a cross).

- American culture wants us to view ourselves as consumers; Christ sees us as givers.

- American culture wants us to see ourselves as "number one"; Christ sees us as servants.

- We are taught—in the college experience—to see ourselves as acquiring knowledge to gain power and mastery; Christ sees us as known by God in order to be enabled to be vulnerable to others in loving them by using our skills.

Jesus was executed because he was thinking differently. But God raised him from death's grip and, according to Paul (Col 3:10), God is renewing *our* minds and assures us that we have the "mind of Christ" (1 Cor 2:16). What does this mind-renewal mean? At the least it means that you think differently or think new things. Jesus gives you something new with which to furnish your renewed mind. He gives you a new way to think and a new subject matter to think about. In fact, the largest part of his teaching was on the subject of *the kingdom of God*. In his many parables, he described what it would be like if God were truly in charge of everything. In his miracles he made that "God in charge" notion actually happen. In his confrontations with religious, political, and cultural leaders, he showed what it is that God wants as he reveals human leaders in their selfish, partial, and perverse plans.

In Jesus' teachings, he sets forth a perspective, a framework that is God-oriented and within which you can make sense out of all of the details and parts and partial truths you learn from your human teachers. Their truths are partial truths because they come from the useful and correct, but partial, perspective of narrow man-made disciplines (e.g., sociology or chemistry or algebra). It is only in Christ that you can grasp a coherent and meaningful wholeness in which all that you learn can take on meaning in relation to everything else.

> **Worldview**
>
> *—a personal and at the same time comprehensive conception of all things: how they fit together, make sense, and provide answers to all of your questions. (If you want to impress, use the more popular German word,* Weltanschauung.*)*

The practically applicable contribution that Jesus as Teacher makes to your college education is that he reminds you how you can use what you learn to meet God's goal for your lives in employing your skills to love others in concrete and helpful ways.

The personal application you experience with Jesus as the one Teacher is that here is a teacher who will love you forever, one who will not abandon or flunk you when you fail. He is patient, longsuffering, and loving. Better than any human teacher.

Who would not want Jesus as their most important teacher? He provides a God-focus for your life; he makes everything fit together and make sense; he shows you the most ethical and loving application of what you learn; and he is the one teacher who will never abandon you.

What Does That Make Us?

Christologies such as Messiah, Son of God, Bread of Life, and Pioneer and Perfecter of our Faith tell what Jesus has done for us. Lamb of God, for instance, clearly refers to Jesus' death on the cross. When Jesus says, "I am the resurrection and the life" (John 11:25), he is reminding us of his conquest of death on our behalf. When the author of the Letter to the Hebrews calls him a High Priest, it is the remarkable *double* reference to Jesus' (a) *sacrifice* of

(b) *himself* for us. All Christologies are about Jesus; most are about what *he* has done for us. We are the passive recipients of Jesus' work.

With Teacher as an important Christology, Jesus is still active, but in a different role. And what does that make you? You become an active recipient in faith. You are now to think through what you are to do as a recipient, as a changed being, as a disciple, as a citizen of the kingdom of God. Having this happen in the college setting couldn't be better. Here you are, doing all that learning and thinking anyway and with all the resources of college teachers and even your peers available. What better things to think about than the most important things of all?[7]

It cannot be emphasized too strongly that if you are going to college you are *not* dropping out of the Christian life. You are *not* exempting yourself from dependence on God, and you are *not* striking out totally on your own on the odd assumption that you can do it all yourself. God claims you in all that you do. Therefore, no matter how much it depends on you—and in college pretty much everything does—you still can depend on him.

Jesus the Teacher taught a great deal that can help you during your college tenure. While the teachings of Jesus are numerous and compelling in many ways, we can best illustrate his significance as Teacher and the significance of his teaching by looking at an example—the kingdom of God.

Kingdom of God

From among a number of possible themes, "the kingdom of God" or "kingdom of Heaven" is one of the most appropriate to the concerns of those wanting to be faithful in their calling in the college experience. Why? Simply put, the college experience is intended to prepare you to function effectively in American life, obedient to the values, hopes, dreams and mores of popular American culture. But that culture is not identical with the Christian faith, nor is America the kingdom of God.

Jesus initiated his public ministry by announcing the imminent arrival of the kingdom of God, an arrival that he cautioned his listeners to take seriously enough to "Repent and believe in the good news" (Mark 1:15). The kingdom of God is the rule of God, his active power real and visible in the world. We become part of it when we acknowledge the power of God

---

7. Buckley, *The Catholic University*, 17–20, describes "Christ as paradigm" and one in whom we most fully can understand both things human and things divine. Buckley quotes Blaise Pascal: "Not only do we understand God only through Jesus Christ, but we understand ourselves only through Jesus Christ. We understand life and death only through Jesus Christ. Outside of Jesus Christ we do not know what life is, nor death, nor God, nor ourselves."

and take God more seriously than we do any other power. God's kingdom or rule has multiple dimensions as it claims governance over our lives in their social, economic, political, and intellectual functions.

Jesus illustrated the notion of the kingdom in his parables—stories that are both numerous and diverse. The Gospels retell dozens of parables, most of which Jesus introduces with, "The kingdom of God is like . . ." followed by an illustration. Parables provide a suggestive and creative richness to the idea of *what it would be like if God were really accepted as being in charge in the world.* Each parable gives a snapshot that sheds some light on that new idea. In his miracles and in his death and resurrection, Jesus demonstrates the kingdom of God in action as God's power breaks in again and again to realms previously governed by powers that have not acknowledged God's ultimate sovereignty.

Let's look at two parables as examples, one fairly simple and understandable, the other more complex and challenging. In Matthew 13:45–46 Jesus tells the following parable:

> Again, the kingdom of heaven is like a merchant in search of fine pearls; on finding one pearl of great value, he went and sold all that he had and bought it.

You can understand this story. A merchant would want to have the best merchandise. He would be experienced enough to know what was the best. So you are not particularly surprised to hear that this merchant "bet the farm" on the one "pearl of great value" in order to get the absolutely and unparalleled best. Admittedly this is a bit of a gamble on the part of the businessman, but you have heard stories where people have made this kind of a gamble, sometimes losing but sometimes winning. And when they won, they were extraordinarily well off. So you can understand the story even if you wouldn't do it yourself.

When Jesus uses this story to lead his listeners to think about the kingdom of Heaven it is not hard to follow him. What do you think that he is trying to get you to understand? Probably that the kingdom of Heaven is so absolutely extraordinary that it is worth giving up everything to get (or to get into) it. That's how much it is worth: everything. This is a parable that says something about the kingdom of Heaven and about what an appropriate response on your part would be. But what is there about that kingdom that makes it so valuable? The answer to that question is provided by many other parables that illustrate in detail what there is about the kingdom of God that you would find compelling.

A parable that offers one marvelous insight is the parable of the vineyard owner in Matthew 20:1–15. This is a story that you can understand—to a point:

For the kingdom of heaven is like a landowner who went out early in the morning to hire laborers for his vineyard. After agreeing with the laborers for the usual daily wage, he sent them into his vineyard. When he went out about nine o'clock, he saw others standing idle in the marketplace; and he said to them, "You also go into the vineyard, and I will pay you whatever is right." So they went. When he went out again about noon and about three o'clock, he did the same. And about five o'clock he went out and found others standing around; and he said to them, "Why are you standing here idle all day?" They said to him, "Because no one has hired us." He said to them, "You also go into the vineyard." When evening came, the owner of the vineyard said to his manager, "Call the laborers and give them their pay, beginning with the last and then going to the first." When those hired about five o'clock came, each of them received the usual daily wage. Now when the first came, they thought they would receive more; but each of them also received the usual daily wage. And when they received it, they grumbled against the landowner, saying, "These last worked only one hour, and you have made them equal to us who have borne the burden of the day and the scorching heat." But he replied to one of them, "Friend, I am doing you no wrong; did you not agree with me for the usual daily wage? Take what belongs to you and go; I choose to give to this last the same as I give to you. Am I not allowed to do what I choose with what belongs to me? Or are you envious because I am generous?"

Here is the easy part. A landowner is confronted with the compelling reality that his crop must be harvested—*now*! Perhaps it is acutely time sensitive, perhaps bad weather is on the way, perhaps the market is just right. In any case, he has got to get the crop in immediately. So he goes out to hire day laborers to do the harvest. Soon it becomes clear that the workers hired early aren't sufficient to complete the work. So he goes out later and hires more pickers. Again, they aren't enough to finish the job. So he goes out a third and a fourth time. Finally, late in the afternoon he hires still more. (Note that the fellows he finds standing around have come out looking for work and no one has hired them. They are in danger of having to go home with *no* money.) So far so good. You can probably assume that the harvest is completed.

But when it comes time to pay the workers, he begins with those hired last and pays them *a full day's wages!* That is hard to understand—especially for those who began working early and worked through the hottest part of the day. They complain but the landowner points out that it's his money and he wants to pay everyone who worked a full daily wage. This mind-boggling aspect of the story (from an American's capitalistic point of view) is surely the point of the parable. In the kingdom of God the landowner, who could be God, doesn't operate by our rules and expectations. In the kingdom of God the rest of us, who could be the workers, don't get what we *deserve* but what we *need*. Indeed, throughout the whole of Jesus' ministry and in many of his parables, people get what they need (healing, forgiveness, inclusion) and not what they deserve. So here we have another example of Jesus' effort to illustrate a concept—the kingdom or rule of God, a concept that we cannot remotely comprehend—with a story that we can (sort of) understand. The kingdom of God [=Heaven] does not fit our expectations. For those in need, the kingdom of God *exceeds* their expectations!

As a college student, studying the world from perspectives informed by the kingdom of God would be the most faithful approach a Christian could use. And it would place what you study in a unique light. When Jesus is understood as the proclaimer of the kingdom of God, and when he is also recognized to be one who exposed the lies, failures, and inadequacies of the kingdoms that oppose the kingdom of God, exciting things happen. Students are enabled to reflect more profoundly on their own lives and on the world in which they live. Hearing Jesus focus on the kingdom of God can clarify your learning. It can place all theories and knowledge in a new context. It can provide an approach to inquiry not available elsewhere. It can place the object of your study in a frame of reference that raises the question of ultimate significance. This *was* Jesus' theme, according to the Gospels, and it continues to be his theme in your life.

You may learn human anatomy from your lab instructor but you know what humans are all about from Jesus. You may research Russian history using written records but you know that Christ is at history's center and will finally be its judge. You may enhance your computing skills in a high-tech lab environment but you know that the Gospel is the most important message ever communicated. Your job is to remember that and work at fitting things together within that Christological framework.

Know Jesus Better . . .
Try a *Daily Bible Study*

To get a close-up and personal look at Jesus the Teacher, a daily reading of the Gospel of Matthew would be excellent. This Gospel is often considered the "teaching Gospel" since it focuses so much on Jesus the Teacher and his teachings. You can divide it up into small chunks (5–20 verses per day) and let it dialogue with you on issues you encounter in your college experience.

Jesus provides the direction for how you are to use what you learn—the skills, techniques, abilities, theories. Remembering that you are to love your neighbor (including your enemies) as yourself, Jesus the Teacher reminds you that each new accomplishment you absorb or develop is for the benefit of others.

Jesus gives you the furnishings for your renewed mind and the hints to develop those thoughts in the right direction. As Teacher he invites your imaginative engagement and application. Jesus teaches that you help others—for example, in the parable of the Good Samaritan or the command to give to those who ask. Are those teachings narrowly and literally limited? Are you only to help those literally beaten and lying by the side of the road going from Jerusalem to Jericho or those who specifically ask for your cloak? (Who wears a "cloak" today anyway?) Surely the Savior of the world who died for all on the cross would not have offered concrete directive that were so narrow and time-bound as to no longer be applicable. You are given resources to help stretch your Christian imagination and live out Jesus' teaching. Your job, as it was for the disciples in the Gospel of John, is to *remember* what Jesus has said and done and then apply that to the moment in which you now find yourself.

Finally, we all need regular reminders that we are disciples and, like the original disciples, are not abandoned to be the individuals that our American culture prefers. We are all in this together. Just as there are many Christologies—descriptions of Jesus—so there are a number of New Testament images of disciples. We call those descriptions or pictures ecclesiologies—from the words for church (*ecclesia*) and *logy*. The body of Christ is a collective, a "priesthood of believers" or "family" or church. All of these descriptions imply a community that has its solidarity in Christ and not in geography, class, race, or team colors. Labels like "saints" and "aliens" suggest that we are not to consider ourselves "at home" in the world as defined by popular American culture. These descriptions urge us to reexamine our self-concepts and we can only do this kind of discipleship thinking if we are in a new frame of mind.

We are reminded that Jesus invites everyone to leave the secular world and accept his invitation to the kingdom of God. That is not simply a momentary and individual agreement on your part to say "okay" to Jesus for a brief "spiritual getaway" from which you immediately return to a life defined by the secular world. It is a major move across clearly marked borders from one "kingdom" to another, from a world of darkness to a world illuminated by Jesus Christ (Col 1:13). We will be examining that new life in detail through the rest of this manual. For the moment, let's commit ourselves to Jesus *the* Teacher.

You have been gifted with a new nature "which is being renewed in knowledge according to the image of its creator" (Col 3:10). This is one of the results of your new life in Christ. The renewal of your nature is a gift of God and it is constantly under re-creation *in knowledge*, a knowledge that is the reflection of God the creator. A re-created nature, "renewed in knowledge," is a marvelous gift for anyone going to college. This is not a guarantee that Christians are smarter than other folks or that you will learn more easily. Rather it suggests is that you are redirected in a way that serves God and all God's creatures.

These have been hints of ways in which Jesus Christ can function as a concrete resource—indeed, as your *Teacher*—in the college experience. He is the means by which you measure that experience and he points in the direction of its best use in your Christian walk. With such a start and the assurance that he is always with you in all of his Christological roles, you can go into the college experience with confidence. This *Teacher* speaks through Scripture and provides you with the whole armor of the Christian tradition. He offers these resources for your continuous growth as a Christian in the college experience. No matter how far those resources take you, their power derives from Jesus, who is at their core and who shows their use. He is truly Teacher and Lord.

Thought and Discussion Questions:

1. Which Christological title is the most meaningful one for you? Which one do you consider the most accurate or true? Has that changed for you over time?

2. Since Jesus did not give a complete teaching on every topic you will face, how can you extend what he did teach to cover what he did not teach (use of birth control, genetic engineering, drone warfare, etc.)? If you *can* do that, *how* do you do it?

3. How can a teacher be a savior?

4. Debate: One group lists a teaching of Jesus; the other side tells how obeying it in today's world might work out.

5. Who is the best teacher you ever had and what were his/her main characteristics? How does that teacher compare with Jesus the Teacher?

6. Can you imagine a new Christological title or label (not mentioned in this chapter) that tells something important about Jesus?

6

Scripture—Your Best Text

Scripture focus

2 TIMOTHY 3:16–17

All scripture is inspired by God and is useful for teaching, for reproof, for correction, and for training in righteousness, so that everyone who belongs to God may be proficient, equipped for every good work.

Paul's letters to Timothy and Titus contain a lot of practical advice from an older, experienced Christian to young persons just entering Christian service in a harsh environment. Christians were up against it. The earliest believers lived in eager anticipation of the immediate return of Christ to wrap things up in this old world and to inaugurate something totally new. Instead, as the years passed, and Christ's return delayed, Christians were required to think more and more about the mundane issues of family, jobs, survival, and getting along with the institutions that disliked them.

Paul's advice hangs on the two hooks of good education: theory and practice. You need to have right ideas to begin with. Then those ideas must be put into practice. When the "rubber hits the road" the wheels sometimes come off. So there is need for correction and its stronger form, rebuke.

Paul assumes that Timothy will be attentive to training and receptive to rebuke. All this is given in love for the purpose of getting the new Christians to do what Jesus had called for in the great commandment: love God and love neighbor.

When you start your Christian life, you don't automatically know what Christian teaching and Christian practice is, so instruction is necessary and everyone can benefit from regular trips "back to the drawing board." The Scriptures to which Paul refers here are the writings of the Old Testament. Paul and other early Christians wrote more, especially Gospels to show us Jesus and letters that applied the new Christian faith to specific challenges faced by believers. These Christian writings are our New Testament. We have received all of these Scriptures with God's blessings and thanks to the struggles of the earliest Christians. We can ill afford not to study them.

Prayer: God, help me to be serious about my studies—especially the study of your Word. Amen.

Introduction: So Many Books!

The last chapter began by affirming that the heart of the college was the faculty—the teachers. That is true. It can also be argued that the heart of the college is found in the books. Books to read for class. Books in the library. Everything in the library! With the magic of electronics, even the smallest of college libraries can connect to systems that will bring literally millions of additional documents to the computer screen in seconds. Such riches in books, journals, news reports, articles, and other items mean that virtually all the facts, theories, and wisdom of all the ages are accessible.

So perhaps your first stop at school ought to be the library. It is a resource with which you will want to familiarize yourself at leisure. It will bring you pretty much any information you might want. Someone joked that it was like "Amazon.com on steroids."

Browsing there before you get to class can be helpful because once you are in class the work can become overwhelming. As soon as classes start, your selection of reading materials will narrow dramatically due to a staggering amount of assigned material for your classes. But wandering about in the quiet of the library, you are in charge. You can skip what you will, stop where you choose, and familiarize yourself with some of the wonderful possibilities.

One of the professor's main tasks is to select just the right study materials for each class. It should be up-to-date, attractive, easy to read, good at conveying the material, and not terribly expensive. And it should encourage a positive feeling toward the class's subject matter on the part of the student. It is an indispensable complement to the teacher. She can use it as a foil to argue against or as a means of extending her content delivery outside of class. Students may want to hold onto a good text as a resource for use later in life—on the job, pursuing a hobby, or for lifelong learning. The textbook should be a resource that helps the student make sense of the subject matter—especially at those points where the professor may not explain things fully.

Early in the semester, you will encounter textbook shock. So much to read! And sticker shock: these are expensive books! But each book goes deep into its subject, revealing so much more about the subject than you ever dreamt existed. Welcome to college: you will be learning a great deal about every different subject, with doors of interest and opportunity opening at nearly every page turn.

> ### Lots to Read!
> "*But these are written so that you may come to believe that Jesus is the Messiah, the Son of God, and that through believing you may have life in his name.*"
> JOHN 20:31

This is exciting stuff. The reality of college is that there is way too much to read. And even if you could read everything that all your professors assigned or recommended, it would not come close to covering all there still is out there to read! However, in the course of all this reading you may stumble upon things that profoundly change your thinking—those four or five books that will become your favorites and to which you will return again and again for entertainment, more information, or new questions.

What Is Missing?

Is there anything lacking in this treasure house of books, articles, films, microfiche, computer files, Internet sites, YouTube—even Twitter and Facebook—that you will use in college? What will you choose as the text for the most important task of all—living your life? Given the fact that you will grow and change and the world will certainly change, is there a textbook or some "how to do it" manual that will prepare and guide you through your whole life with its certainties and uncertainties? Let's face it—you probably don't know all you need to know yet about living the Christian life faithfully. Who does?

The Christian Scriptures contain a comprehensive message that covers pretty much all that there is to life. The college courses you take can fill in a lot of the details, but Scripture contains the big picture—the comprehensive world view of how everything comes from and goes to God and fits together in him. It provides a comprehensive framework within which everything has its appropriate place and where everything makes sense. What is Scripture? Why is it the best textbook? How should you use it?

The Hebrew Scriptures begin with the Law, or the Torah (= God's guide or words of direction for his people). Later, Psalm 119 praises those Words of God and shows how seriously the psalmist treated that expression of God's will. Here are some of the verbs that describe the psalmist's attention to God's word/ promise/law: **observe, guard, treasure, declare, delight in, meditate on, fix my eyes on, not forget, keep, learn, choose, set before, cling to, run the way of, keep, long for, hope in, seek, revere, hurry to keep, love, incline the heart, fear, hope in, not swerve from, stand in awe of, rejoice at.** *The psalmist is totally serious about reading, studying, paying attention and living according to the Word of God.*

What Is Scripture?

The first Christians' original Scripture was the scripture of the Jews—what we know as the Old Testament. These writings told them of God's love and promise of care. That promise was fulfilled in the coming, life, ministry, death, and resurrection of Jesus. It was the early Christian struggle to apply that new faith expressed in the twenty-seven independently written documents that eventually came together (by about 367 CE) to comprise the New Testament. With that, our Christian Bible was complete.

First and foremost, Scripture is your story. Scripture tells you of all that God has done to make the world (including you), and to provide answers when the human story (history) turns tragic. So continue to do what you have been doing all of your Christian life—absorb that divine narrative and pray that you might be at the center of the life it reports. Scripture is a *story*—the story that all Christians share, around which we all gather, over which we struggle about interpretation and application. That is its objective, "out there" reality. It can become *your* own personal story, the drama that guides your life toward meaning and fulfillment. That is its subjective, "in here" reality (I'm pointing to your heart).

The twenty-seven documents that make up the New Testament originated in settings where the Christian faith was coming into contact with strongly opposing views. After all, the people who rejected and killed Jesus were still around. His triumph over death certainly didn't change their negative attitude toward him or his followers. Those twenty-seven documents were written by and for Christians who found themselves adjusting to life in a fundamentally hostile world and in need of guidance for that struggle. Those documents were helpful to the earliest Christians because the Jesus Christ of whom they spoke had answers for the problems that they faced every day.

The four Gospels—Matthew, Mark, Luke, John—tell us Jesus' story. It is not just a story of the past but it is also the story of the Jesus who is alive for us now. The twenty-one letters address particular problems that Christians were facing in the early days of the movement when they were up against Jewish opposition, the occupying Roman army, *and even* internal conflicts *within* the new churches. One book of history (Acts) and another of comforting assurance in a poetic and coded language (Revelation) round out the twenty-seven different documents of the Christian New Testament.

Scripture reveals the experience of the first Christians struggling *as* Christians to understand the presence of Jesus in their lives and to live faithfully in the alien atmosphere of the Roman Empire. It is a church-made and church-approved record of experience, a standard of faith and behavior, embraced by the church that produced it. It is the witness of the whole church to the reality of God in Jesus Christ. Christians believe that it comes with the blessing of God and the full authority of God and the church.

The first Christians had to learn a new story, have a new outlook, be a new community. Christians had a unique understanding of the world. In the face of a world that confronted them with a different story (i.e., Jewish and/or Greco-Roman)—reinforced by all the social pressures and rewards stacked against them—Christians were faced with the need to really understand their own unique Christian view. The reason we have Scripture is so that we—as Christians—can read this new sense-making story and work toward fitting our lives into it. This is terribly important since you, as a college student, will be in a minority seeking to thrive in the midst of other more powerful groups with markedly different understandings. How do you get that story working for you?

Obviously the New Testament is not a road map or design for higher education. But it can serve to diagnose dangers. It can also serve as a prescriptive resource to suggest how faith might approach specific problems. It is *not* a book that dropped out of the sky, although Christians acknowledge its divinely inspired nature. It is *not* a book that was written last year in English with a private message exclusively for your own personal benefit. As you will see, the problems confronted in Scripture have many similarities with the challenges you face in the college experience. Scripture also provides all the information about Jesus to keep you from the perennial temptation of modernizing him and turning him into your pal, errand boy, or sugar daddy.

Why Is Scripture Our Best Textbook?

The first and best reason to have Scripture as your primary text in college (or anywhere else) is that it is your primary source for the words of your Teacher, Jesus Christ. It brings you the original version of his life story and it puts you "in the picture" when it comes to the church's first responses to Jesus as Lord and Teacher. So if you want to know what Jesus the Teacher said, you read Scripture. If you want to join in the conversation among Christians, since that conversation all started with Scripture, Scripture is where to enter the conversation.

Scripture reveals God's call to God's own children and points out an appropriate response. College textbooks aren't usually written to elicit response and commitment on the part of the readers. In fact, one of the dangers of college is that you might go through the experience without a serious challenge for your commitment beyond the decision about a possible vocational choice. So Scripture is the best textbook to call you to the appropriate commitment of your life.

Scripture provides Christians with a common reading. There are so many books in the world that it is often the case that two people could go through college without ever reading the same text. *One school I know well has the same prescribed curriculum for all but two weeks in the junior year. For a lot of students that is too much regimentation. But imagine, all students read the same authors so if they want to talk about school, they really have a common experience to talk about.*

In contrast, there are many schools—I taught at one of them—where it would have been possible for two students, say a boy and a girl, to attend for the full four years and not share a class or a reading assignment. Later, they get married. Can they talk about school? Yes, but not very well about anything they studied. Christians who take Scripture seriously as their text for life will have a common set of readings that can connect them not only to peers, but also to all other Christians who have ever lived. So Scripture gives us one common text that we all share in community and continuity through time.

As new discoveries bury old truths under the weight of their evidence, your college teachers will have to search out new textbooks to keep current with the new information and the changes that new information necessitates. Your "curriculum" as a Christian has a simple, unchanging content: Jesus. He is the same today as he was yesterday; and he will remain constant in his love for you into every tomorrow. There is no need to seek an updated version of Scripture—except that you might look for *the* one of many translations of Scripture that you feel most comfortable reading.

How Should You Use It?

Probably the first thing that you would like to know is, "What is the correct interpretation of Scripture?" or "What is the correct way to read Scripture?" Textbooks aren't always easy to read. One of the most important things you can learn in college is *how* to read—that is, *how* to read for understanding.

Reading Scripture is much the same. You read in hopes of understanding the subject matter—Jesus, your Lord and Teacher. That means that you can't read it in just any old way. But since it is written for your benefit, you do have to read it as it applies to you in your situation. In fact, historically, Scripture has been read "correctly" in a variety of ways with a number of different techniques. It would be unnecessarily limiting to suggest *the* correct technique for interpreting Scripture since faithful Christians through the ages have come out pretty well using everything from allegory to numerology in seeking the meaning of Scripture.

> **Hermeneutics**
>
> *The "how" of interpreting a text: the use of the best methods and principles of explaining any text—even or especially Holy Scripture.*

More important than method is attitude. If you read Scripture with an eagerness for it to speak to you in your situation, you are likely to find God's help there. If you read in a mood to listen to Scripture rather than simply to have it back up your pet ideas, you are more likely to find Jesus teaching you. If you read with imagination you might be able to see what our Lord and Teacher has in mind for you. Whether you read regularly in the morning or evening, or irregularly, with others or alone, it should be the most important book in your book-filled life.

A "correct" reading is a reading that takes into account the purpose for which Scripture was written, collected and preserved in the church, as well as an approach that takes into account your needs—the needs that drive you to seek its help. A "correct" reading would have you be silent before the text, so it can interrogate you. The "correct" way to read is to have Jesus at the center as you read.

There is the story of the old Jewish rabbi who had taken on a young student aspiring to the role of rabbi. The mentor would periodically insist that his young disciple learn from *everything* the rabbi did. Memorizing texts as well as memorizing lifestyle was all a part of becoming a rabbi. One night, in the middle of the night, the old rabbi and his wife were asleep. But a sound awakened the old man; it had come from under the bed. Cautiously arising and peeking under the bed he found . . . his student! "What, in the name of the Holy One, are you doing there?" cried the rabbi. Defending himself, the student protested, "But you told me that I must learn from *everything* you did."

This may just be an apocryphal story that tries to make a point about of the extent to which faithful Jews tried to bring every detail of their lives under the rule of God. But that type of audacious seriousness should not be viewed as a joke. In a supportive response to people who were utterly serious about living faithfully as Jews, the Jewish law goes into excruciating detail to spell out exactly how everything—from how to dress in the morning to how to wash the dishes before bedtime—should be done; and, oh yes, while you are asleep you are still under God's care and his will.

Despite his criticism of the Jews' practices, Jesus never intended to deny the utter seriousness that the Jews placed on their joyous obligation to bring the whole of their lives into obedience to the will of a loving God; he just thought they were doing it in such a way that it excluded some people whom God wanted to include. So we read Scripture with the eagerness of the young "wanna-be" rabbi and with the seriousness of the Jewish lawyer because we know that the God who made us wants everyone to enjoy the fruits of living in his love. The New Testament could be said to be the assigned text in which Christians find their curriculum. If you read Scripture in this way, you can be transformed by your "working out" (Phil 2:12) of your own salvation. Scripture provides the narrative into which you can project yourself and play your part.

Throughout this manual, Scripture is employed to offer examples of how it can serve you in your college experience. You will find individual passages as well as some broadly drawn themes that offer ways to understand and respond to what you will encounter in the college experience. The real goal is that you will feel so firmly located in sacred Scripture and so adept at reading that you can apply it faithfully and usefully to new situations—not addressed in this book—that will inevitably arise in the future.

No amount of pre-planning can prepare you for all the things that will come at you, but we want to help as much as we can. Let's close this chapter by looking at a few examples of how Scripture can do this for you.

The most serious way to read Scripture would be to read one of the sixty-six separate "books" as a whole—like you read a college text, or like you would read a story. That is how Scripture was written in the first place. The twenty-seven "books" of the New Testament (Gospels, letters, history) were written by different authors at different times, in different places, responding to different audiences in different situations. Each was composed with the intention of solving some problem(s) by bringing the work of Christ to bear on it. Reading a "book" of Scripture in this way would be the best way to allow each separately produced piece of Scripture its own integrity. This focus on one "book" at a time is a step toward a more complete interaction with Scripture.

> **ism alert—*Literal+ism***
>
> *Limiting your reading of Scripture to only dictionary definitions of words and ignoring unique features of the original languages, the translations (now so many), editing, and the artistic choices made by the human writers; for instance: allegory ("speak in another way" [Gal 4:24]); hyperbole (exaggeration [Matt 6:24]); metaphor (figure of speech [Gal 4:21–31)]; metonymy (designation of one thing by another associated with it [Rom 5:9]); polysemy (word capable of two meanings); puns, similes (1 Cor 3:10); synecdoche (use of the part for the whole [2 Cor 3:15]) or the whole for a part [Col 3:15]).* **Don't be confined by literalism.**

For example, the Gospel of Matthew gives the longest and most detailed picture of Jesus' entire life and particularly about his career as the one Teacher for all Christians. Paul's letter to the Colossians—a group of Christians who wondered about the relationship of their faith to things intellectual—is a completely different writing. Both of these "books" address matters of interest to Christians like you who are trying to be faithful in the college experience, but they are different matters. One is about Jesus the Teacher; the other is about Christians and the way they think about Jesus Christ and the world. Perhaps the best way to utilize this approach would be to commit to a disciplined, regular reading of one or another "book" of Scripture over the course of a semester. In any case, it is crucial to seek out Scripture that promises some correlation to your particular situation in college. Another valid way to read would be to take a look at some of the broad themes and main topics of Scripture. There are a number of such themes that characterize the biblical story. A theme is a centralizing idea that can be found in a variety of places throughout Scripture. It is a collection of word pictures that cohere into a central and powerful message. Some examples of biblical themes include: love, mercy, justice, hope, forgiveness, and creation.

These are not values to be praised in the abstract. They are topics or themes that are expressed in numerous specific actions of God, Jesus, the prophets, and the faithful. These ideas are central to many biblical stories in which they assume concreteness. (We saw just such a big concept in the last chapter when we looked at the central theme of Jesus' teaching—the kingdom of God.) The following theme is an example that can be helpful in forming a faithful understanding of your place in college.

> **Scripture Goes to Hollywood!**
>
> *1 Corinthians was written 2,000 years ago to a problem-ridden church at Corinth. But it will give you great insights on how to survive in an American college. And with all its sex, pride, and conflict it would make a great Hollywood movie!*

Discipleship

That theme is discipleship. It is appropriate to anyone going to college. *Discipleship*—following Jesus and being attentive to him, to his teaching and to his actions. The term "discipline" is closely related to the term "disciple"; the disciple is one who is disciplined into Jesus, his life, ministry, death, and resurrection. Jesus provides the curriculum; Jesus *is* the curriculum.

In the college experience, the curriculum is the mechanism whereby students are disciplined into thinking about specific subjects in certain ways. The discipline comes through the course structure, the reading and lectures, the quizzes and the study demanded; and through doing research and writing papers. After a great deal of discipline, one acquires the skills and the habits of the practitioner, the expert, the professional. This is obvious in terms of learning to play the piano or speak a foreign language; but it is also the case in every serious discipline. Students may start the college experience as novices, but by graduation you will be seen as fledgling biologists or accountants, with the traces of professionalism beginning to appear as a result of the discipline to which you have submitted.

I spent a sabbatical leave—a study leave college teachers can earn after seven years of satisfactory performance—at a famous university that had an even more famous basketball coach. One of my sabbatical year teachers would point out that, if you want to understand discipleship, you should look at the basketball team and the way that the coach inspired and taught his players.

It was only through discipline that the individual players with their variety of skills had been able to come together to be a cohesive team—and win national championships.

There may be discipline in a more personal way. Students often become the disciples of particular instructors. This occurs because of the instructor's mastery of material, her fame, charm, or her personal care for the student. The personal and professional bonds that thus occur can have an amazingly formative influence on students.

But being a disciple is a risky business. To whom does one become a disciple? The choice is crucial because discipline to the wrong person, cause, or subject matter would be a tragic waste of commitment.

As Christians, you hear Jesus' call to follow him as his disciple. The Sermon on the Mount reminds you of your discipleship to God to be perfect as your heavenly father is perfect (Matt 5:48). Discipleship is part of the Christian life; it could be seen as the framework of the Christian life, that pattern of thought and behavior within which each is called to walk. In Romans 6:17 Paul refers to this as "the form of teaching to which you were entrusted."

According to the New Testament, Jesus selected his disciples with no apparent regard for their qualifications, past histories, or future promise. They were a random lot, taken from across the political and economic spectrum of the Palestine of Jesus' time, fishermen and tax collectors, untrained as preachers or physicians, but nonetheless empowered to be the bearers of the message of the kingdom of God. He invested his energies in their "education" but there is little evidence that they learned much.

- After seeing him rescue many from their physical dilemmas, the disciples found themselves in a boat in a storm and feared that Jesus had no regard for them (Mark 4:38).

- After hearing Jesus predict his own impending suffering on the cross, Peter urged him to choose a different course (Mark 8:32).

- After promising to be with Jesus in his time of distress, they abandoned him to return to their former life (John 20:10).

They did not seem to get it; yet they were the ones he chose and they were the ones who eventually did carry the Christian message to the world. The nature of discipleship, therefore, is not simply the story of great potential developing into distinguished performance. Instead, it is a story of unknown potential that may show little development. It is the story so familiar in Scripture: God chooses, redeems, and uses the ordinary and flawed. Human incompetence is turned into divine success.

This is just one biblical theme with practical consequences for those going to college. It holds a mirror up to your life. What you see there should give you pause to consider the worth of your choices in selecting mentors whom you would have "disciple" you. It will also remind you of what is required of one who would be good at what he or she does, be it basketball, philosophy, electronics, or the life of faith.

Verses as Mottos

Moving from large units (books, Gospels, letters) and overarching themes, you can also find help in small units of Scripture; this is how most of us hear Scripture anyway—a verse or two on Sunday morning or in a discussion to support an argument or illustrate a point. While a single verse does not convey the big picture of a whole book or theme, and can be dangerous if abused, it is short enough to help you focus on a particular point. It need not be *Scripture lite*. It can be a key to remind you of the larger issues of the Christian life. When used carefully, one verse can serve as a summary, even motto or slogan, of what you are up to. It can become a shorthand rallying cry and reminder of the common purpose shared by all Christians. It can serve the Christian life just as a college mission statement or traditional college seal cryptically points you toward the goal of a higher education. Such a verse could even become *your* motto or seal for your college experience. Here are a couple that have kept me focused. You will come up with your own verses from Scripture that bring Jesus the Teacher into a living relationship with you in the midst of the college experience.

1 Thessalonians 5:21—". . . test everything; hold fast to what is good."

Paul's admonition to the church at Thessalonica to test all things is part of a list of admonitions related to the topic of prophecy. There are two aspects of prophecy. The definition that fits that activity throughout the Scripture is that prophecy is primarily the expression of the will of God. Whoever prophesies is claiming to express the will of God. That is a reckless claim if not made with care. The second feature of prophecy is that it must be helpful and upbuilding to the church (1 Cor 14:3). In both cases, prophecy is something that has significant application to the whole life of Christians since prophecy makes claims that impact your whole life.

Thus it is not a stretch of interpretation to apply this text whenever you hear claims to truth, whether by another Christian (in a sermon or devotional reading) or by anyone claiming to pronounce truth on any topic. As a Christian in the college experience you are constantly exposed to claims of all kinds that have to do with important matters. Paul invites careful consideration and analysis *and* then a commitment to that which is good. The Christian is both critical and committed. College life offers too many opportunities to be uncritical (tolerant) and uncommitted (lazy). Testing all things might sound like a lot of work but it is important and it can prove very interesting!

John 8:32b—"... and the truth will make you free."

"But I am free!" you might object. "I am an American and I am at college. How much freer can you get?" Like the Jews to whom Jesus spoke in this Gospel passage, you would likely respond that you are not in bondage, so why do you need to get free? But, of course, no one is completely free. We are all in bondage or indebted to someone or something. We are all tied up and burdened with responsibilities. The real issue is that of the identity of that which rules us: Who is it that you submit to? When you go to college, you are promised liberation from the provincial constraints of the particular influences that have formed you and that have held you captive. Occasionally, the new truths you are offered are even couched in the words of this verse: truth that will make us free.

You need to look at the whole sentence: "Then Jesus said to the Jews who had believed in him, 'If you continue in my word, you are truly my disciples; and you will know the truth, and the truth will make you free'" (John 8:31–32). It is not just any truth that sets you free. The real meaning of this verse is that it is only *the* truth—Jesus Christ—that makes you truly free.

Application

Christians seeking to live faithfully in the college experience have their best, most comprehensive and best textbook in the Christian Scriptures. Two and a half millennia ago, the Jews suffered a terrible disruption in their lives. Invaders destroyed their Temple, the holy geographic center of their religious life, and carried off the nation's leadership into exile. While it could be said that they never fully recovered from that tragic event, it is also more important to note that it was from that cataclysm that a new form of religion emerged. What had been a geographically settled, politically organized and Temple-centered faith was transformed into a religion "of the book." Instead of having to relate to God primarily through Temple rites and worship, faithful Jews could be faithful *anywhere*. The promises of God could be carried about in a book (very portable!) and the community of God's people could live scattered across the face of the earth.

Now you can carry that text to college—not for defense or as protection to hide behind, but as something to engage and digest. After all, what's in it is your story, not a weapon with which to confront others. Jesus speaks through it to strengthen and transform you in your quest to live faithfully. The idea of using the Bible as your resource in college is as simple as it is bold.

It is *simple* because there is consensus among Christians that the Bible, and particularly the New Testament, is our main guide for "faith and order"—what we believe and how we behave. If that is so, then the Bible should be the most important resource consulted with regard to any problem or opportunity that you face.

And this is a *bold* proposal because Christians have often been hesitant use the Bible thoroughly and seriously as a resource in shaping their lives in the arena of higher education. But you need not hang back. In faith, you can take Scripture seriously, use it regularly and systematically to inform your thinking and growth in your vocation as a Christian student. In the following chapters you will be invited to share in exactly that kind of thinking.

Thought and Discussion Questions

1. How is the Bible the *same as* and *different from* other texts you use in college?

2. In a group, let each participant find his/her own significant passage (whole text, themes, memory verses) and expand on its significance for the college experience.

3. Apply one of these biblical themes to the college experience: creation, sin, forgiveness, justice, judgment, redemption.

part two

The Curriculum

ROMANS 12:2

*Do not be conformed to this world, but be transformed
by the renewing of your minds, so that you may discern what
is the will of God—what is good and acceptable and perfect.*

After spending eleven chapters telling his readers about the wonderful things God has done for us in Jesus Christ, Paul opens the last part of his letter to Roman Christians saying, "Okay, here it is—what you ought to do—unlearn the self-destructive falseness of 'the world' and let your minds have a complete make-over so that you understand the kingdom of God."

Here, as everywhere in Scripture, you are called—you have a *vocation*—for radical change. This is not a matter of learning more stuff (although that will certainly happen in college), but it is a matter of something like a mind or brain transplant. Christians are asked to let God completely take them over—heart, soul, *and mind*! College can help if you pray . . .

Prayer: God, transform me so I may know and live according to your will. Amen.

Finally! We come to the stuff that college is about: studying and learning. Here you will uncover the most subtle and most profound challenges to faith. While most warnings about college dwell on the extra-curricular things—especially the social life—the focus should be on what college teaches, especially in the implicit, under-the-surface ways that have the biggest potential to sneak under your faith radar and insinuate un-Christian convictions in place of solid faith. Remember, there is no such thing as "losing your faith" in college. You can't lose your faith like you might lose your room key. If faith leaves, something else takes its place. Since faith deals with everything that is important, your thinking about everything important doesn't just leave. Instead, other thoughts take over. You can't simply drop all the ideas and commitments and hopes and beliefs that you had about who you are and what makes like worth living and what is right; you don't stop thinking about why there is beauty, what really causes war, and what is the meaning of your own life. If faith goes, something else comes in. Jesus understood that there is no such thing as a vacuum in our lives—see that strange parable in Matthew 12:43–45. All the questions that you would have answered by faith are now going to be answered by . . . what? Everything else is a poor substitute.

The *curriculum:* that is the subject matter you study, from art to zoology. It is the lectures, discussions, quizzes, internships, term papers, labs, service-learning projects, field trips, independent studies— everything that the college can think of to help you to learn what you need to learn in order to get the college's approval of your worthiness to receive a degree. This is the place to start because this is where most of the explicit and implicit substitutes to your faith will come up.

In order to get you into this environment, we will offer an arrangement of topics so that you can get a general idea of the kinds of things the college will offer you to study. But these will be things you will be able to critique from your position of faith because we will also point out the hazards that might await you in those studies, and the help that Jesus the Teacher and Christian Scripture offer to deal with those challenges.

1) Beginning with "the academic basics" in chapter 7 and "the generals" in chapter 8, we look at your movement through the curriculum from the beginning as a raw freshman who may need some help with English, through the general requirements to the major field of study in which you hope to receive your degree.

2) At each step, there is explanation of the college's intentions in offering (or sometimes requiring) these courses or programs.

3) In addition to a description, there will be a warning. Christians need to know that with each area of study there can be challenges to faith's understanding of things. This is where "the curriculum" gets interesting because it (the curriculum) does *not* just consist of all those lectures, and readings, and quizzes, and term papers, and projects. It *also* consists of *everything*

that *is* and that *happens* at college; it *all* affects you; it *all teaches* you. What you are told will happen is the *explicit* curriculum; what you are *not* told *happens*—and this is called the *implicit* or *hidden* curriculum.

4) The warning is not meant to frighten, but to prepare for a Christian look at the subject at hand—particularly from a Christological perspective. Remember Jesus the Teacher? We can also look to Jesus the Word and other Christologies—ways of understanding who Jesus is—that will help you see this particular piece of the college experience from a Jesus point-of-view.

5) And with that perspective will come some suggestions for the Christian student to consider: alternative approaches, substitutions, or ways to take the college's secular offering and transform it into a useful tool for faith.

6) Finally, a few thought-provoking discussion questions are offered to help you (and your sister and brother Christian) ponder your situation and develop strategies to ensure that the college experience is fueling your faith and not frustrating it.

Paul's challenge in Romans 12 to be transformed means that you think about the topics taught in a Christian, not a secular, way. This is hard work, requiring an understanding of what happens in college. The curriculum is central because you will be spending the major part of your college time and energy on it and it can be at once the most dangerous most helpful part of your college experience. I know you will learn wonderful things.

7

Basic Skills

Readin', Writin' & 'Rithmetic

"Most of the occasions for the troubles
of the world are grammatical."
—Michel de Montaigne (1533–1592)

"Not seven times, but, I tell you, seventy-seven times.
—Matthew 18:22

Scripture Focus

John 1:1

*In the beginning was the Word, and the Word
was with God, and the Word was God.*

"Sticks and stones may break my bones, but words can never hurt me."
That was part of the protection you used when other kids taunted
you. Of course now you know that it's not true. Words *are* powerful. It
is said, "The pen is more powerful than the sword." That pen is powerful
because it writes *words*. Apparently the writer of the fourth Gospel, who
wanted to start his account of Jesus at the very beginning of God's story,

believed in the power of the word. His portrayal of the very beginning of everything is that it started with a word, God's Word.

The most recent scientific view of "creation" is more dramatic. (People seem to prefer the dramatic.) According to today's scientists, the universe suddenly emerged from almost nothing in a fraction of a nano-second and expanded at incredible speed to become the ever faster expanding universe we now inhabit. We call this idea the Big Bang theory. And we imagine it not only as quick, but as loud and violent.

Another dramatic creation narrative is one of the earliest. It was a competitor to the biblical story; it was the Babylonian story in which creation occurred when the hero (Gilgamesh) whipped out his sword and sliced a monstrous dragon in half, with the bottom half becoming earth, and the top half the heavens. We do seem to like explosions and blood and gore in the movies, but isn't it really more dramatic when it takes only a word to make something amazing like the creation of the universe happen?

Words are powerful. The Word that was God, the Word of God, was sent by God to humankind in the person of Jesus who exerted great power through his miracles and through his own words. That was amazing. That person, Jesus, the Word of God, and his words, live on to inspire and direct us today. Christ's words remind us that God, the most powerful force there is, was the first and most powerful employer of words. And God has given us the gift of communication. What a shame it would be to squander that gift.

Prayer: O God, who speaks to us through Jesus, help me to read and hear and speak aright. Amen.

The College Experience: Getting the Basic Tools

To do anything right—if even just to play a game—requires some preparation. A lot of preparation goes into getting ready for college: getting clothes, a checking account or credit card, a cell phone, a required medical exam, maybe even a car. The list goes on and on. No matter how much stuff you pack or how many preparations you have made, you probably can never feel completely ready for college. You may be thinking, "What have I forgotten?" Your folks may be thinking, "What have we overlooked?" This kind of anxiety—thinking something was left out but not being able to put your finger on what it is—is to be expected. You can't think of everything and you can't ever be totally ready for college.

One of the things that you can't be completely ready for is your academic preparation in the form of the basic tools needed to do college work: the skills of reading (and understanding what you read), writing (and communicating your well organized thoughts to others), and mathematics (the ability to measure, compare, and calculate). Whatever your interests, whatever your future major, even if you have no idea what your major will be, there are some basic tools that everyone needs in order to do the kinds of work that college involves. They are the tools that enable you to acquire information, organize it, analyze and evaluate it, and communicate your understanding clearly to others. These are the traditional "three Rs" of reading, writing, and arithmetic.

> **Bad News About Basic Skills**
> *The Higher Education Research Institute finds that half of all college teachers think that their students are inadequately prepared to do college work. 2012 ACT and SAT test results show a decline in the basic skills on the part of high school graduates. Sixty percent of recent high school graduates are at risk of not succeeding in college because they lack the basic skills required.*

Some students may think that they will not need much more work on these basic skills. *I vividly recall instances where students went to the dean to plead to be let out of freshman year requirements. One said, "I'll be a business major, I can't see why I have to take English." Another plead, "I'm going to teach English, I can't understand why I need math." I always marveled that a nineteen-year-old college student would already know what he would NOT need to know during his next fifty years.*

Other students may worry that they do not have nearly enough of these basic tools. *During a Sunday school class session with students and parents discussing their concerns about attending college, one high school senior told of her visit to the college of her choice. She had met the instructor who was going to teach her English class. She learned he had graduated from a prestigious university. Even though she had been an honor student all through high school, she was deeply worried that she would not do well in his class. She felt unprepared.*

Whatever your *feelings* about your level of English and math readiness, it is a fact that a substantial number of all college beginners lack the basic skills to do college work.[1] Because that is the case and because colleges want

---

1. *Almanac 2011–12*, 38 points out that 20 percent of first-year college students took a remedial course during the last year for which statistics were collected.

to enroll all the students they can, many schools have undertaken to provide basic English and math classes.

That is good, because you can never have too much in the way of English and math skills—whether for doing college work or for meeting the challenges of life in today's world. Your college will want you to master these basic skills and will test you to ascertain your skill level. If you fall short, you should not worry. Your school will likely provide special, remedial classes designed to help you catch up.

If you are identified as one of the students in need of such classes, consider yourself fortunate to be able to take them. Instead of seeing these classes as burdensome and delaying your entry to college, look on them as providing "languages" that will open windows of communication and understanding. After all, the demands on you to practice all three skills— reading, writing, calculating—will only increase as you acquire more information, process it, store it, communicate it, and use it to solve problems of all sorts in studies, your job, and personal life.

Is There a Problem?

Yes, there is a problem, but it is not in the fact that some students are not sufficiently skilled for college in the basic skills necessary; that can be fixed.

The problem is that there is an attitude problem: there are so many folks who don't seem to care about students being prepared with basic communication skills to do college work. How often have you heard someone—even an adult who should know better—say, "I never was any good at math," or "I did terrible at Spanish [or German, or English] in high school"? American culture in general seems to tolerate poor communication and calculation skills. Worse yet, when people admit these shortcomings, they do so in a way that humorously seeks to invite listeners to agree—agree that they aren't much good at these skills either *and* that it's okay not to be any good at them!

There are two kinds of institutions in America that say that these basic skills are important. One of those institutions consists of the businesses— where you may one day be hired to work—that regularly proclaim that the main thing they look for in prospective employees is the basic package of communication and math skills. This is routinely affirmed as even more important than knowing the specifics of how to do the job for which you are applying. That is so because the particular skills needed in the job you may get will undoubtedly change over the course of time; we live in that kind of world. The company can teach you what you need to know for that job. But the company cannot teach you how to speak well, listen well, write clearly, or calculate with skill. So business affirms the need for basic skills. But the world of business is not in a good position to teach America's youth those skills. That is up to the American educational system.

The other institution that trumpets the importance of communication and calculation skills is the educational system—of which we are all products. And it has not done the job. Critics lament the lack of rigor with which students are trained in the basic academic skills.

Our task is not to solve this lack of rigor in the system, but rather to help *you* understand the implications of this situation for your college experience.

But sorry to say, students can be a problem here also. There are a lot of folks who don't take these basic skills seriously. These are folks who are sloppy in their speech habits—with bad grammar and imprecise ways of expressing their thoughts—and don't seem to care much about trying to get it right. By "get it right" we mean developing habits of careful communication so that you will be able to understand pretty much any other American and be understood by that person—hearing them or reading what they have written.

That brings us to your college, which may (or may not) be one of those schools that is really trying to solve the problem for their students. Usually colleges are aware of the possibility that incoming student may need bolstering in the basics, and special classes, sections, or labs are available. That's the good news.

The bad news is that colleges aren't always able to carry through with the delivery of those skills and students still fail to get them. Sometimes it is the case that colleges don't treat the need to teach basics as seriously as they treat the need to teach advanced subjects. It is also often the case that these classes are offered as a kind of afterthought, using part-time faculty. The colleges' message seems to be: "We say that learning basic skills is important but we don't really mean it."

Then there is the situation with the faculty who might feel a responsibility to help new students with their "basics." Usually, faculty feel that preparing students with the basic skills to do college work is somebody else's job. Science teachers and history teachers and music teachers do not usually feel obliged to help students with their writing. Nor do they see it as their job to work with them to improve math skills. In some cases, where they do take that responsibility, they may not be well enough prepared themselves. Sometimes those who are qualified—the English teacher and the math teacher—don't want the science, history, or music teacher telling students how to do *their* basic skills. The basic skills experts don't always trust teachers in other departments.

And finally there are attitudes that some students—perhaps even some of your peers—have about college work. One such attitude is that these basic skills are not all that important. *"I can get by with what I have."* Another attitude with serious consequences is that college is seen as consisting of a list of requirements each of which in turn is measured by some formal criterion—contact hours, minutes in a classroom seat, passage of a test. Looking at it this way, a student simply needs to turn up and be counted, get the credit, check it off the list, and move on to the next course without necessarily *learning* the needed skills. Courses are like items to consume; it is like going to the grocery store for milk or bread: just consume the class and "check it off" or "get it out of the way." While it is true that some of what we learn is not going to be remembered, isn't the point of an education to learn and not just check requirements off of a list? Especially if basic skills classes are seen in this light, the student won't have the skills to do all the other learning that will be required later.

A group of us went to our professor in charge of a particular program in which we needed to pass an exam and asked for a checklist of books or facts or theories that we would have to get through before we could be sure of passing in the program. He stunned us by saying, "I won't give you any such list. If you study, you will know when you are ready to take the test." That was totally depressing. I had to figure out when I had learned enough. (What a drag, I thought.) According to him, learning wasn't simply completing a list of someone else's requirements. It involved studying and accumulating and remembering what had been accumulated and then learning more so that we finally knew enough to know whether we knew enough!

It is the case that basic skills are demanded by colleges but not always taken seriously enough by schools that require them and by students who need them. It is also the case that some college professors who agree that having those basic communication skills is important don't always help to make sure students acquire them. And it is even the case that the very students who need the knowledge are too often content to shun the work needed to learn them.

So here is the first problem: Everyone is aware that basic skills are important for doing college work. But not everyone takes responsibility for making sure that every student in college is fundamentally prepared to do the work.

There is a disconnect. Colleges seem to be saying, "We insist that the basics are critically important; but we don't really take it seriously enough to make it happen." Saying one thing but not doing what is said. Worse, maybe we have all gotten used to living in an environment where there are two realities: saying one thing but actually doing another.

Perhaps you already have this sense of confusion or betrayal. Your nation tells you everyone is equal; and yet you know that some people don't get a fair deal. TV tells you that a product can solve your problem; and yet you know that it can't possibly. Your folks may have told you that if you try hard enough, you can do anything you want; but you tried really hard at something, and you weren't able to do it. You may be getting used to living in this kind of a world. Welcome to college: colleges tell the world that they will prepare students to achieve their dreams; colleges tell the public that they run "clean" athletic programs; college vouch for their faculty, that their published research is original and true. These and similar claims are not always true.

Maybe you should get used to this kind of—what is this?—hypocrisy, deception, lying, deceit. Just overlook it? If so, then *you* run the risk of being deceitful, hypocritical, a liar. You run the risk of accepting the value represented: it is a value embedded in the college environment; and it is a value held in popular American culture; it is *not* a Christian value. (Remember: Christians don't have *values,* they have *faith.*) Don't let it become your value. What is this value of approving that it's okay not to do what you say you will do? *Insincerity? Irresponsibility? Hypocrisy? Pretense? Lying? Deceit?*

Saying that something is important to do and then not doing it has bad consequences. First, it suggests that those calling for training in the basics of communication and mathematical skills don't really mean what they say. Or perhaps it means that they feel it is important to *say* that having the basics is crucial even though they really don't believe it. Second, whether colleges, faculty, students, and employers don't really believe in the importance of the basics or whether they only think it is important to *sound like* they are for them, it makes it okay for students to slough off the importance of these basic educational tools. For a Christian, to accept and adopt such an attitude would be a terrible way to begin your college experience.

For the sake of putting a handle on this problem (and perhaps learning a new word), let's call the problem *dissimulation*—being okay with saying one thing but doing another. This is a value, but it is a value with only the most limited use. It may be acceptable in casual conversation, for example, when someone asks, "How are you?" and even though you are on your way to the dentist or just found out your team lost the game you respond, "Fine, how are you?" We all know that we are *dissimulating* in this case; it is a formal, silent agreement that we all make.

But, *dissimulation* is not okay in college, or in a courtroom, or when taking marriage vows, resolving labor disputes, or conducting international peace negotiations, or telling your grandparent that a prescribed course of treatment can cure his terminal cancer. Telling the truth as clearly as possible and telling it convincingly and meaning what you say are extraordinarily important. Any valuation of *dissimulation* with regard to reading and calculating to find truth and expressing that truth clearly cannot be tolerated by the successful college student—or by a Christian. Success in taking the most positive advantage of the college experience means that it is not okay to *dissimulate* when it comes to the basics. They are important. You better be sure to have them.

My daughter was really excited about attending a particular college. She had read up on it and was excited to know that it had a history of reaching out to students (for instance, women) who had not originally been welcome at most schools. It had also been active in the Civil Rights movement in America. She wanted to be in a place that was really forward-looking and acting. When we went for an introductory interview and she was asked why she was interested in that school, she told them how impressed she was with the school's past—a past about which she had read in the school's own brochures. The admissions counselor was somewhat surprised: "Oh, that's interesting."

My daughter enrolled and guess what? The school was nothing like she expected. It had radically changed in the 100-plus years since the stories told in the brochures had occurred. The college had lied. It had been deceitful. It had said one thing, and changed into something else. No wonder it didn't work out for my daughter.

So yes, there is a problem. When important expectations are created and not met, there is a major problem. When the most important tools for college success are expected and promised but not taken seriously, you—the student—are in big trouble. When you find yourself in a place where promises are not fulfilled you are in a place you don't want to be. Does the Christian faith offer help?

Christology: The Word of God

Anything the Christian faith tradition has to offer must begin with Jesus Christ. Jesus Christ is our Teacher and is also much more. Christians will take these basic skills of English and math seriously not just because they are fundamental to the success of their vocation as students but because Jesus Christ is the Word of God.

God is a God of words and has shown himself in words. From the very beginning, when God said, "Let there be light" (Gen 1:3), God was a God of words powerful enough to bring order to the chaos of the universe. God spoke to humans in the Garden of Eden, then through angels and prophets and in the words of (what we know as the Old Testament) Scripture. Finally, in the New Testament, God spoke definitively in Jesus, *the* Word of God, who, in his turn, spoke what God wanted us to hear by means of his earthly life, works, and words. And Christians will want to read all about it and understand it.

"In the beginning was the Word." So writes John (John 1:1), the author of the fourth Gospel. He presents Jesus as the wisdom and the creativity and the mind of God become human flesh. In becoming flesh and living among us, Jesus spoke to us in human language. That was all written down in Scripture. Jesus, the Word of God, continues to deliver his message today, in human language through Scripture. And you will want to have the skills to read it and understand it.

Jesus, the Word, delivers God's truth in a variety of styles or literary formats: commands, prophecies, prayers, revelations, proverbs, arguments, and—especially—parables. He and his words occupy the central place in the Gospels. If you want to know truth (not deceit), you can hear it in the words of Jesus. It comes in the most ordinary and truthful language. Predominant is the parable that uses every day and well-known objects or situations to tell about God and particularly about what it would be like if God's authority were acknowledged by everyone. The parable was a way for Jesus to express the inexpressible by referring us to something we could comprehend and then draw a comparison. This fact gives us a strong reason to treat words with respect. Because Jesus, the Son of God, used words to tell us God's truth, he sanctified words so we must treat them with reverence. Because Jesus is Word we must treat words with care.

Jesus, as the Word of God, not only used ordinary language to tell God's truth. He also often gave words new, special meanings. We might say that he rescued words and language from abuse by humans. Every day we see how language is used to deceive, dissimulate, and to damage, to separate and condemn. Jesus deflated some language; other, more humble vocabulary, was given more significance. For example, he clearly deflated language referring to the rulers of this world and upgraded servants and service. We learn that language is to be used honestly and with clarity: "Let your word be 'Yes, Yes' or 'No, No'" (Matt 5:37a). His story—his life, death, resurrection—was something new. It was astounding. Not surprisingly, some people began to take his words seriously, remembering them and applying them to their lives, and commenting upon them in written documents. This gave rise to the documents that now comprise our New Testament. Christians remembered, treasured, and lived by his words. Beginning with Jesus, a whole new language emerged: Christian language. It was needed to tell the Christian story.

We enter into this Christian story and find it makes more sense to us than other stories we have heard. We have heard other stories but find that they are inadequate. For instance:

- The story that we can pull ourselves up by our own bootstraps is a story that simply doesn't work for a lot of people.

- Or the story about how you can achieve whatever you want if you work hard enough and believe in your dream only seems to work for the few who wind up on top.

- Then there is the patriot inspired story of "My country right or wrong."

Many, many possible narratives vie for our approval and adoption. We are the audience at what one writer called a "tournament of narratives"[2] where many stories battle for our attention and allegiance. You need to read for understanding if you are to pick the right narrative for your life.

In order to know our Christian story well, we need to take language seriously. Ours may be a religion focused on a person, but we know who that person is through a book, the Bible. In many ways, ours is a religion of the book. So we better know how to read and know what we have read because other languages and other stories are clamoring for your attention. They will have to be read (because professors assign them for class) and you will need to be ready to understand them—critically. Because you are a student *and because you are a Christian* you need to be prepared understand, critique, accept or reject their claims on your life.

Our Christian story is a unique story, written in a new vocabulary. Its words are not a part of the college's typical vocabulary. That is because the college experience incarnates and promotes a different path with its own array of values.

It might help if you thought of yourself as "bilingual," working in college with one language and living the Christian life with a richer, larger, more powerful language that makes more sense because it explains more of life in a more helpful and more meaningful way. Approached bilingually, your educational experience is richer. Neither language—Christian or secular/job-related—comes without effort in learning and a lot of practice in using it.

2. McClendon, *Systematic Theology*, 143.

The Christian Use of Language and the Use of Christian Language

It has been said that our world—the world accessible to each of us individually—is limited by the language we use. One language confines us to one narrow world; two languages expand the world in which we can live. Going to college is all about learning new languages (the language of chemistry, the language sociologists use, etc.), each with a new vocabulary that will change and sharpen the way in which you observe the world. The new language you acquire in your major will be a specialized vocabulary, the main tool for understanding a new field, a discipline, a trade—perhaps your life's work. This kind of special vocabulary is what is called a jargon. Such jargon is necessary because of the highly specialized nature of what you will be doing. Words like "whatchamecallit" or "thigamajig" will not do when fixing a computer or performing brain surgery; to say "you know what I mean" when conducting a contract negotiation or finalizing a peace treaty will not work. You will need the specialized jargon for the specialized work you will be doing.

But the special and necessary jargon you need for your future job can also separate people, dividing the elite specialist from the rest of us who lack the specialized knowledge and the vocabulary to communicate that knowledge. The more specialized your language and the more you depend on it to understand your world, the more risk you take that you will isolate yourself from others who do not speak that jargon.

As a Christian you need a language that meets several criteria. It must be universal (accessible to everyone), and it must give an account of truth. It must be uncompromised by the values that dominate the worldly college experience. In pursuit of these high goals, Christian faith has two contributions to make.

The Christian Use of Language

English teachers these days lament the current lack of interest in speaking and writing well. We are language sloppy in our culture. Thus the Christian insistence on a Christian use of language may come as a jolt.

The first aspect of the Christian use of language is the seriousness with which Christians take all language. Christians have great respect for the "word." Since God became "the word" in the person of Jesus and since Scripture offers us God's powerful words of self-disclosure, Christians want to use language with care because that is the vehicle God uses to communicate with us. Indeed, are we not obliged to have a reverence for God's gift of language and a humility for the fact that of all God's creatures are given this gift?

Use of Christian Language

In addition to a serious appreciation for using language and all the related skills of clear communication, and the ability to understand what others communicate, we have the additional gift of "Christian Language." It is the language of God's power, God's love for God's own creation, God's longsuffering and mercy, God's judgment, God's will for the creation. Christian language has a peculiar sound because it is the language of sin and redemption, of judgment and grace. It is the language of faith! The secular world does not use the Christian vocabulary because it does not know the realities that the Christian knows and so neither needs nor knows the language necessary to name those realities.

Christian vocabulary is at once both specialized and general. It is specialized in that it relies on specific terms to express the unique features of faith. For example, humans are *creatures* of God; we rely on God's *grace*; God *reveals* himself to us in Jesus. Such terms are specific to faith but ignored in other technical or cultural jargon. For this Christians are sometimes criticized as sectarian, insular, holier-than-thou, or self-righteous. But it is precisely those special terms that enable us to name features of the Christian experience that other language cannot name. Christians need our own language in order to speak the wonderfully new and different message we believe, because the secular world lacks those insights and has no words for them. The communication vehicle of modern American culture is not adequate to bear the weight and express the nuances of the Christian faith.

But this Christian language has a wonderful universality. Our jargon refers to the reality of *all* human experience—all people *sin* and God's *grace* is for everyone. Christian language is not a new vocabulary, a "jive" current with some new cultural fad, or a dialect that appeared in some previously undiscovered backwater of the world. Ours is an old vocabulary, rooted in the Word made flesh in Jesus Christ. It goes back still further, fashioned first among the ancient Israelites as they reflected on their experience with a God who saved them from slavery and made them into a blessed and blessing nation.

Our vocabulary was further enriched by the Christian experience with the risen Christ and enriched as Christians moved out from the Holy Land into the wider world where that vocabulary was tested and refined as Christians encountered, and explained themselves to other peoples with other languages. Ours is a powerful language into whose simple words and phrases are packed understandings of immense power and consequence, fabulous riches and promises, terrifying critiques and judgments. As it developed throughout the past 2,000 years, millions of believers have used it to reflect on their own faith and to explain themselves and their faith to others.

Ours is neither an insular nor an insulating language. It is too old and universal for that. It has a powerful vocabulary, which is worth a brief review in order to remind us of its scope and its applicability to the college experience. The following ten words are only a selection but can serve as a kind of vocabulary *deca-logue* or language resource for your college experience. These are terms foreign to the common currency of college vocabulary and so they not only express central Christian truths but also fill a really unfortunate and ultimately crippling vacuum in the language you will find dominating your campus. You already know these words, but perhaps you have not thought of them in a college context. Having a Christian vocabulary at your immediately disposal gives you better ability to express your faith and to criticize or complement what you will be taught in college.

i. *creation*—We are creatures; that means we are made by someone or something else. The universe and all that is in it is "creature"; that is, it is *made*. Scripture may not reveal all the mechanisms of creation—that's one reason to go to college. (You can learn about the "how" of creation in science classes.) We are convinced that God is responsible for the creation. The maker, the source, is God. God made it good and God made it for a purpose. The implications of this are powerful.

- First, we are not in charge of anything; we are only servants dedicated to the care of what (and who) exists.

- Second, what there is is *good* and demands our care, whether it is our own bodies, those of others (*all* others), the rest of the entire natural world, or even a speck in the farthest reach of outer space.

- Third, what there is is *conditional*, not necessary; it is transitory, not permanent. The created, physical world—wonderful as it is—changes and ultimately will be gone. We cannot ultimately rely on any permanence from it. If we long for what is permanent, then the created world, the world we know around us, is not what we ultimately seek.

ii. *eschatology*—This refers to the whole business of purpose and gives us a word to affirm that there is a purpose in God's creation. In achieving that purpose the world as we know it is going to end and be replaced by whatever it is that God might have in mind for later. That means that whatever it is to which you are committed stands under an ultimate judgment beyond any judgment known to our own understanding. You go to college with a purpose. College offers an opportunity to clarify and refine that purpose in light of God's ultimate purpose.

iii. fall—As in *the* Fall. This is another way of talking about sin without suggesting that sin was the original condition of the creation but rather something that happened *after* God had made it all good. Humans caused the Fall; God did not *drop* us! The result is that the human race suffers from a self-inflicted wound; a self-centeredness, a ruinous discontent, a poisonous pride—it can be called by many names. The Fall is shorthand for sin. What seems in constant need of retelling is that we humans are responsible for our own mess. I am responsible and you are responsible, not God, not someone else. God made all creation good. Then there was this moment, this decision, this event in which humanity rejected God and went off, went down, on its own: the Fall. Each of us replays this decisive and sad moment in our own lives.

Many academic disciplines struggle to understand why what we consider bad things happen—war, abuse, exploitation. Christians already understand a lot about those kinds of damage to God's creation: sin is the ultimate cause. College helps you understand the mechanisms that move the bad stuff from its origins in human sin to the specific expressions of sin that we find in the world.

iv. forgiveness—"I don't get mad, I get even," reads the bumper sticker. According to American culture, forgiveness is a sign of either weakness or stupidity. But forgiveness is one of the fundamental characteristics of the God who self-reveals to us in faith. This is an astonishing characteristic, particularly in the fact that we ourselves can be forgiven for our fall, sin, transgression—call the problem what you will. We pray about this in the Lord's Prayer; we confess its reality in the Apostles' Creed. To the extent that this characteristic becomes characteristic of us the astonishment continues. Here is a behavior, an attitude that is almost totally lacking in American culture from the individual level to the level of international relationships.

How can this be a resource? Those who know forgiveness in their own lives know the liberation they experience. Those who practice forgiveness toward others know the lightening of their own load of ill will. Forgiveness is something that helps the forgiver and the forgiven. Here is another word that describes a reality that can be known only in the naming of it. But don't look for forgiveness as part of your academic program in college. Your professors may be nice but forgiving students for not learning is not what they are paid to do.

v. grace—This is a word that has virtually disappeared from American English. In Christian usage it refers to a number of things ranging from prayer before meals to God's sending of Jesus Christ for the salvation of the world. It, like forgiveness, is a characteristic of God. In acting with grace, God is not just behaving in a fine manner; God is always moving toward us, though without force, in love and forgiveness, offering us what we need. God precedes us when necessary because we don't always acknowledge our need. He follows to clean up after us when necessary. Grace is a resource for us because it is the infinite capacity of God to do the right thing for us. It enables us to say what we need but what our worldly language can't help us express.

vi. incarnation—To embody. The Incarnation is another unique Christian way of affirming that God knows our human experience. God does this by experiencing human life in the person of Jesus of Nazareth. The resource it offers is not only that God knows what it is like to be who we are, but that he has taken it upon himself to rescue us from our hellbent ways.

vii. judgment—Lest we fall into a Santa Claus way of thinking in which we see Christ and God as powerful genies with Teddy Bear personalities, pushovers to do whatever it is that we want done, we are reminded by this term that God is a God of judgment, of serious evaluation of human action, and of judgment of whatever befouls the creation. We can't just have a "designer God" that we make up. While God is love, God has no patience for the evils we do and we need to know we are in great peril in our sin.

   With great care, the notion of judgment can be a resource for us. The secular equivalents—*critique, assessment, evaluation*—are important but wimpy compared to God's judgment. The Christian is invited by Paul to test all things and hold to that which is good (1 Thess 5:21a). It is this "testing" capacity that you can exercise in college and from which you can expect great results. We do not exercise it at a whim or out of our own concerns, but as Christians, using Christ as the standard. You are invited to evaluate all things—ideas, persons, actions, institutions, processes, technologies—in terms of how closely they accord with Christ's will for each of us. To the extent that they accord with Christ, we judge them good; to the extent that they are used sinfully, they deserve being named and unmasked for what they are, then rejected.

viii. repentance—This "change of mind" involves *un*-learning and disarming the rebel within our hearts. This act of changing our mind puts us in position to receive God's self-revelation. Repentance as an admission of error, weakness, and need is not frequent on college campuses. However, it comes to us as a welcome gift to deliver us from the serious dilemmas into which we can get ourselves through pride.

ix. sin—The Greek word for sin means something like "missing the mark," as when an archer shoots her arrow and misses the target. It is an appropriate term in describing the human condition for here we are, failing at what God created us for—creative and intimate fellowship with one another. Instead, we want to re-create ourselves *for* ourselves; we compete, we don't cooperate; we destroy, we don't create; we want more and different and are not satisfied with the givenness of who we are and what we have. We not only sin but we have created—and a perverse kind of creation it is!—a sinful environment for human life. The world is tainted with our sin and we cannot run from it nor can we fix it by ourselves.

Sin is a term often misused. Sin, the condition into which we place ourselves, is often fragmented and turned into *sins*. Then we can reduce and sanitize them: "Gossip isn't all that bad"; "I couldn't resist the urge to . . . [do whatever it is you did]"). Pretty soon, there is nothing left but a bad habit or a social goof.

And it is not only we ourselves who sin but it is everyone. *Sin* is what everybody does and has; *sinful* is what everybody is. This is a non-discriminatory, equal opportunity aspect of the human failure. It is not our intended condition; that original condition was very good (Gen 1:31). But now we are sinful; that is not good and it is our own fault.

The naming of sin is powerful. Sin is normally not something named or acknowledged in the college setting. The idea that sin—removing ourselves from God—might affect our thinking and pervert it is almost beyond imagining. But if sin is rejecting God, then the thinking we do away from God is affected. The result is what one writer calls "the epistemological consequences of sin."[3] The idea packed into that phrase is that our sinfulness, or our willful separation from God, affects everything in our lives, including our intellectual abilities—how we think, what we think about, and how we know what we know. Sin affects everyone in college and it affects them at the point of the way they think. The point is: Beware. There are many hazards on the road through college.

America's great institutions of higher learning desperately need the humility that can come from the acknowledgement of sin. The Christian is the one who, living out the life of faith, can bring the rich, penetrating, devastating, and cleansing critique of sinfulness to the college experience.

---

3. Moroney, "Sin Affects Scholarship," 443.

x. gospel—Here is another term seldom used, but with specific meaning in the Christian tradition. The essential meaning is that of the good news that God has sent Jesus Christ to address the world's problems. This good news is a constant antidote to the stream of bad news that fills the newspaper pages and TV broadcasts. It is good news to counter the bad news we occasionally receive in our personal lives. It is the truly good news not available elsewhere in the college curriculum.

Take note: this Christian vocabulary is not spoken in the day-to-day activities of the American college. (A recent survey of terminology used by commencement speakers at forty US colleges showed that none of the ten Christian terms in our list was featured in those addressed.[4])

However, these terms provide an excellent resource for the analysis and understanding required of Christians in the college experience. That is because they can name realities for which there are no terms in current secular language. These terms are tools to use in the academy where the dominant philosophy is profoundly different (secular) from a Christian understanding and is communicated in different terminology. The use of Christian language provides tools for our deeper understanding of faith and for constructive criticism of the inadequacies of the academy. It provides a vocabulary that expands the limits of your world. Care in how we communicate is an act of faithfulness and it fits with being the best student you can be.

Hey, What About Math?

Okay, there may be a Christian language and a Christian use of language, but is there Christian math or a Christian way to do it (like getting the right answer every time)?

This is not the right question. Sorry, but there is no Christian Math. The result of 2+2 is going to be 4 whether you are a Christian or an atheist.

Does Jesus, our Teacher, tell us anything about math? Actually, Jesus did not do much math. He probably could have, but he didn't. In fact, the Jewish and early Christian tradition had relatively little interest in mathematics. Even among the Greeks and Romans of biblical times, math was still more philosophical than practical and it remained so until about 400 years ago. It was not until relatively modern times that mathematics became the practical subject it is today.

Still, the ancient Jews were intrigued with the mysteries that numbers held for them. Those who wrote the Bible had a fascination and respect for the mysterious power of numbers.

4. *NYT* (Saturday, June 11, 2011), 22.

While they did not "do math" in ways that we would recognize, they did believe that numbers held riches of information. Some of the obvious examples of the significance of numbers for the first Christians include the emphasis on there being only *one* God and the *one* Teacher, Jesus Christ. *Six* represented imperfection and *seven* perfection. There were *ten* command-ments and *twelve* tribes and disciples. In the difficult-to-interpret apoca-lyptic books of Daniel and Revelation, numbers of years and the number of people constituting groups were important. And, of course, we cannot forget Jesus' admonition to Peter to forgive others *seventy* times *seven*. This reverence for numbers is a caution to Christian students—even those of you who still struggle with the basics of math—to respect and trust their significance. You can learn from that not to dismiss what you don't yet un-derstand. Respect for math—as respect for the Word—is a most appropriate tool for the vocation of Christian student.

Application

Jesus, the Word of God, comes to us as the truth in a world that is confused, and often confuses us. Because of that, Christians respect language and care about precision of expression. Reading and paying attention to what you read and getting the point of what you have read—these are skills that Christians use to know God and themselves better. It so happens that they are the basic skills you need for success in college.

James graduated with a history degree, went to law school, and became a successful lawyer. I had gotten to know him in college because he had taken several Bible classes from me. Years later we were chatting and—out of curiosi-ty—I asked him what was the most important class he had taken in college. He said it was my class on the letters of St. Paul. I was flattered and—wondering which of my brilliant insights had been so memorable—asked his reason for selecting that class. His answer deflated me and pointed toward the impor-tance of those basics we have been discussing. He said, "That class was really important because we learned to read the text—to see what was there, printed on the page, and to notice what was not there. That was very important in preparing for law school and for being a lawyer."

Respect for the basics—that's what the Christian faith imparts to you through the person and work of Jesus, the Teacher, the Word of God. You can use that respect and that seriousness about the basics to make your col-lege experience work well and contribute to your growth in faith and life as a Christian.

Thought and Discussion Questions

1. Pick one "Christian" word and tell its significance to you. Can you see how it might help in enriching your college studies in any particular subject?

2. Name a subject in which you feel unprepared or inadequate. What would it take to help you feel ready to do college work in that area?

3. What are similarities between written communication and mathematics?

4. Can you think of examples of the specialized language or jargon you expect to encounter in any of your classes? Can you think of any similarities or parallels between that and "Christian language"?

5. Share an example of the time that something important that you were given to expect was not forthcoming. What were your feelings of anger or disappointment? Can you understand what had happened to have caused that failure to "come through" on the part of whoever made the promise?

8

Everything, but Connected?

General Education

"Things fall apart; the centre cannot hold."
—W. B. Yeats

". . . in him all things hold together."
—Colossians 1:17b

Scripture Focus

Colossians 1:15–17

He is the image of the invisible God, the first born of all creation; for in him all things in heaven and on earth were created, things visible and invisible, whether thrones or dominions or rulers or powers—all things have been created through him and for him. He himself is before all things, and in him all things hold together.

*A*ll is a little word but a big concept. "All" is beyond most of us. If you have ever tried to collect *all* the matchbooks, to know *all* there is to know about the Beatles, or to be better than *all* other players at chess—it just doesn't happen.

In college you may begin to get a glimpse of "all." You soon realize that you can't read all the books in the library and that all the books in the library are not really all the books there are and that all the books there are don't contain all there is to know. If you can't learn all you need to know in college, you can go on and get a master's degree. Or how about a doctoral degree? (A would-be comedian commented that a doctorate is the degree you receive when you have learned more and more about less and less until you know *all* there is to know about nothing!)

Colleges offer the study of the parts of knowledge (art, biology, chemistry, dance, education, French, zoology). Most colleges will require that you complete a number of courses on at least some of these subjects. Colleges want you to have a wide exposure to at least some of the "all" that there is to know. But the mutual interconnections or interesting relationships of those pieces are seldom explained in a way that would make sense of how it *all* might fit together and be meaningful to you, the student. Because professors are more focused on their own research on their own particular narrow part of the whole, they often leave those sense-making connections up to you the student.

General Education is supposed to do that; it is supposed to give you the "big picture." But most students, faced with the difficulty of fitting each required "gen ed" class into some understandable whole decide simply to "get it out of the way." Rather than try to find any coherent connection among all the different requirements, students routinely dismiss these classes as a necessary but bothersome evil—like flies at a picnic. Usually colleges leave this most intellectually demanding job of all—the job of understanding how all things somehow might make sense together—to students who at this stage of their careers are ill-prepared to do it. One might ask, if the faculty won't or can't show students how the gen ed classes make sense together, why should students be expected to do so? But not to panic.

We usually resort to Jesus only in a crisis—to bail us out or to put things back together. Now, in college, touching base with Jesus the Teacher should be a daily event. In such an environment, is it possible for Christians to know if Jesus is really a player in a secular college environment? Paul, writing to the Colossian Christians who wondered about the relation of Christ to other claimants for their religious faith, quotes a powerful Christian hymn. The song hails Jesus Christ as primary (image of God, first born of creation) and as that which integrates everything, holds the entire cosmos together, and gives it all meaning. We may no longer know the tune of this early hymn, but the central message of a Christ who makes sense of everything is an incredible blessing—especially to anyone in the college experience.

Prayer: Help me to hold to the center, to Christ, and to know that he is at the heart of all my understanding. Amen.

General Education: The College Experience

Does the world make sense? Why don't your parents approve of your choice of clothes or music? Why do bad things happen to good people? To what extent are you responsible for climate change? Is there life on Mars? (And what if there is?) And do these questions and the answers to them have anything to do with one another?

General education is a phrase that captures colleges' attempts to begin to suggest answers to these and about a million other puzzling questions. General education is that program or set of requirements that all students, regardless of major, must take. In these days of emphasis on job preparation, general education is the only time other than the "big game" (see chapter 12) and graduation that all students will share the same experience.

I wrote earlier of the possibility that two students could attend college together, meet, date, fall in love, graduate, marry and live together happily forever after but still have taken only one class together during their entire time in college. If each took a different major it would have been possible for them to have spent their entire four years together geographically, but separated academically, since there was only one class actually required of all students. One of the sad results of this scenario would be that despite all they had in common, there might be virtually no common teachers, readings, great ideas, and specific skills that they shared. In a sense, they might not have much of educational substance to discuss.

There are many reasons for your college to require general education. Students in your school should have some common point of discussion; all students—regardless of their major—should know something of the breadth of human thought and experience. All students ought to sample a bit of this and a bit of that—they might even find something that they like but had not been aware of before. Any educated person needs to have studied certain subjects—specifically the ones required in general education. These high-minded goals are supported in an astonishing variety of ways in different schools. At your school you may find anything from a list of classes to a complex system of options from across the curriculum. You can anticipate that somewhere between a quarter and a third of your college studies will be general education classes; that's the equivalent of one whole year of school!

The intention of these classes is to broaden, to free, to expose—all desirable purposes of the college experience. Each of us needs a broader perspective—to see how the other half lives or how things happened before we came along. Each of us needs to be freer, liberated from the narrow provincialism of family, high school, hometown, ethnic or cultural group. Each of us needs more exposure, particularly to things that are challenging and to the possibility of things that are unifying. Each of us needs to be prepared for the unexpected since that is exactly what you can expect in the future.

However it happens, you will be required to study "outside of the box" of your own comfort zone in the hope that something unexpected and good might happen to you. So you will learn something about literature and the arts. You will be exposed to statistics about mental disease, physical illness, or social movements. You will meet new people—heroes, founders, inventors, villains. You will look in through the window of science at your DNA and out through the window of history to the past and where you came from. Your college will assist you to search for the whole organic interconnected unity of everything. Your college hopes you can see the deep, underlying connections that tie everything together and that you can begin to answer the *big* questions.

Is There a Problem?

Unfortunately, the efforts made to convince students that general education is a great idea too often are ineffective. With speed toward degree completion a central concern for many, it is unlikely that students will take more than a required detour from job preparation studies to enroll in Persian poetry, Arctic biology, or advanced algebra. General education doesn't seem to be on the "fast track" for most students. They can't understand why they need all those classes that are not a part of their major. It can seem like a stupid bureaucratically imposed detour on their way to a job.

You may be asking the same question that popped up in the last chapter: If *it* (the basics, or general education) is really important, why doesn't the college make sure *it* gets done? In answer, the responsibility lies in several places. Let's follow the lines of responsibility to see what the problems might be and see what you miss out on as a result and what problems can arise that Christians need to face.

First, the general education program is almost always the product of the deliberations of the faculty at that specific institution. You would hope that the highest principles and goals would be the primary goal in the development of the program, its aims and requirements. Some possibilities along those lines would be:

> General education at "Center College" aims to create the person that best represents the history, character, and values of "Center College"; or General education at "State University" gives each student an exposure to all the information that every college graduate should have.

But faculty members haven't always done the best job. Well, actually, the problem is that they *have* done *their* jobs—historians teach history, biologists teach biology. But they have not shown students how the two go together—or why a student who is heading for a career in business should have to know both history and biology. Faculty often see teaching of general education classes as they might see teaching the "basics"—as a distraction from the time and energy they need for their own research. If you were to look behind the scenes and see how the faculties of colleges develop the general education programs you would be reminded of the admonition that if you are going to eat hot dogs, you should definitely not watch them being manufactured—the process is not appetizing.

A cynic might argue that the most practical reason for general education is the faculty's need to guarantee employment for itself. With students focusing more and more on business, fewer students enroll in art, poetry, music, and anthropology. So who will enroll in those courses? If those subjects are required as part of general education, teachers of those endangered subjects are virtually guaranteed employment. Sadly, the fact is that when colleges develop their general education curricula the process is more political than educational. Faculty can end up arguing and negotiating the inclusion or exclusion of courses on grounds other than their academic value and the list of classes composing the program is a result of politicking rather than educational vision. The long and labored debates over general education could boil down to something like:

> *Professor Jones: I support the inclusion of Professor Smith's class as a general education requirement. (He's thinking: So that Professor Smith will vote to include my class.)*

> *Professor Smith: I'm glad you agree. Professor Jones's class should be required of all students also. (She's thinking: That should ensure that he'll vote to include my class.)*

When it comes to general education, it looks like faculty tend to focus on their *part* of the whole of knowledge rather than on helping students see some coherent wholeness. That focus on the part leads to exactly the kind of *fragmentation* that general education is intended to overcome. The focus on the *part* to the exclusion of the *whole* can lead to a kind of idolatry—making that part which is not ultimate the most important thing; that's *idolatry.* That is a problem both for those who seek a total, integration of all knowledge and for Christians who know that idolatry is a no-no (Exod 20:4).

Parents—or whoever pays the bills—don't always like general education either because it seems to extend the time spent in college unnecessarily and thus raises the already high cost. It is common knowledge that, as you go through life, most of people will change jobs and probably even change careers. At the rate things change, even if one were to stay in the same job for a lifetime, the job itself would probably change enormously. You simply don't know what will be changing. *At an off-campus enrollment session, I was astonished to hear a father whisper to his eighteen-year-old daughter as she approached me to help her schedule her classes for the coming semester, "Don't let him make you take any classes you don't need." How did she—at eighteen— know what she would need to know when she was thirty, or forty-five, or sixty? How did her father know?*

With the pressure to get on with it and in the absence of the college "making a case" for general education, students are often unhappy with the requirements that force them into classes they see no reason to take. You typically will hear other students express this unhappiness with the query: "If I'm going to be a brain surgeon, why do I need to take literature?" or "Why do I need biology? I'm going into computing." So each in her own way—student, parent, faculty—may lack enthusiasm for what is really a well-intentioned aspect of any college education. The result could be that the college ignores the *big* questions and sets the student up for an idolatrous and myopic focus on her major exclusively. That student will simply be reinforced in her bias that the world is ultimately fragmented and that nothing is connected with anything else in a way that ultimately makes sense.

This is not to say that colleges, faculty, and parents are consciously part of some evil plot to skip the possibility that everything might be able to make sense. The downplaying of general education is probably driven by the felt economic need to get on with it—move along, hurry up, finish school. Or worse: maybe it is because since education is so governed by a secular vision, there is really little hope that coherence, sense, and unity are possibilities. But Christians already have a hint of the possibility that there is ultimately meaning (God) and purpose (eschatology). And some good examples of how that practically works by taking a history class or a physics class would help to enrich your faith.

General education is still usually a requirement, and as the saying goes, you can't beat city hall. So, you will hear students adopt a fallback position, tighten their belts, gather their courage, grit their teeth, and face general education with a determined: "Let's get these basics *out of the way.*" The college student who adopts this "get them out of the way" approach to general education accepts and affirms several secular values and misses out on firming up her Christian faith.

First, she accepts life as fragmented, chopped into small pieces; and she accepts chaos as normal. More importantly, her college experience embodies an atmosphere in which the lack of coherence and the absence of a center that holds everything together is acceptable.

Second, this attitude of "getting it out of the way" reinforces the values of *tolerance* and *consumerism.* You will encounter facts that might disturb you and ideas that may threaten some cherished belief. If you don't take gen ed seriously you may not feel the need to engage those facts or ideas with any seriousness. All you need is to do enough to pass the test. All you need to do is *consume* the class—check it off your list of requirements. This confirms the secular value of *consumption* and develops your sense of *toleration.* Toleration may be a pretty good skill to use in superficial dealings, but it will not get you very far in terms of life's most important issues. Learning to tolerate new ideas will not really achieve one of the positive goals for general education—that of liberating you from the narrow and provincial views with which everyone initially comes to college. To tolerate is to "put up with" but not to take seriously. To tolerate is to acknowledge the existence of something but not necessarily to try to understand it.

Propelled by the feeling that you need to hurry on through college and only take one thing seriously—to prepare for a job—you might settle for accepting such values as *toleration, fragmentation,* and *consumption.* Instead of this kind of toleration, a Christian would practice hospitality—take the new and strange in and treat it with consideration and respect—check it out seriously. Instead of this kind of fragmentation, a Christian would further investigate what it means for Jesus to be at the center of everything. Instead of being a consumer, the Christian would try to cherish and retain what is offered for later use.

Despite the politicking and the inability of the college to provide the means to try to make everything cohere, fit together, and make sense, there is a great benefit in your college wanting you to study what you would not study if left to your own devices. It may sound harsh, but when you go to college you are admitting that you do not know everything and you are submitting yourself to the much more mature and educated minds of those who know a lot more than you do.

Despite the problems, the *purpose* of general education is definitely good—especially when viewed from the perspective of faith. Paul urged the Christians of Thessalonica to "test everything; hold fast to what is good" (1 Thess 5:21). Perhaps the Christians faith can make up for some of the shortcomings of the way in which the typical college general education program is seen. Instead of you getting it out of the way, let it *get in your way*. You will be astonished what you might run into!

Christology: Head of the Body

Who is this Jesus? He is the one who holds it all together; he is the one who makes sense out of everything. He holds it all together because he was in on the creation of everything that exists. He makes sense of it all because everything holds together in him. He connects and interconnects everything. He is the glue. He is the nerve center to and through which all information passes. He enables you to know that everything hangs together; how it hangs together; and what it all means. As such, this Jesus is a definite player in your college experience.

> *Faith enables you to see and embrace a Christology of Jesus as the GLUE that holds it all together.*

In an early Christian hymn (Col 1:15–20) you get a kaleidoscope of prepositions that relate Christ to the creation—*through, for, before, in*. This is a shower of notions about the deeply complex involvement of Jesus Christ with the whole cosmic scope, breadth, and depth of all that exists. He is asserted to be at the center of everything. So if you want to know about something, you eventually have to come to him to have a full and fundamental understanding.

This does not mean that Jesus can substitute for your physics, art, or sociology teacher; it does mean that after those professors describe their subject matter and argue the strengths and weaknesses of the disciplines' basic theories, any final understanding of the ultimate significance of those subjects—how they all fit together—depends on the framework offered by Jesus Christ: agent, planner, purpose, and maker of all that is.

We can see a bit of what that will be from the assertion that Jesus is the Lord and Teacher and that his main message is the kingdom of God—a universe in which all things finally and perfectly fit into the role for which God originally designed them.

When I was in college I signed up for a course in creative writing. By a wonderful stroke of providence, the great American novelist and Nobel

Prize-winning author William Faulkner was "in residence" at my college; and he was teaching the class! Faulkner was the teacher; but he was the teacher who was also the great author. He was a teacher who had "been there, done that." I don't think that I have ever paid so much attention to a teacher as I did to him.

Jesus, as our Teacher, is the Teacher who is not simply confined to telling us *about* things. He is the Teacher who actually was there (at the creation) and is (yes, currently) involved in it in the most profound ways. While the physics professor can describe the universe mathematically and the art professor can describe it in suggestive shapes and astonishing colors, it is only God in Jesus Christ who can give us the whole picture.

Perhaps a clearer Christology—more human and less cosmic in scope—is that of Jesus the Teacher as the Head of the church or the Head of the body of Christ. The body of Christ is an excellent metaphor for the church (cf. 1 Cor 12:12; Eph 4:15-16; Col 2:19). Paul uses the expression in writing to the Christians at Corinth, a church where everyone was doing their own thing and no one felt the need to connect with anyone else. St. Paul's basic idea was that each person was unique—like an eye or a foot—but in order to be the best eye or foot they could be, they needed to be connected—like all the parts of the body are connected. And Christ is the Head—central command, overseeing the smooth interaction of all the parts.

When you study personality and consciousness, it is interesting to ponder what part(s) of you could you do without and still be yourself. Cut your hair and fingernails or pull a tooth and you are still you. Amputate a finger? Still you. Two fingers? Three? Remove a lung or kidney? Still you. We know that humans can be deprived of a lot of parts and functions and still be *who they are*. But cut off your head and it's all over.

Jesus the Teacher as the Head is a Jesus Christ who we cannot do without. The body—constituted by the rest of us—would not be able to function. We could not connect with each other. We would have no connection that would make us fully who we were meant to be.

So what did Jesus teach? He taught about the kingdom of God—about what the universe would be like if everything took his/her/its appropriate place as a creature of God and lived out the purpose of his/her/its respective natures. The topic or theme of the kingdom of God is useful in learning more about the world in which you live. It protects you from the idolatry of worshiping a *part* (e.g., job, poetry, food, money, computers, biology, sex, winning) and lures you on—with Jesus' help—to the fullness of the *whole* in which the part finally finds fulfillment.

Wholeness in Christ the Head of the body fulfills and connects the parts; it does not obliterate or devalue them. Coherence in Christ the Head of the body overcomes the dangers of fragmentation and utilizes the meaning of each part in a grander significance of the whole. Worship of Christ the Head of the body increases in meaning at the same time that it protects you from a fragmenting idolatry that can seduce you away from God to a commitment to only one part. When it comes time for you to select a major, be careful. A major—biology, business—is only a part of God's world. Don't let that part absorb you so completely that you forget about the whole; that would be idolatrous.

Holding to Jesus the Teacher as Christ our Head provides assistance at the point where the college experience presents you with the dangers of fragmentation—something that inevitably meets you at virtually every step of the college experience. Thus Scripture can remind you that Christ is to be at the center of what you do. If Christ is at the center, as the agent of creation, as the principle of coherence in the universe, then you will not be lost when it comes to seeking coherence and connection within the changing jumble of what college offers, what students are required to study, what teachers are required to teach or what life might present you.

For example—and each of us faces this—picture yourself with a career and a personal life; one is fairly public, the other fairly private. Each has its own *place*, each has a (probably different) cast of characters, each fulfills you in different ways. Will you be able to integrate the two so that you are essentially the same person, with the same interests, morals, goals, personality, enough so that the disinterested observer will be able to say that you are a person of integrity? Or will your life and your thoughts about it be fragmented and lack integrity? The college experience is not one that favors integrity. Certainly something to think about.

Clinging to Jesus as the *glue* that holds all things together provides guidance at the point where you may be tempted to tolerate and accept something that doesn't seem to fit. Rather than disregard or "blow off" the new, strange or apparently objectionable, you are invited to see how it all finds a connection through Christ.

Instead of taking these required classes and checking them off of your list—like they were some bad-tasting medicine you were forced to endure—you might see them as investments in understanding more deeply what this complex miracle of life is all about. These aren't classes to be consumed and checked off; they are experiences to be savored. Don't be in such a hurry. When you think you need to hurry through your college requirements you might remember Jesus the Teacher, who did not hurry toward achievement of his own goal but allowed himself to be interrupted constantly by people with *their* problems.

And remember Jesus' visit to the two sisters, Mary and Martha (Luke 10:38–42), who responded to him in different ways. Martha busied herself serving and doing the necessaries required in entertaining a guest. Mary, on the other hand, sat at the feet of Jesus, oblivious to the chores calling to be done. Note Jesus' assessment of the situation: Mary had chosen the better thing, *the* thing: Jesus at the center, the only focus. We are reminded in the Mary/Martha story, as in Colossians 1:17, that Jesus is absolutely at the center, whether it is at the center of your personal life or at the center of an unimaginably huge and complex cosmic reality. Whether you experience the cosmos as too unmanageable, with no center or no frame, or whether the wheels are coming off of your life and things are coming apart at the seams on a personal level, there is something stronger and something that provides meaning and centers everything. The college experience can seem like a welter of distractions to the Martha within each student, running from this assignment to that activity, from this report to that test. Christ is the answer to the Mary in you when you seek the one best thing.

> *Connections: Hell is a place where nothing connects with nothing.*
> —T. S. ELIOT

Finally, you need to remember that Jesus—the one in whom all things come together and make sense—is the truth who makes you free (John 8:32). It is he who moves you beyond the barriers that isolate you and will move you toward freedom from the local, the false, the partial, and the cultural boundaries, but more importantly a freedom for true communion with and service to others.

Application

You will have an advantage going into your general education program because you know *that* it is important, *why* it is important, and *how* all the components—whatever crazy combination of classes is thrown at you—finally fit together. So instead of joining in the complaints ("Why do I need this?" or "I'm going to *get this out of the way*"), you can approach these educational experiences with eager anticipation since—again, whatever they are—they will reveal one more part of the grand reality that God offers you through Jesus Christ. You will have the confidence that there is a final culmination in which all things will come together in Christ.

So: general education. Something to "get out of the way"? No. Instead, your prayer might be, *Lord, let my general education classes get in my way.*

Instead of my wondering what I can do with them, help them do something with me; let them do something to me. Let them help me see Christ as all in all and let me know that I am never alone. Amen.

Thought and Discussion Questions

1. Review reasons that Christians would prefer understanding to tolerance, commitment to consumption, coherence to fragmentation, and valuable to cheap.

2. How far ahead in life can you see (a week, two months, five years, ten, twenty-five?) and do you feel prepared for all that will happen in that time frame? Why not? Is there any way you could?

3. List three things about which you would like to know something, even though they may not be in your planned major. List three that you really don't care about. Why don't you?

4. List several connections that you can imagine between science and literature, or between history and music, or . . .

9

Thinking About a Major?

Humanities

"Play it again, Sam."

—Attributed to Ingrid Bergman as Ilsa in Casablanca

"No prophecy of scripture is a matter of one's own interpretation."

—2 Peter 1:20b

Scripture Focus

Mark 4:13

Do you not understand this parable?
Then how will you understand all the parables?

Jesus' main teaching vehicle was the parable. A parable is basically a comparison between something you know (for example: a steel trap) and something you have difficulty describing in ordinary language either because it is otherwise unknown or extremely difficulty to describe (for example: the mind). The result: He has a *mind **like** a steel trap*. The "like" sets up the comparison. The listener is led from his *mind*—that which needs description—to *steel trap* and one or more of the characteristics of a steel trap: tough, quick, tenacious. Jesus used this parable form to communicate his extraordinary message of God's kingdom. We know dozens of his parables from the Gospels; he probably told many more that didn't get written down.

Jesus' concern in the passage quoted at the beginning of this chapter was that his disciples understand his parables. He had just delivered the parable of the sower (or seed) and he wanted them to understand what he was saying about the subject of the parable. The disciples all understood about farmers (they scattered seed all over their farms during the planting) and seed (it responds differently depending on where it lands). What they did not yet understand was how that bit of agricultural information illuminated the subject matter of Jesus' teaching—the kingdom of God. The task for the disciples was to *understand*.

Notice that the task for the disciples was *not* to run out and *do* something. We really short circuit Jesus the Teacher when we take what he is telling us about God and what God does and then turn it into something *we* are supposed to do. That misunderstands God, Jesus, his teaching, and our own situation.

- It misunderstands God because it is God who rescues us, not we who rescue ourselves.

- It misunderstands Jesus because he saw his task as living out the love of God toward us.

- It misunderstands his teaching because Jesus' teaching is primarily the proclamation, explanation, illumination, and illustration of the kingdom of God.

- It misunderstands us because we mistakenly think that our salvation is based on our own performance.

So we place ourselves in several mistaken roles. First, we set ourselves up as super interpreters of Jesus' words by turning them from the description of God's work into *rules* that we incorrectly pretend were made for us to perform. Second, we reverse the role of faith so that we become the ones who cause salvation by our own performance, while God's role is reduced to that of a clerk whose main job is to check up on our performance and enter it into the heavenly records. There are too many mistakes here for us to make all at once!

So let's not make *any* of them. Anyone who takes the parables and changes them from Jesus' description of God into something that we must *do* has really missed the point and misinterpreted him badly. Jesus does not ask us to perform; he asks us to understand and appreciate. Jesus does not compel us to act; he invites us to imagine. What are we supposed to do? Well, nothing. Nothing, that is, except try to understand what the picture is that he is verbally painting. Nothing except let our imaginations be carried on his words into realms that haven't been explored before. Elsewhere he cautions that there are some who listen but really don't hear. So—let's *hear* him.

Prayer: Free my imagination and let my listening to Jesus be so focused on him that I finally begin to understand. Amen.

The College Scene: The Humanities

Now that you have taken the "basics" seriously and have figured out that college's gen ed can enrich your faith-based conviction that Jesus is really at the center of things and can make sense out of the big picture, you are ready to get on with the specific academic areas where you will find your major.

What is your favorite subject? Can you admit that your favorite subject is . . . *you*? You are that unique, complex, amazing human being who is always near to if not in the center of your own spotlight. That was simple, wasn't it?

Now, what are "the Humanities"? That is a little more complicated; at least, the list of possibilities is longer. "The Humanities" is a term for the various ways of studying that human being that is you (and, of course, all other human beings). According to the US government's 1965 National Foundation on the Arts and the Humanities Act, "The term 'Humanities' includes, but is not limited to, the study of the following: language, both modern and classical; linguistics; literature; history; jurisprudence; philosophy; archaeology; comparative religion; ethics; the history, criticism and theory of the arts; those aspects of social sciences which have humanistic content and employ humanistic methods; and the study and application of the Humanities to the human environment with particular attention to reflecting our diverse heritage, traditions, and history and to the relevance of the Humanities to the current conditions of national life."[1] That covers a lot of territory (different courses) but all of it is about what it means to be a human being.

The most likely encounter all students will initially have with the Humanities will be in classes on literature, music and art, history, religion, and philosophy—probably as a part of general education. These courses

1. National Foundation on the Arts and Humanities Act of 1965, sec 3(a).

are characterized by study of the imaginative products of women and men throughout the ages—otherwise known as the *classics* of literature, drama, music, and art.

Originally, the reason such study existed was because it was believed that the classics taught lessons of fundamental importance about life. "Classics" is a general term that could include religious texts, drama, poetry, and fiction. Music and the visual arts were also included because they speak without words (one picture is worth 1,000 words). Classics can be read (seen, heard), reread and revisited with the expectations that they will continue to inspire, soothe, challenge, or otherwise pay new dividends. The classics engage us in struggles over big questions, offering different perspectives that people through the centuries have considered worthy of consideration.

Perhaps you will major in the Humanities. In some cases, there is definitely a linear progression in the training. If you study language, you will begin with present tense, move to simple past and future, then to perfects, subjunctives, and the more complex subtleties. In music, you learn simple notes and rhythms and move later to the more complex. Much study gets you from A to Z, from square one to some concrete, measurable skill. In computer class you start with the on/off switch and end the semester creating programs. In science you begin in ignorance and end up knowing how to differentiate cells or produce chemical reactions.

While it is true that in music or art or language you might learn skills, the interesting thing about this kind of study is that you can return again and again to the same material, learning more each time. It is not so much a matter of learning information as it is of plumbing the depths of feeling and the heights of imagination. This requires constant return to the text or portrait or melody; it means seeing *Hamlet* produced several times by different actors, Beethoven played by another musical group, a painting revisited five years from now, after you have had a baby, lost a parent, been up Mount Everest.

A group of three faculty—Dr. Jones (a musician), Dr. Smith (a chemist), and I (a theologian)—team-taught a seminar for a group of ten freshmen. They were the brightest students in the freshman class, and we believed that there would be some great benefits for the students (and ourselves) if we could join forces to bring our particular expertise and individual academic perspectives to the class—letting the students see how experts could interact, and provide multiple layers of insight, and draw the students into the conversation. Our chosen subject was a famous piece of music—a piece of music written by the great Johann Sebastian Bach.

Dr. Jones was to help us understand the work as a piece of music. I was to examine the religious themes in the libretto (words). Dr. Smith was to place the

*whole piece in its contemporary historical, political, social setting. We thought
it would be a great experience.*

*From the start the students objected. They could not see where the
seminar was going—what its outcome would be. It seemed to them that there
were no skills to be learned that would help them in future careers. They were
suspicious that just conversing with three instructors would prove more ar-
gumentative than informative. The student frustration seemed to culminate
in the defiant challenge of one student: "You can't make us take this class; it's
unconstitutional!"*

This incident is an extreme example of the disconnect students sometimes experience. They want to get on with things. The Humanities seem to
slow you down—like when you are required to study the same poem twice.
Students want to know how to prepare (fast) for a job; the Humanities invite
you to slow down and they try to help you understand what it means to be
a human being.

What's wrong with taking things slowly? Even repeating something?
You usually don't mind doing things you like more than once: eating grand-
mother's cookies, going to the mall, listening to your favorite song. As a
human being, you really enjoy repeating pleasant experiences. These experiences seem to be what life is all about—or at least what makes life fun.

But you live in a culture that wants to consume and move on. In college, students want to learn what they need to know and do not want to stop
along the way to "smell the flowers" or to have to learn something that they
think (at this moment) that they will never need to know. If there is some
requirement to study some music by Bach, the tendency is to want to "get
'er done" and move on—as if the class were a fallen tree blocking the road.
Even the college interested in providing the best learning experience would
be hesitant to invest three—count 'em, three—teachers for one class that
seemed irrelevant to the students enrolled.

But what may appear at first to be irrelevant may be peculiarly human
and engaging once you get into it. You do listen to your favorite song again.
And again and again. Why do you do it? You do it because it is beautiful.
Or because it moves you in some way. Or because it conveys a message. Or
because it reminds you in strange ways of other times and important people.
What is your favorite song? How many times have you heard it? Would you
listen again? Why?

In the 1942 Oscar-winning film *Casablanca*, Humphrey Bogart and
Ingrid Bergman are in love and *their* song is a tune called "As Time Goes By."
At one point in the movie, she asks the piano player in the bar Bogart owns
to, "Play it, Sam." Why play it again since it had already been played earlier
in the movie? After all, the audience knows it and the audience knows that

the characters in the film already know it too. Why play it again? Because it is something expressive of the love relationship shared by Bogart and Bergman. It brings to mind the love relationship that is being threatened by misunderstandings and war and suspicion.

Incidentally, that movie, like a handful of others, has itself become a classic. It is recognized as a classic because it addresses issues of profound human interest: growing up, thwarted love, war, patriotic duty. As a classic, it is a film that people will view again and again, despite the fact that repeat viewers know the plot, much of the dialogue, and how it will end.

Finally, it is interesting to note that the most famous quote from that film is Ilsa's (Ingrid Bergman's) line, "Play it, Sam." That line has become famous *not* as "Play it, Sam" but as "Play it *again*, Sam." The word "again" is actually not in the movie, but the notion of repetition definitely is and over time those familiar with the movie supplied (in their own memories) the word "again" because they knew that was what Ilsa really wanted—to hear the already familiar and emotionally powerful song repeated. That is a notion that we can all understand because we continue to return to those works of imagination that help us to feel and to understand more deeply.

The classics give us resources with which to deal with the overwhelming questions and emotions of life: love, broken relationships, death. Why do we go over and over such problems as death? *When our daughter died we knew the physical cause. The science of medicine explained it; we understood the scientific explanation. We never had to ask again about the specific cause of her death; it was all too clear. But why* her? *Why did she have to die? That was the real question and we kept asking it and trying to find answers when there were none. You'd think that you wouldn't want to re-ask hard question— especially ones with no answers. But we do and that is all too human.*

Death is one of life's imponderable facts, about which we cannot stop thinking just because we thought about it once.[2] The Humanities encompass the study of the great products of human imagination and deep pondering of life's most impenetrable questions. In your acquisition of basic skills (chapter 7) and our exploration of the vastness of knowledge (chapter 8) you discovered that you can read, study, and learn. The arts push the limits of language in poetry. But sometimes you have to abandon words and allow music to express your feelings. Other times it is something visual. What

---

2. Another problem: colleges seem to prefer to ignore death. Carlin Romano (a philosophy teacher at Temple University) wrote "When Death Breaches the Campus Walls," and asserted that death had no place on college campuses. "On campus," he wrote, "we outlaw it from our minds whenever possible."

Sorry, but death does happen; it happens all the time on college campuses (car accidents, suicides) so students must deal with it *in* class and *outside* of class.

happens when you fall in love? You resort to poetry or you may "say it with flowers." Humans *feel* more deeply than there are words to express those feelings. You *question* more than there are answers. And you *rejoice* more than there is laughter in you. The Humanities offer assistance in doing these profoundly human activities

Is There a Problem?

You might say: *Yes, there is a problem! Can I ever get a job if I major in something like Medieval French Art or Ancient Greek Philosophy or Hippie Poetry?*

Relax. Generations of students will answer: "Yes, you will get a job; that isn't a problem." You may not get the job as curator of Medieval French Art in the Louvre in Paris or Professor of Philosophy at Harvard. However, if you get that humanities degree, consider what you have accomplished: you have mastered a great deal of material by means of rigorous study; you have met the expectations of experts in that field and have proven yourself to be someone who can perform at a high level.

Humanities Majors Can Get Good Jobs![3]

Name	Major	Job
George Bush	History	President of US
Carly Fiorina	Medieval History	CEO, Hewlett-Packard
Katie Couric	American Studies	TV news anchor
Bruce Lee	Philosophy	Movie actor
Sally Ride	English	Astronaut
J. K. Rowling	French	Author: *Harry Potter*
Willard Scott	Religious Studies	TV meteorologist
Clarence Thomas	English	Supreme Court Justice

Your prospective employer will want to hire someone who is capable of meeting the high standards of a university program. Your future employers will want to hire someone capable of learning the company business; you will have to show that you are capable of *learning*. Your college accomplishment—regardless of your major—will show them that you will be able to make the grade because you already have made the grade.

3. http://kaarme.com/Celebrity_College_Majors.

No, getting a job is not the problem. The main problem is the challenge to faith—the temptation to forget your limits as a creature of God and think you are the ultimate authority. The Humanities introduce you to the world of amazing human achievement—the *Mona Lisa,* Plato's *Dialogues,* the Sphinx. Such achievements strike us as inspired, nearly divine. Because the Humanities tend to focus on the best and the most beautiful of human creation, you might be blinded to the divine by the intense light of human brilliance. You might focus totally on making movies or practicing with your band and forget the whole picture God paints.

Protagoras, a fifth-century BCE Greek philosopher, claimed that "man is the measure of all things." One way to understand that is: the highest level of perfection is set by humans; ours is the highest authority and the ultimate standard. Christian faith has a problem with that. Christians believe that God, the creator of all things, is the ultimate reality and the measurer of all things. At most that makes humans the "penultimate"—next to the ultimate.

Penultimate: second place in the creation. That's not a bad place to be. The Psalmist puts it this way in Psalm 8:4–6:

> . . . what are human beings that you [God] are mindful of them . . . ?
> Yet you have made them a little lower than God . . . ,
> You have given them dominion over the works of your hands;
> you have put all things under their feet . . .

In fact, it is most helpful to know that we are so close to God. It suggests that among the responsibilities of your Christian vocation as a student is to be responsible for coming up with the best interpretation of whatever you encounter in college, in the Humanities, indeed in all subjects. It is both your opportunity and your responsibility to be as imaginative as possible.

But there is always that lingering temptation to see yourself as the ultimate judge when it comes to offering your opinion when interpreting what you read, see, or hear. This is the age of hyper-individualism. It is more and more the case that each person is encouraged to measure things in his or her own individual way. There is the danger of forgetting that God is the ultimate judge; you might also think that other humans—even your professors and other experts, even *all* of the experts—can be ignored. You will encounter those who feel that their opinion is better than anyone else's. In such an environment, you might begin to think that any opinion is equally valid and that each of us can believe as we like regardless of facts, well-tested theories, or the wisdom of others.

A common label for this kind of thinking is *post-modernism.* This is the current new thing in philosophy and many of your professors will speak of our being in a post-modern era or "age." You may have heard of the "golden age," the "enlightenment," "romanticism," "modernism"; if you haven't yet, that's okay; you will hear about them in college. Each label tries to convey the sense of the real core of a particular period of time—in particular, the way in which the leading thinkers of each era thought of themselves comes through. Most people who take this seriously would probably put us at the end of *modernism* (when we thought everything was figured out and settled and there was really one best way to think about what humanity had created) and at the beginning of post-modernism, in which everyone is encouraged to have their own personal answers to important questions and where no absolute truth that is the same for everyone can be counted on.

Post-modernism is really hard to define because everyone can have a different view on what it is. That may be the best definition of this new period—it is whatever you think it is. It is a time in which everyone's ideas have a claim to be just as good as everyone else's ideas. There is no such thing as absolute truth; instead, truth is thought of as a social creation—we make it up ourselves. If we disagree on what truth is, that's okay—each of us can have our own truth(s). Thus one of the notable characteristics of post-modernism is *relativism*: what's true for me needn't be true for you; what's true for you doesn't need to be acceptable to me. This is the ultimate assertion of humans over against God's self-revelation in Christ. And that *is* a problem because Christian faith leads us to trust and hope in a God who is the same—yesterday (from the beginning), today, and forever (Heb 13:8).

The independence of each of us asserting the truth is good—to a point. But ultimately our personal whims must be checked and balanced by other arguments, opinions, traditions, and facts. In an age of individualism, study of the Humanities opens us to two things that could tempt a person of faith. First, it invites us to focus on human creativity. That creativity is good but we must not ignore the God who created all of this human potential in the first place. Second, we are tempted to become enamored by our own opinion and ignore those of others. To be uncritically satisfied with your own views, regardless of the views of others, is to elevate independence and your own opinions to the level of an ultimate or final authority. Do you really trust your own opinions so much?

But the Christian is in a good position to avoid idiosyncratic opinion and thus to seek understanding outside of himself. He can ask critical questions: what did the author or composer intend? What interpretation is held by the community in which this classic (or classic-to-be) is most at home? What are the accepted rules governing this genre? (For example, a sonnet has sixteen lines, no more, no less; and country and western music has no half tones.)

You want the key to unlock the meaning of what you study. This is not only the case with the Humanities but with anything that you might study in college. There you are, sitting in class, and (just as the Psalmist said) recognizing the total majesty of God the creator of everything and of your own fallibility. The professor asks you a question. What you need to find is a balance between feeling totally worthless (on one hand) and feeling like the world's greatest know-it-all (on the other hand). You need a well-considered, informed answer, an interpretation that is solid because you have considered the evidence, evaluated the argument and only then come to your own conclusion.

Jesus gives us an example of humility; but he also shines as a practitioner of the interpretation of the facts around him; with that he combines imagination, artistry, insight, and storytelling about the facts of faith and the reality of the kingdom of God.

Christology: Jesus the Artist

There is an old saying: "Those who can, do; those who can't, teach." It does not apply to Jesus. Jesus was the Teacher who could truly perform. When it came to literature, Jesus not only taught the Scripture, he also created picture stories that still live vividly today. If you are thinking, *Sounds like there is another Christology here*, you are exactly right. In order to have a good Christology—an understanding of the significance of Jesus—you don't need a label found in Scripture. But there is certainly a picture of Jesus in Scripture that suggests that he is a masterly and imaginative creator. (You might see this Christology as a sub-category of "Jesus the Teacher"—he is a teacher with a way of telling stories that brings you into a totally new world view experience.) This is clear in the truly unforgettable pictures he offered to help us get our minds around the notion of the kingdom of God.

> ### What Do Humanities Professors Believe?
> *Sixty-six percent of Americans believe in God, but only 23 percent of college Humanities teachers do.*
> —TOBIN AND WEINBERG,
> *PROFILES OF THE AMERICAN UNIVERSITY*

Who is this Christ, the Artist? He is the one who expresses the inexpressible (the kingdom of God) by using human resources. His main tool was the parable—stories of the ordinary—by means of which he explained that which is extraordinary. He took the raw material from his own cultural environment and fashioned stories that have survived and become shapers of our thinking today. Some examples are the Good Samaritan and the Prodigal Son. He used his imagination to prompt us to use our imaginations to seek and discover what is true and important.

There are some themes that Jesus the storyteller employs with regularity. One of the most frequent includes servants as the central figures. These characters demonstrate a range of understandable characteristics from faithfulness to cowardice to sheer nastiness. Related to servants is the topic of masters (kings, landowners) who are depicted "lording it over" others, ignoring the needs of others or, alternatively, having extraordinary patience, forgiveness, and generosity. Agriculture is another topic Jesus uses with frequency. He uses food, trees, fish, seeds, crops, and fields as features in his parables. The point is that Jesus uses the materials of the world around him to create pictures of what we previously could not even imagine.

When Jesus speaks about his favorite topic he says, "The kingdom of God is *like* . . . ." And then he goes on to compare or illustrate it by means of something about which we probably know a lot more than we do about God and/or God's kingdom and power. Some of these things are pretty commonplace: The kingdom of God is *like* . . . yeast, a pearl, a farmer, a mustard seed, a king. But it doesn't get easier.

Instead, we are called upon to use those Humanities-like skills of imaginative involvement. What is there about yeast, or a pearl, or a farmer that can shed some light on the kingdom of God? Why would you want to know? As a student you ponder imponderables and as a Christian you ponder the nature of God. Who is God? What difference does it make if there is a God? What is there about the kingdom of God that would make it so important that you would want it more than anything?

Some of these things are not so easy to figure out. The kingdom of God is *like* . . . a bad employee, a businessman who sells his entire inventory to buy one pearl, a shepherd who abandons ninety-nine sheep in perilous territory in order to try to locate one that had gotten lost.

> Here's Another
> Christology to Ponder
> —*Jesus the Hermeneut—this is the Jesus whose hermeneutics come from God. He interprets Scripture . . . and everything else so we can understand things faithfully.*

In parable after parable, Jesus the Teacher builds a picture—tentative, partial—of that which God is and what God wants us to experience. (Remember: It is something God is doing; not us.) We are invited to imagine the possibilities. As you add one parable to another and build a montage of glimpses of what Jesus is talking about, you get an amazing picture of Jesus' vision of God's plan for his creatures.

Jesus is an imaginative teacher who is also a storyteller who liberates and stimulates our imaginations. "Liberal arts" is a term occasionally used for that portion of college study outside the major. It really means "liberating" arts—studies that can lift us from our inherited notions and challenge us to think more broadly. (Is this still another possible Christology? How about "Jesus the Liberator"? With his stories he certainly takes us out of our "boxes" and gets us to think in new ways!) College ought to do that; Jesus certainly does that for us. Jesus who teaches and who pushes us beyond the limits of our imagination is not one to abandon us if we fail to grasp things.

It is not only the stories that Jesus told but also it is the entire story of Jesus that Jesus invites us to imagine. Let's face it; the notion of someone overcoming death is pretty mind-boggling. That is Jesus' story. It challenges us and stretches our imagination. It invites us in.

"In" doesn't mean that we somehow go back to Jesus' day. There is no great benefit—and probably a lot of silliness—in trying to speak Aramaic (or Greek), giving up your car in favor of a donkey, and preferring a monarchy to a democratic form of government. But there exists the possibility that the story experienced by the first Christians can transform your life into one shaped by the gospel in Jesus Christ. And you can use what you learn in the Humanities to enrich your understanding and grow in your faith. Jesus does not leave you on your own to read his stories, his miracles, his life in any way that might please you. His life, ministry, death, and resurrection provide the main context that helps you interpret his teaching of God's eternal truth. That teaching should be interpreted in the context and with the fellowship and insight of his community, the church, the ongoing family of faithful Christians who seek to live within Jesus' story. You read the Scripture within that community that surrounds, supports and nurtures your reading, and to which you in turn contribute. If the feeling in college and particularly in doing the Humanities is that you—when it comes to finding, defining and committing yourself to the Truth—are the Lone Ranger, then you are on the wrong track and are not going to find yourself as part of Jesus' story.

You read Scripture in order to let Jesus' interpretation define who you need to be; in this sense you allow yourself to be reformed by the text and ultimately by Jesus himself. The text discloses a new and different "world" to you from the one the secular college leads you to accept. Jesus invites you to enter his world. If you do, you can be transformed—not, of course, by the text, but by the God whom the text takes seriously. The transformation is not something final, just as any particular Scriptural reference to faith is not finally exhaustive of all the possible meanings of faith. The transformation is an ongoing "working out" (Phil 2:12) of the scripturally embodied story in your own ongoing life. Through such imaginative attentiveness to

Scripture you are armed against the college's culture of fragmentation and individualism.

In Christ the Artist and in Scripture (the writings of the original Christian community), you have some basic tools with which to (1) use the Humanities creatively in your own education, and (2) do your interpreting of the Humanities (or any other college course materials) in contexts in which you are comfortable in taking the experts' and the community's understandings seriously.

Application

God is extraordinarily creative and imaginative; after all, just look at the cosmos—giraffes, octopuses, and a million other marvelously inventive creatures. How about yourself? You are created in God's image. The study of the Humanities is a great way to work at developing your own imagination and understanding. Jesus occasionally acknowledged that people listened but didn't really hear, looked but didn't really see (Matt 13:13), and spent a lot of time with him but failed to understand (Matt 15:16). Don't be caught not understanding—or at least not trying your best to understand.

The study of the Humanities exercises your imagination. Jesus calls for you to imagine the possibilities of a world with God in charge. When Jesus asks the disciples if they understand his stories, isn't he asking you also? Being exposed to the Humanities, listing to the stories, watching the plays, seeing the pictures, hearing the songs, focusing on what they have to say—all this helps you develop skills of listening so that you hear, and seeing so that you understand.

"Without knowledge of self there is no knowledge of God."[4] "Without knowledge of God there is no knowledge of self."[5] The more you know about yourself, the more you know about God. The more you know about God, the more you know about yourself. You learned as far back as Genesis 1:26 that you were made by God in God's own image and that you are very good (Gen 1:31)! Don't forget the three truths packed into these Genesis verses: you are (1) made by God, are (2) made in the image of God, and are (3) made very good.

The Humanities have produced astonishing works of imagination. But there must be room left for the even more astonishing: God. Any failure to take that seriously guarantees a view of humans that is faulty. But allowing

---

4. Calvin, *Institutes*, 35—the very first words in Calvin's great theological treatise.

5. Ibid., 37—this is the heading for the second section in Calvin's *Institutes*.

your God-given imagination to interact with the highest expressions of human creativity and in so doing find out more of the truth about yourself, the world and the creator, will speed you along your vocation as a student.

Thought and Discussion Questions

1. If you could be proficient (or even a raving genius!) in any of the Humanities, which would it be? And why?

2. If you are still lacking in enthusiasm for the Humanities, but you will need to take at least one Humanities course as part of your general education program, which would be the one course that you would settle for? Why that particular course?

3. We can agree with the words of the chorus, "Jesus loves *me*, this I know," and still be very critical of the value of individualism. Explain.

4. How would you balance being "a little lower than God" with being a responsible critic/interpreter of ideas, books, plays, movies, philosophy, etc?

10

THINKING ABOUT A MAJOR?

The Sciences

"Science without religion is lame;
religion without science is blind."

—ALBERT EINSTEIN

"You killed the Author of life,
whom God raised from the dead."

—ACTS 3:15

Scripture Focus

COLOSSIANS 2:2–3

*. . . God's mystery, that is, Christ himself, in whom are hidden
all the treasures of wisdom and knowledge.*

*W*isdom and *knowledge*—they may sound similar but they are two different things. According to Scripture, knowledge has to do with intimate relationships. Adam "knew" Eve (and she had a child); God knows Israel; we are known by God. God reveals himself (and knowledge about himself) to those whom he knows.

Wisdom, on the other hand, refers to practical insights about the world. It is information derived from practical experience. The Wisdom writings of the Old Testament (Proverbs, Job, Ecclesiastes) contain the learning—the savvy, the "street smarts"—gained through close observation of the world.

In Jesus you encounter both knowledge and wisdom. Being God, he knew us and as an astute observer of the world he was wise in all matters. Thus Jesus *is* both wisdom and knowledge.

Can we have both knowledge and wisdom? Do we need both? Before we answer, we need to remind ourselves that these days we define both wisdom and knowledge differently than the biblical writers did. For us, college provides knowledge about computers, speaking Arabic, playing the clarinet, ancient history, statistics, personnel management, and all the rest. Wisdom has to do with what we can learn about the best way to live our lives. Whether we use the biblical definitions or our modern ones, these terms point to different but equally important things.

To live wisely and use our knowledge in the best way, we certainly need Jesus as Teacher. The fact that he is both wisdom and knowledge gives us assurance that our trust in Jesus is trust in someone with roots in the very origins of reality and the very immediate presence of God. Jesus is a "been there, done that" teacher. There is no one like him.

Prayer: I pray that I might acquire the knowledge I need and that you will grant me the wisdom to use that knowledge according to your loving and gracious will. Amen.

The College Experience: Science

Nothing characterizes the content of a college education today better than the claim that *"knowledge is power."*[1] The knowledge that you seek in college is primarily knowledge of the physical and social worlds—these are the worlds where you will work and over which you may want to exercise some control. Knowing *how* the world works enables the knower to exercise some control over it. If you know how it works you may be able to manipulate the mechanisms that drive the world and perhaps change things, maybe even for the better. This power puts humans in (at least some) control of the world. The tool is Science (and her active cousin technology).

1. This famous affirmation was made in 1620 by Francis Bacon (1561–1626), a writer whose primary claim to fame lay in his outline of what has come to be understood as the "scientific method." His linking of knowledge with power changed forever our understanding of the nature, potential, and use of knowledge. No longer would it be about intimate personal relationships; now it would be about hard facts.

Science encompasses a multitude of college courses: biology, chemistry, physics, sociology, psychology, politics (political science), economics, and more. All Science courses share one key element: method. Since the goal of Science is precise knowledge, the method of gathering that information must be careful and controlled. It is to be done in a way that is objective and not biased or contaminated by any personal prejudice on the part of the investigator. What you will learn in the Sciences is not necessarily final truth, but at least the current status of what useful theories have been able to demonstrate convincingly to those who study the subject. No one can reasonably doubt that we have learned a lot about the world and as a result gained a lot of control over it. The ability to cure and even eliminate certain diseases is an area in which Science has been the foundation on which we have achieved spectacular results.

These advances in our knowledge (and power) began back when some ancient Greek philosophers set out to discover what the world was made of. The crucial factor was not the answers they came up with. (Those answers included the notion that the world is made of water, or, another, that it is made of air!) The important thing about their quest was the method they used. Instead of being satisfied with traditional or religious answers, they set off to solve the riddle using their own powers of observation and reason.

When colleges were young and Western Science was just beginning to emerge as a distinct field of study, the practitioners studied the world in order to understand what God had made. As time passed, and more was learned about the world, the role of God as the ultimate explanation receded. Today, religious faith is often unwelcome—and almost universally seen as unnecessary—in the neighborhood of Science. That secularizing of Science—taking religion out of it—was probably a good thing because belief in God was impossible to include as a useful part of contemporary scientific methods. Religious belief often supported theories it had no business defending: that the earth is flat; that the sun revolved around the earth; that witches caused disease.

Just what is Science? Science is more a method than a subject matter. It is basically a procedure. In order to discover the nature of something—a bodily organ, a society, an economic system—you have a theory about it and you test that theory by doing experiments. If the theory works out as you expected, then you have an experiment that can be repeated with the expectations of the same outcome. If it doesn't work out, you might fiddle with one or other parts of the theory until you get it to work. Either way, you have learned something.

This procedure can be used on the material world (physics, chemistry, biology) or on the human or social world (sociology, psychology, economics). The former is often referred to as "hard" Science since that kind of Science performed on the physical world and in the controlled environment of the laboratory yields more precise (solid, hard) results. Less precise results are attainable in the social sciences, perhaps because analyzing live human beings, in the real, outside-the-lab world is not as easy and clear-cut as analyzing physical matter in the laboratory. In the outside world, it is more difficult to measure public opinion, tax returns, or school dropout rates and then get general agreement on what the results mean. Nonetheless, the results of these sciences can be marvelous and can lead to all kinds of improvements in our lives. If you are considering a career in one of the sciences you will have numerous rewarding and helping options from which to choose.

Studying Science—even if that should not be your major or career goal—helps you to understand how most educated people understand the physical and social world.

Is There a Problem?

There is a problem if you take Science too seriously. To "take Science too seriously" means to believe (!) that Science explains everything or that you take various aspects of Science so seriously that your focus on God is compromised. If you take the methods of Science as the only methods or at least the most reliable ones to get at truth— as your guiding epistemology[2]—then you are in danger of cutting off other sources of truth about much of reality (for example, the approach taken by the Humanities, or by your Christian faith). Taking Science as the main or only pathway to truth places you in danger of taking as real only that which Science presents as proven. In such a case, would love or hate be real? Would memories and hopes be real?

> ### Do Science Teachers Believe in God?
> *While about 66 percent of the American public believes in God only about 28 percent of college Science teachers do.*
> —Tobin and Weinberg, *Profiles of the American University*

Along with relying on Science as your best or only source of truth, the idea that the physical and material world is the main or even the only reality there is can pose a problem. If you put total reliance for your knowledge of what is real on what you find in the material world, then you are relying on an approach variously called *materialism, empiricism,* and *positivism.* These

2. Epistemology: the understanding of how you know what you know.

terms refer to the notion that the material world is all there is and is the best source for truth.

The Christian faith claims that there is more to reality than the material world and more avenues to truth than the scientific method; so to value empiricism, materialism, or positivism more than, or to the exclusion of, the Christian faith would be a problem.

ism alerts!

Material-ism (n.) is a worldview in which physical matter is believed to be the only or fundamental reality and that every being and process and phenomenon can be explained as manifestation or result of matter. Positivism (n.) is a belief that knowledge is based on natural phenomena. Empiricism (n.) is the reliance on experience or observation alone to find real truth.

Objectivity—The best Science results when it is done with *objectivity*; that calls for the least interference in the scientists' application of their methods. It is hard to ensure complete objectivity; actually it seldom happens. Complete objectivity would require that scientists remain unaffected by everything that might bias or contaminate their work. Because scientists are human and operate in specific physical and social environments, perfect objectivity is almost impossible. Valuing objectivity is a worthy habit, not only in doing Science but in doing any project aimed at discovering truth. It is always realistic (and humbling) to acknowledge that objectivity is a value that is beyond anyone's reach to achieve fully.

Assumptions and Presuppositions: Everyone who does Science has beliefs. They may not be called beliefs and they may not be recognizable as religious, but no one can do Science without at least assuming something and assuming it with real conviction. The scientist assumes that she can trust her perception of what she studies. The researcher believes that what she studies behaves according to some (perhaps not yet fully understood) reliable pattern or "law." Social scientists may consider "normal" what Christians may view as sinful (for example: war). Teachers of business may assume (believe?) that capitalism is the natural default for an economy. Every psychology teacher begins with some basic assumptions about human beings and the mind.

The criticism of the sciences made by Christians is not that the sciences, in their proper place, may lure students away from their Christian faith. The criticism is that Science is *not* bias-free or faith-free. The criticism is that when Science is taught, the foundational assumptions—basic beliefs—of Science ought to be taught so that every student is clear about those basic beliefs.

For example, you may find that one narrative is offered (assumed) to be the norm (what is good, natural)—let's say "health" is the norm and the narrative is "I am normally and basically healthy." Then in the course of your study you might conclude that illness (and even death) is an abnormal and a bad narrative. The Christian, of course, does not have such a negative view of death; it is a fact of life and something through which God promises to care for you. Or in studies of disease, Science has typically preferred to use the male as the standard or "normal" and the female as "different"; only recently have such studies began to see females as just as "normal" as males. But Science is so powerful that such biases can go unnoticed and unchallenged for a long time.

An ancient philosopher claimed that if he had somewhere outside of our universe to stand, he could move the earth. There is a debate today between those who think they have found that place (unaffected by prejudice, bias, religion, or even by having a bad day) and those who are convinced there is no such place. College professors may claim that they offer you only facts, not opinions, and that they are not biased in any way; in short, that they are objective. They are either smart enough or well-trained enough so that you the student can't really make a good judgment on that claim. But even where they try to be perfectly objective it is really, really hard to be so.

> *Patrick Byrne's passion for science might seem to compromise his ability to "do" good Science, but he believes that God so passionately loves the whole world and everything in it that God's love for him as a believing Christian and as a physicist invites him to love God in return and to love to "do" Science without any fear of what he may discover.*
> —BYRNE, "WHOLENESS THROUGH SCIENCE"

To value objectivity is important and each of us should seek to rid our thinking of prejudices. Failing that, we should be able to acknowledge the prejudices we can't get rid of. To claim to have achieved perfect objectivity, however, is to claim that one is nowhere—that is, without any specific "where" or place—and without the point of view one would have from being in that particular place.

Uses and Misuses: There is a problem if you think Science is the absolutely best or only source of truth. There is definitely a problem if you think that scientists produce absolutely objective truth. There have been too many times when matters were "settled," only to find that the old truth had been supplanted by new and better Science. Examples would be the truth settled in the nineteenth century that assured us that men were more intelligent than women and that Caucasians were a superior "race."

There may not be a solution to every problem and not every solution limits itself to solving only the problem for which it was developed. Often there are side effects, some of which are dangerous. The "solution" of DDT (dichlorodiphenyltrichloroethane) was put to work in 1939 and was found to be effective against malaria and typhus; after World War II, DDT was used to control agricultural pests—until it was discovered that it could negatively affect wildlife and caused some cancers in humans. It was banned in 1972. So much for that scientific idea. Science can do a lot, but it cannot do everything.

We have learned how to make people well, but not how to make them good. We can make them well, but we can't keep them from dying. And then there is the matter of ensuring that everyone benefits from the achievements of Science. Discoveries are not equitably shared; preference is often given to men (over women), rich (over the poor), and Westerners (over dwellers in the Third World).

Science can seem so exciting that some people use it to prove just about anything—even the existence of God (or in the non-existence of God) or the rightness of the Christian faith. In seeking for a harmonious relationship between religious faith and modern Science, some people have fallen into the trap of relying on a scientific approach to support their religious beliefs. There are two major problems with that.

First, if we need Science to prove anything—such as the existence of God—it makes God dependent on Science rather than making the world and its secrets dependent on God. Second, if Science is the support for truth, what happens to the truth when the Science changes as it occasionally has? If we use Science to prove things that it cannot prove, that is a problem. *Proof* is nice to have, but sometimes it is impossible to achieve. To overvalue proof could mean that other things—the existence of God, the reality of love—are undervalued.

Control: Our support and admiration for Science comes in large part because Science promises the possibility of control: control of diseases with medicine; control over distance with modern communications; control over enemies with powerful weapons. There is a problem if we value *control* too highly. The fact is that any control we have is limited. Being in control is a great value to us moderns. Control is pretty valuable in connection with handling volatile chemicals, but not so helpful in terms of interpersonal relationships. Separating the arenas where it works and where it doesn't seems to be pretty hard for a lot of folks.

Ignore at Your Peril: On the other hand, not taking Science seriously enough can lead to difficulties. We ignore the results of Science and the consensus of the scientific community at our peril. Again, examples in medicine are the clearest. If you do certain things with or to your body that God created, certain results are likely if not inevitable. Science can give us tools to care for God's creation.

The coach was teaching a physical education class and the topic was preventive medicine. He was giving data on the difference between men and women in the frequency of their visits to a doctor for a checkup. Women do so more often. Reaching into his own experience, he recollected that his own father was not good about checkups and had in fact died of a heart attack at a relatively young age. Then, instead of using this personal example to stress the importance of checkups, he went on to share his own personal attitude and practice: He did not get regular checkups either.

Here was a teacher and coach, the authoritative figure for many of the athlete-students in the class, lending his own personal authority to the practice of the average male: don't get checkups. He was ignoring the weight of scientific data as well as the personal experience of his own father's death. He was sending a really bad message to his students. He was a bad teacher. To value some kind of unfounded personal belief that flies in the face of what truths Science offers is to value personal pride and ignore the best current results of human inquiry. Not a good idea.

An over-enthusiasm for Science might lead to the over valuing of empiricism, materialism, positivism, objectivity, proof and control to a degree unwarranted by the Christian faith's humble appreciation for the full mystery of God's creation. But undervaluing Science is just plain foolish.

> *Contextualize* (verb)
> —*to locate something (an idea, a thing) so that its meaning or significance is determined or controlled by context. For the Christian everything must be put in a context or a place where God in Christ is in control—putting faith around the problem and putting Christ to work solving it.*

Yes, there are risks with any commitment to Science as a source of knowledge, of wisdom or of a life's vocation. An idolatrous commitment that focuses exclusively on Science, an over-blown trust in its methods or assumptions, and an overly optimistic faith in its possibilities challenge fundamentals of your Christian faith.

In bringing a Christological affirmation to bear—in pointing out that Jesus as Teacher or Poet or Word is at the center of our faith—you are placing one or another part of the college experience (in this case Science) in the *context* where it belongs: into the context, framework, and at the service of your Christian faith. When a particular Christology is suggested as a point of reference for your faithful consideration, you are taking that thing that God intended for good in your college education—again, in this case, Science—and you are letting God redeem it from its secularity into the service of your Christian vocation. Let's call this "contextualizing." We have been doing this over and over throughout these chapters so that you can see how a Christian can embrace aspects of the college experience that might have become secularized and thoroughly disconnected from any faith understanding.

Christology: The Author of Life

What does Jesus offer as you study the various sciences in your college experience? Who is the Jesus who accompanies you? Which Christology is really helpful in understanding Jesus' guidance and contribution in your understanding of the sciences?

One temptation is to think of Jesus the miracle worker—one who could "break" a natural or scientific law in displays of divine power. He could be the super-hero who trumps Science. But that would position him as an opponent to the fundamental activity of Science, namely the orderly process toward understanding. We see from Genesis that orderliness is an attribute of God that God step by step imposed on chaos during the act of creation (Gen 1:3, 5, 7, 9, 11, 14–15, 16–17, 21, 24). Later, Jesus cautioned against coming to him on the basis of his miraculous acts, indicating that it was more important to come to him because of faith than because of the "proof" provided by miracles (John 20:29b).

Another avenue to seek a Christology that can help you with the challenges of Science would be to repeat the assertion that Jesus is the Word. Instead of emphasizing the communication aspect of "word" a different

> A *"Christocentric universe"* is what excites Ilia Delio, who found her original student vocation in chemistry and at the center of chemistry she found . . . Jesus Christ! Christ did not come to the world as an afterthought just to atone for sin but because he was at the very center of the whole of creation from the beginning. And she knows that he continues to act in bringing fulfillment and the new creation of which Scripture speaks.
>
> —Ilia Delio,
> "Christocentric Universe"

aspect could be explored: the creative power and reasonable orderliness of God's Word. The Scriptures describe Jesus as the Word that was with God at the creation of the universe. (Paul picks up on this in the famous hymn quoted in Colossians 1—the world was made through and for Christ.) The term *word* in Greek carries overtones of "logic" and "reason." In the original Hebrew of the Old Testament, the term translated "word" conveys the creative power of God's spoken word. So when the fourth Gospel writer speaks of Jesus as the "word" he is suggesting the *power* that created the cosmos and the rational *orderliness* Science finds in the material universe.

Without the assumption of order, no one could do Science. It is also clear in the creation story of Genesis that the main thing that occurred was that God (along with Jesus, the Word) imposed *order* on the disorderliness of matter. Clearly God (along with Jesus the Word) is the source of power, meaning, order, and creativity in the universe.

In Colossians, a letter to Christians who had a deep interest in questions about the basic principles and fundamental truths of the universe, Paul describes Jesus as the one *through* whom and *for* whom the universe was made and *in* whom it holds together (Col 1:17). The Colossians were particularly interested in something they called the "elemental spirits [or building blocks] of the universe" (alternative translation: "the rudiments of the world"). This was the ultimate stuff, the foundations, the basic principles of the universe—what we might see as the "final" frontier that Science is still exploring today. Paul presents Jesus Christ as more fundamental than this ultimate "stuff"—whatever it might finally turn out to be.

In the Christological hymn quoted by Paul in Colossians 1:15–17, Jesus is connected to the universe and every aspect of it with prepositions. Those prepositions—tiny words

> ## A Christological Foundation for Doing Science . . .
>
> *One of the early post-biblical Christologies (not in Scripture, but originating in the second century as Christians sought to connect with the pagan, Greek world) is that of Jesus as logos—Jesus as a rational principle underlying the entirety of the universe. Logos is the Greek word for "word" and it carries a rich cargo of meaning, including philosophical notions of reason and order. Thus Joseph L. Spradley, in "Christological Influences on Science" can claim that this early Christian idea that Jesus was the logos ensured that the world would not reject Greek Science, but affirm an ordered, orderly, and intelligible cosmos, and provide the basis for Christians to have a positive view of theoretical Science.*

though they may be—describe Jesus' deep, fundamental and original involvement in the ultimate "stuff." The *in, at, through, around, for, with* denote relationships.

Like the ligaments that hold us together, Jesus is the one who makes, connects, and makes sense of all things. You get the big picture from Jesus the Author of Life. Science is working to fill in the details.

An area of particular excitement in the hard sciences today is what is loosely referred to as the "genome project." This is the effort by a worldwide network of scientists to "read" the genetic code or DNA of human beings. This genetic code is like a blueprint or assembly manual that explains how the basic material elements composing your body are directed to develop. It is like a long "how-to" manual of incredibly detailed instructions. The genome project's goal is literally to write down every piece of information that has already been inscribed or encoded in us.

> *Christina Vanin is a Christian and a college professor who studies and teaches ecology. She believes that the scientific story of the universe is a holy narrative that helps us to truly know who we are. It is a story of God-created diversity that she embraces.*
>
> —Vanin, *"Attaining Harmony."*

Science is the window to the details of creation. How do you find out the answer to that other question—Why? Faith answers: Jesus Christ, the Author of Life, "wrote" it. (In the original New Testament Greek, the word translated "author" means originator, founder, leader, beginner.) What a wonderful picture: Christ authoring the creation, writing the book of life that would be "published" in the creation of the cosmos. Science is what opens up the details for us.

Jesus also helps you understand the work of social scientists in describing God's hopes for individuals and communities in his many parables. The pictures painted by the parables portray images you can compare or contrast with the charts, graphs, data, experimental results, and theories you will study in sociology and psychology.

How does Jesus the Teacher answer the problems that can confront you in the college experience with Science? Those problems can be embraced by faith as you let the prior reality and creativity of God in Christ put them into the framework and context of Christian faith. There is no need to think that what Science does happens outside of the realm of God the Creator or Jesus the Author of Life. In Christ you know that you cannot be content with the limits posed by positivism or materialism. Christ, the Author of Life, not only helps you to know the truth about this world but delivers you to the wider reality of the eternal and divine. How does he do this?

He does it through his teaching and through his miracle working. But primarily he does it through his resurrection from the dead. The realities of this world—its materiality and its processes and laws—were ignored (not broken!) as God raised Jesus beyond the confines of this life into life eternal. Those "scientific" limitations were irrelevant in the game-changing response of God's reversal of the human condemnation of Jesus of Nazareth. God's will in the resurrection was to declare his "Yes!" to overthrow the "No!" with which sinful humans rejected Jesus when they crucified him.

All values associated with Science must be contextualized by dealing with them in the context, framework, or worldview of faith. That means that as important as these values are—and they are indispensable for doing Science—they are not absolutes when it comes to the broader and more important issue of faith. For example, objectivity is a sought-after virtue that is achieved when you have all the facts and can view life from a bias-free perspective. In the actual everyday world in which you live you never have the luxury of such a clear view. Nevertheless you have to make decisions; you have to make commitments. No one can be objective and detached forever—even if all the facts aren't yet in. (They will *never* all be in.)

Jesus could not waver between serving God and succumbing to the earthly authorities. Jesus could not be indecisive in dealing with the needs of outsiders and the rules of the religious leaders who would separate themselves from those they considered unacceptable to God. Jesus took sides, committed himself, and his

> ## What about the Theory of Evolution? Don't Worry About It
>
> *Just a word about a topic that seems to scare Christians in college more than any other: EVOLUTION. It is likely that you will encounter a professor or a text book that asks you to learn something about Charles Darwin's theory of evolution.*
>
> *The primary thing you need to know is that this is a theory used by scientists when they do Science. Theories are one of the tools scientists use when they do Science. When they are doing Science they are not doing Christian faith because Science and Christian faith are two different things.*
>
> *The issue is: How do Science and faith relate to each other? Christians both before and after Darwin have no problem with their belief in God. If your vocation is in Science, you will continue to examine the relationship between Science and faith and—in particular—what to do with Darwin's theory.*
>
> *For now, however, don't worry about it. The theory of evolution can't get rid of the Author of Life any more than could his enemies who have tried in the past.*

enemies executed the Author of Life. Except that God had the last word, in the resurrection and vindication of Jesus' commitment. And that leads to the secular value of control—something at which Jesus just didn't excel. From the fact that he let others continually interrupt his life with their problems to his final submission to execution on a cross by Roman authorities, Jesus did not seek control. Instead, he started by allowing God to control him ("Thy will be done") and by submitting himself to the needs of others and the laws of the land.

Christian faith brings additional ways of thinking about the college experience of Science so that when you contextualize your studies in Science (or any other field) you can do so in ways that insert commitment, submission, awe, wonder, appreciation, and even supernaturalism into the mix of your thinking. Your embracing of these Christian virtues (commitment, awe, etc.) will not compromise your learning wonderful things in the labs and lectures of college Science. Instead, they are characteristics of the Christian life that will help you to learn as a student and grow as a Christian.

If you remember that Science tries (and does a pretty good job) to explain *everything* except where it came from, why it's here, and where it's going, you won't get into any major conflicts.

Application

The sciences direct you toward God. "Doing Science" is in many ways retracing the creative work of God. Knowing nature will not exhaust your knowledge of God. Instead, it will enrich your knowledge of God. Study of the sciences and knowing Jesus the Teacher and the Author of Life (in whom are all the treasures of wisdom and knowledge) incalculably enriches your faith. That knowledge is almost as wonderful as knowing that you are known by God. Remember: The fear of the Lord is the beginning of knowledge (Prov 1:7a) and the expansion of that *knowledge* can happen in the college experience and can make your God-given *wisdom* a down-to-earth, practical virtue.

Thought and Discussion Questions

1. Illustrate with examples the differences between knowledge and wisdom.

2. Discuss how Science and faith challenge each other. Don't limit your discussion exclusively to evolution.

3. We have assumed that Jesus had/has a lot to do with the "real world" of politics, history, culture, economics, and psychology. Some would argue that the Christian faith should be confined to spiritual matters, and exclude all of the "real world" issues. How would it be possible to extricate Jesus in his many Christological *personae* from the material and social world of everyday life? How would you describe the Jesus who remains?

4. Choose any one of the secular values discussed in this chapter (control, materialism, positivism, objectivity, proof) and discuss its strengths and—from the perspective of your Christian faith—its weaknesses.

11

Thinking About a Major?

Business

[Disciples] "What must we do to perform the works of God?"
[Jesus] "This is the work of God, that you
believe in him whom he has sent."

John 6:28–29

Scripture Focus

Matthew 4:19

Follow me, and I will make you fish for people.

The transition to college can be hard. Part of it is all the new stuff. New people. New places. New responsibilities. New opportunities. But what about the old stuff—friends, family, activities, places? Do you keep connected to them? You can't just up and leave it all behind. Or can you? You'd think that there are things that can't be dropped: family, for example. But other things can, and you may be surprised at how many things can be left behind. Going to college forces you to do some reconsidering about how your life as a Christian and a disciple of Jesus in college will look. How much of your old life is brought along? And in what way(s) is it brought with you?

For four of the first disciples—Peter, Andrew, James and John—the transition from living at home and working at fishing with their dad on the one hand to going off with Jesus on the other is instructive. While it is not necessarily a model for everybody, it could be helpful for college-goers. There were things that the disciples left behind and things that they kept with them as they went off with Jesus.

What they left behind was equipment—tools, technology, material items. Peter and Andrew left their nets. Without nets, there was no way they would catch fish. It was a definite break. James and John left their boat. Again—no way would they catch fish without a boat.

But they also left their father. That was a major reorientation of relationships; in the New Testament we find a new set of relationships opening up to Jesus' followers in the new "family" of the church.

What they did *not* leave behind was their calling or vocation. Their vocation was to catch fish in order to earn a living—but also, on a deeper level, their vocation was to feed people. Jesus took that call and transformed it—to catch people for the kingdom of Heaven and to feed them with the good news of the gospel.

Prayer: Lord, help me to listen to your call and discern what I need to let go and what I need to keep. Amen.

The College Experience: Business

In a memorable scene from the movie, *The Graduate* (with seven Oscar nominations in 1967), a worldly wise and successful adult whispers knowingly to the young graduate (played by Dustin Hoffman); he says one word: "Plastics." That one word has signified for many Americans what college—indeed, what life—was all about: getting the right job and working one's way into financial and social success.

The word for the magic key to success today may no longer be "plastics." Maybe it's "computers" or "pharmaceuticals" or "finance" or "management." Whatever the word is, college is definitely the place to prepare for the job that can provide the path to social and financial achievement. While many college students will study to become English or math teachers (see chapter 7), or writers and artists (see chapter 9) or social workers, doctors, scientists, or counselors (see chapter 10), more college students these days indicate a preference for majoring in one of the many fields that can be grouped together as business.

The courses, majors and future careers found in this category vary widely—from accounting to hotel management, from electrical engineering to computer graphics, from investments to sales, from real estate to data services. And the list goes on. And it will go on, constantly adding and changing to accommodate the need for workers in new fields that weren't even thought of a few years ago.

> In 2012, 88 percent of college freshmen agreed that getting a better job was a top reason to attend college; that was the highest percentage ever!
> ALMANAC 2013–14, 36

College education in America continues to be intensely responsive to the job market. (Remember our discussion of the purpose for colleges in chapter 3?) Is there a need for more computer analysts? Expand the program. What about persons skilled in speaking Arabic or developing wind generated power? Establish a program. When one author called American higher education a "vast job training program" she was not alone in thinking of the college experience as a vocational training program. Since the beginning, colleges have responded to economic and market needs. Today the array of programs and courses available is astonishing in its breadth. This is all for the good because we live in an increasingly complex world in which more and more ways to provide for people's needs require more and more specialized experts to produce and manage all the goods and services demanded. The world needs well-trained folks to run things. College is pretty much a requirement any more for learning the kinds of skills that are in demand. When anyone decides to attend college and prepare for a career in one of the many business fields, he is almost guaranteeing two things: he will be well equipped to do things that the world needs; and he will earn a lot more money over the course of a lifetime than he would if he were not to complete college. This is particularly true in the areas of business.

But as you already know, business is not the only area where college graduates will be looking for a job. So though we will focus on business as a major, we are also looking more broadly at your future job. The complexity of today's world demands specialized skills. Just as the needs that originally motivated the rise of colleges were met by the training for religious and political leadership, today's needs are determined by a modern global economy: managing people and information, and the production and distribution of goods and services. The breadth of needed skills reflects a complexity never before known. This is what runs the economy, produces the jobs, provides the high standard of living and all of the good things that we think we need. It is all very exciting, very demanding—and it can be very useful in serving the needs of a whole world full of people.

Is There a Problem?

Business is about providing goods and services to people so that their lives are sustained and enriched. That will involve inventing, designing, buying, building, marketing, selling, advertising, hiring, capitalizing, investing, shipping, assembling, repairing . . . and these are only some of the activities and factors that make up life in the world of business. When it all works and everyone is satisfied, we have success. What is *success*?

Success—In American culture, success in business is usually measured in terms that are used in the motto for the Olympic games: swifter, higher, stronger. Swifter service; higher profits (and salaries); stronger companies and markets. How are these goals pursued? Individuals compete for jobs and companies compete to attract customers. It is hoped that such competition produces the best in workers, companies, products and services. *Competition* is valued in achieving success in business. (We will consider competition in the next chapter.) Success is highly valued in American culture, and the kind of success sought in business (or any other vocation) demands that at least three other values be brought into play to achieve success.

Vocationalism—The first is the value of *vocationalism*—the idea that one's job is of supreme importance. Vocationalism is one of the main values that dominate the college experience (and American culture in general). Some, rather than thinking that they work to live, have come to believe that they live to work. The focus on job preparation supports the idea that the entire college experience is about jobs.

It seems obvious that Jesus knew that everyone needed to "make a living" and "pay the bills." He offered neither praise nor blame for vocational choices. He never suggests that a person *is* what he *does*. But the college experience is tilted toward preparing you to seek your identity in your work. How often do you meet others with the identifying question, "What do you do?" as if the answer to that question gives the identity of the

> **Definition:** *Idolatry*
> —*An immoderate attachment to anything. For Christians: an immoderate attachment to anything other than God.*

stranger. Why not ask, "Are you a child of God?" or "What are the main motives that underlie your life?" If a "job" is your goal, then college only prepares you for the 40 or so working hours of every 168 hour week. What preparation will you make for the rest of life? The college experience in business can have a dangerously narrowing effect on your self-understanding.

Just who are you anyway? It is interesting to note how humans have been identified by concise phrases. These phrases are shorthand ways to single out the main or unique characteristic that identifies us. For example, the familiar modern classification of all life forms put humans at the top of the charts—humans, of course, being the ones who invented these lists!—as *homo sapiens* (intelligent or rational humans). If you were to make a judgment on the basis of vocationalism, it might be the more serious and practical *homo faber* (the human who works or makes things). Is that what God intended you to be? There is a problem with a college education that is primarily focused on teaching work skills to the disregard of seriously preparing you for life's many other demands and opportunities.

Unless you contextualize your study of business and position the work part of your life within the more inclusive realm of Christian vocation you might just become what you do, a workaholic, separated from everything else. That is a problem. Because from the very beginning, Scripture tells us who we are:

> So God created humankind in his image,
> in the image of God he created them;
> male and female he created them (Gen 1:27).

There is a problem if you let your identity come from your job. That may work in the secular world but it cannot ultimately explain who you are. Be sure you benefit from everything your college offers—not just your pre-job major.

Specialization—The second value required for success in the American work culture is that of *specialization*—the idea that it is best to reduce work to its component parts and get experts to perform each of the different, specialized tasks. As almost everything—from medical procedures to energy production to government bureaucracies—gets more complex, more and more specialization is required.

For example, at one time, one worker could make and sell a broom. Then there was a change, and brooms were mass produced—one person measuring and cutting the stick, another cutting the bristles, a third fastening them all together, another delivering them to various stores where they were finally sold. Then someone invented the carpet sweeper—more complicated and requiring more steps to manufacture and sell. If someone started another sweeper factory, it became necessary to add advertising and trained salespersons to convince consumers that one sweeper was better than the other. Then along came the vacuum cleaner. Still more parts (electric motor, vacuum bags, tubes, pulleys, filters—then better motors, lighter weight components, healthier filters), more competition, more employees requiring more skills. And so it goes. Not just for brooms to vacuums but in virtually every product and service. Specialization is valued in business since it is impossible for one person to have all the skills necessary to run a complex operation.

Along with specialization come several other features of business that are valued. One is the specialized language or *jargon* necessary to conduct business. The more complicated, sophisticated, and specialized a service (like brain surgery) or product (a jet plane), the more precise the terminology is that is needed to provide the end product. In turn, this specialization and jargon can produce a special person or group of persons uniquely qualified to provide the particular goods or services. They are the *elite*—those special people who are the only ones who know how to make or provide what we want. They are special; they are in specific ways set aside as different. Are they better? There is a temptation to consider the ones who provide specialized goods using special language as elite and special (and better?) people.

The mere fact of this proliferating specialization, its jargons, and its elite specialists almost inevitably leads to *fragmentation* and *isolation*. The isolation of spending a lot of time with your nose buried in one subject, with one group of people, speaking one job-related jargon, results in thinking that life itself is divisible—one arena for work (and its own morality, jargon, associates, values) and another (or others) pretty much unrelated, for personal, family, and social life (or lives?). A century ago, children could still see dad leave for work, get on a tractor and plow a field within sight of the house. And the children knew what dad was doing. Today, when a parent "goes to work," the child often has no clue where the parent goes or what she does.

When you allow your life to be fragmented into parts—the personal/family part and the job part being the two main ones—you may need to ask: *Who am I?* Or, *Which "me" is the real me?* For example, you might treasure love, cooperation, and leisure in your personal/family life and seek competitiveness, success, and specialization in your job life. If that is the case, *fragmentation* is another value with which you begin to feel comfortable. You might even think, "I've got to be practical; when I'm at work, I can't let love and kindness get in the way of competitiveness and success."

Specialization and fragmentation can mess you up. If you take them too seriously they can lead to your focusing only on your piece of the pie—your specialty and your fragment; this can be idolatrous because it threatens to replace the only worthy object of your faith and hope with something that is only a part of reality.

Pragmatism—That brings us to the third value that seems necessary for success: *pragmatism*—the ethical view that you need to live in what some call "the real world" and that you must "be practical" and "realistic" and "do what takes" to achieve success. Such a commitment to "the job" commits you to a morality that differs significantly from the Christian faith's view of life.

This problem can arise beginning in your college days as you prepare for that job. In almost all of the programs offered in college, there is one glaring omission across the curriculum: the teaching of ethics. You have probably heard of at least some of the scandals in the business world that have resulted in jail time for convicted business executives, loss of money for investors, loss of pension and medical insurance for retired workers, or product liability suits filed by injured consumers, and a general betrayal of the public.

By and large, college classes pay little attention to the matter of *how* the skills learned for a career are to be used. Using business as our example, should advertising expertise be used to sell an adult product to underage consumers? Should accounting skills be used to "cook the books" and cheat some while others gain? Should design skills be used to produce a cheaper but less safe product? Of course, it is not that simple. But that is no excuse for students not to learn to do things in an ethical way.

But wait! The real problem is that morality *is* taught—but no one notices it. While the college teaches skills, it does so in the particular setting (the context of that college, with all of its local culture and values) and by means of the teaching done by particular instructors (with all of their loves and hates, commitments and prejudices). Students not only learn the skills but they learn the context—how those skills are viewed, valued, used by authorities (the faculty).[1]

The teachers who teach you those job skills may seem to do so without any particular set of values or beliefs, but that is impossible. Each of them has values, beliefs, commitments, prejudices, and biases that are conveyed overtly or covertly in the course of a class, a semester, a college career. Each college has its own commitment to goals and each has a mission that is

---

1. Ethics and skills are contextualized and you may not even notice it. This is the *hidden* curriculum at work.

conveyed by the employees, its history, and its tradition and setting. There is no way that a college education comes without a whole range of values and understandings that are communicated to students. (That is the "value added" of which you read in chapter 3.) It is as if these ideas were germs, existing at a real but invisible level in the system, powerful in their effects, moving from you to others or from others to you in invisible patterns. Are these good germs—er, ideas—or not? Do you want to be infected with these particular ideas or with some other, different—say, Christian—ones? The point is that what goes on within the college experience is already infused with values, notions, and beliefs that are powerful. You read of those values in chapter 3. They should be called religious values, notions, beliefs and ideas because they exist and operate powerfully at a very deep level in the lives of the people who live by them.

The chairman of the business department had his office next to mine and we conversed about college matters frequently. I had gotten interested in co-teaching a class to senior business majors on the topic of business ethics. The chairman lamented that waiting to teach ethics to seniors in their final year of college was too late. Besides, he added—and he was not being cynical—most students wouldn't recognize an ethical problem if it stared them in the face.

That incident occurred years ago. Today most business programs have at least some instruction in ethics; every professional organization has a code of ethics; and most businesses can be found to have codes of ethics displayed in a prominent place. But the problem may still not be solved.

More recently, I was discussing the establishment (finally!) of a course on business ethics with the chairman of the business department at a different college and we got into a disagreement over whether the course was a busi-ness course ("What's good is what's good for business") or an ethics course (using ethical principles that transcend the values of success, vocationalism, fragmentation, and pragmatism). We never did resolve the disagreement. He wound up assigning a business teacher who knew a lot about accounting but who knew little about ethics to teach the class. Even though there would be a class in ethics, it was more likely that business would be the subject matter, not ethics.

So . . . there is a problem. In fact, there are several problems. The secular values that typically underlie business studies in particular and job preparation in general are many and pose serious challenges to the Chris-tian student seeking to be faithful. The value of vocationalism as a way to achieve success and self-identity ignores a Christian understanding that we are children of God. The value of specialization tempts you to detach yourself from the one universal people of God into a fragmented isolation. It tempts you to intensify the focus of your concern to the exclusion of the rest of the whole; again, that can be idolatry. The value of pragmatism can lead to an attitude of "doing what it takes" with no regard for your methods or their impact on other people.

All of these secular values are made to seem necessary and not worth questioning because of a higher goal: success. This kind of success is of course the social and material success valued by the general secular culture of America, not by the Christian faith. The value of success is calculated in largely material terms—salaries, status, possessions, market share, profits. While the college experience does something important in the development of your skills, such vocational learning must be placed in a broader context than simply that of your future work. Your reliance on college to help prepare you for *any* career must be contextualized so you evaluate it in the framework or worldview of a critical Christian faith. Then you can keep the good stuff from college—whatever will "fit" with Christian faith and help you fulfill your vocation in a way that truly honors Christ and serves others. Unless you see this, you may wind up thinking that work—the job—is all there is to life. And you may think that there is no need for a context larger than the job. If you are serious about your faith, you can see the conflict.

Christology: Servant/Master

Jesus worked. As any Jewish boy of his time did, Jesus grew up (probably) learning the trade of his father, Joseph; the New Testament variously describes Joseph's job as carpenter or "technician." Jesus knew that people had to work to earn their living. As far as we know, Jesus' disciples were working people whom he called to leave their original trades or professions to become his disciples.

Most of Jesus' parables were about people whom he identified by their work instead of their names: masters and servants. Jesus described himself as a servant; Christians refer to him as Lord (master, boss, in charge). Perhaps the most helpful Christology to address issues of business and, more broadly, vocation would be the combined title of master/servant or servant/master—or, in modern jargon—boss/worker or worker/boss.

Not surprisingly, Jesus' understanding of these titles does not coincide with our own. He was critical of the typical master for "lording it over" others and for insisting that others serve him (Matt 20:25). Instead of seeing servants or workers as unfortunate people who deserved what they got, or who needed to overthrow their masters, Jesus placed himself in the role of servant. Why did he not resent the role of servant? Because he saw the fundamental purpose of life to be one of helping others. Servants in his day did the most menial tasks—all without the help of modern appliances and other aids. They had little protection from their masters. Yet Jesus is pictured as one who voluntarily gave up the trappings of high office to become a servant who finally suffered the humiliation of a criminal's death (Phil 2:6–8).

But, there is remarkably little in the story of Jesus or in the entire New Testament about work. Apart from the occasional mention that Paul the apostle had a skill that he employed so others would not be asked to support his work as an apostle, there is almost no concern with the (obvious) necessity to work. Even Jesus did not seem to be uneasy about the fact that his enterprise as a travelling teacher and miracle worker (accompanied by a group of disciples) was supported by others (who were mainly women)! The most direct and explicit directive about work came from John the Baptist who, when asked by hated tax-collectors and soldiers what they should do, said only that they must not to use their positions to exploit others (Luke 3:12–14). Notice that John did not advise tax collectors or soldiers to change jobs to something more "Christian." He knew that pretty much any work can be care-full of others.

As Jesus the Lord and Teacher (boss and teacher) calls people from a variety of professions—fishing, tax collecting—to be his disciples and to learn the role of servant, he is indifferent to the particular skills each of us has, but he sees those skills (whatever they are) as useful in his service and in the service of others.

What do we learn from Jesus the Teacher/Worker/Lord about how you might view the career preparation you receive in your college experience? First, Christians already have a built-in, ready-made ethical framework within which to locate (contextualize) the skills learned: Love God and love your neighbors. Jesus calls you to servanthood and to serve others. Christian *ethics* are clear and explicit. They are applicable to all of life, not just a fragmented and segregated (Sunday) part of it.

> *J. Michael Stebbins studied philosophy in college and became an ethics professor. His interest is in business. To him, business is a cooperative venture with the potential to do good for everyone. His "ethic of achievement" asks "How can we do better?" It is his way of carrying on the mission of Jesus and the Holy Spirit.*
> —J. MICHAEL STEBBINS, "'REAL WORLD' OF BUSINESS,"

Whatever specialization you might be required to learn, Jesus never lets you separate yourselves from others. You are always an indispensable part of the body of Christ, connected intimately with all others through Christ. Defining yourself by your work is—in the long run—impossible since you are first of all a child of God and brother or sister to all other children of God. You cannot be reduced to what you do. Throughout the New Testament we are always described as members of one another. You cannot see success or "making something of yourself" as a task since you are already made well and pronounced "very good" by God in Genesis 1:31. You are already a success.

You are ready to take the vocational skills you will acquire in your college experience and live the life for which God has created you. If you are still concerned about work, listen to the words of Paul, writing to the Ephesians (2:10): "For we are what he has made us, created in Christ Jesus for good works, which God prepared beforehand to be our way of life." The work you are to do has already been prepared for you by the Creator! You have no need to define yourself by your work, to focus only on your vocation, to allow the drive for success to isolate you in some self-centered project of re-creation. God did it right the first time; your task is to unlearn the secular values—be born again!—and learn who you truly are (created in the image of God) and use your college experience to develop that God-given vocation.

Application

As Jesus makes clear in his call to the first disciples, you are called to follow him and to utilize your secular work. Such a calling, in the case of the first disciples, was quite consistent with the will of God. In the case of Peter, Andrew, James, and John it was that people needed to be nourished and they already knew how to catch the fish for them to eat. They used those skills to "catch" people for God where they could be fed with a nourishment of the eternal good news of the kingdom of God.

Christians can take what the college experience offers because training for a career can equip you for that vocation through which God calls you into the service of others. The vocationalism and specialization so necessary in today's world can be a blessing when employed to love your neighbor.

Thought and Discussion Questions

1. Discuss different models for living as a Christian in the job you hope to have after college.

2. Do you think you can work in the secular world according to Christian faith? If so, name several aspects of faith that you might want to employ. Explain your choices.

3. If Jesus chooses not to fight or use force to get his way, and if he doesn't choose to compete for jobs and business and a piece of the action, what is left of him to be of any value to you in the "real world" of post-college, secular employment?

4. "If you want to be successful in business (or whatever career you pursue) you have to be . . ." Take turns filling in the blank with various actions or qualities to complete the sentence. Then evaluate as many of the choices in your completed sentence as you can from the point of view of Christian faith.

part three

The Co-Curriculum

Scripture Focus

GALATIANS 5:13

For you were called to freedom, brothers and sisters; only do not use your freedom as an opportunity for self-indulgence, but through love become slaves to one another.

Your Christian vocation is fundamentally not to a particular career through which you can serve God and others but it is to freedom. The only real issue for the committed Christian life of faith is: How will you manage that freedom? And we do not mean simply that free time you might find after a day of serious academics. Or your staying out later than you had promised yourself before a big test. We mean the freedom to commit yourself consistently to the master who will govern your life.

The secular view would place you in the center of your small universe and urge you to use your freedom for yourself. Are you sure you are smart enough to use freedom in a way that is going to benefit yourself in the best way?

The Christian promise is that if you use your freedom to love God and others you will be doing the right thing, the most effective thing, the most joy-filled thing. As you read through these next chapters on those aspects of the college experience most associated with freedom, remember this: the key to a great college experience is found in the answer to the question: How will you use your freedom?

Often called "extra-curricular," the social aspect of the college experience teaches a lot. In fact, if you listen to college graduates, they will usually say that they learned more outside of class than inside. They learned from their peers in the ordinary give and take of daily life together and they learned from each other in the intense sharing of concerns, questions, and occasional personal crises (death of a grandparent, divorce of parents, etc.). So rather than refer to these important teaching/learning experiences as *extra*-curricular—somehow happening outside of your explicit learning experiences—it is best to see them as co-curricular. These are powerful learning arenas; simply other ways in which the *implicit* curriculum functions. These are dimensions of college that seem to terrify some parents and many writers of survival manuals. But as we shall see, there is still much in the co-curriculum that will surprise in its (positive) challenge to your Christian faith.

We look first at something survival manuals actually never—really, *never*—look at: the athletic scene at the college level. It is something one can almost never escape from and it is powerful in the way that it can influence the student mind.

Then—finally—we get to the *sex and alcohol* part of the college scene. You all know what the problem is there and that you are not supposed to mess up, so it is important to emphasize the flip side of that whole scene: what a wonderful time you can have in college with all of the gifts and opportunities it offers.

Finally—and no one should actually say "and finally" when it comes to thinking about the good or the risky in the college experience—we have to wrap up this guide and give you some final travelling tips for one of life's most wonderful, intense, and finished-too-quickly experiences.

12

Sports

It's Not Called "the Big Game" for Nothing

"Winning is the only thing . . .
finishing second is like kissing your sister."

—Attributed to professional football
coach Vince Lombardi.

"Outdo one another in showing honor . . ."

—Romans 12:10b

Scripture Focus

Mark 9:35

*And [he] said to them, "Whoever wants to be first
must be last of all and servant of all."*

Oh to be FIRST! It seems to be the goal for so many of us. Jesus' disciples were pretty concerned about being first also. Moments after he had told them he would be crucified the disciples were deep into a discussion of which of them would be first in the kingdom of God. (Talk about insensitivity!)

Jesus had the answer, but it was probably not the one they were expecting. If you want to be first, you have to be last. That meant being a servant— a servant in the kingdom of God. Was Jesus confused? Did he think he was judging a contest for best servant?

It was pretty clear that Jesus did not play by our rules. It was not clear that he played by any rules. In fact, it looks like he was making up the rules as he went along. The last shall be first? Wash his students' feet? You've got to be kidding!

Prayer: Lord, show me what it means that the first shall be last. Amen.

The College Experience: Athletics

Basketball. Football. Baseball. Soccer. Lacrosse. Wrestling. And the list goes on. Now this is something that really turns everyone on, and turns everyone out—to see the big game. The enthusiastic commitment on the part of the whole campus in support of *the team* is an interesting phenomenon. You have seen the TV scenes of half-naked college students with the name of their college painted on bare male chests, or wearing basketballs on their heads, waving wildly and screaming about how great their team is. While they may be a lunatic fringe, most of the school—fully dressed—can also be mobilized to a rally, to the game, to a frenzy of cheers for the good plays and boos against referees for allegedly bad calls. The collective desire for athletic victories can result in this kind of extreme behavior on the part of students. On the dark side, fan enthusiasm can bring on pressure to fire the coach.

What's the biggest building on campus? The library? The administration building? A dormitory? Chances are that it is the football stadium. While most campus rooms, or even buildings, could not accommodate most students at one sitting, football stadia often will be able to accommodate two or three times the total number of students and employees of the school. While no university in America has more than 73,000 students at one campus, there are at least four schools with stadia that hold more than 100,000 each.[1]

When a good friend arrived at a major university where she would spend a year pursuing graduate studies, she was astonished to find that the entire department in which she would study took up only one end of one floor

1. These are the University of Michigan, Penn State, the University of Tennessee, and Ohio State University.

under the grandstand of the football stadium. The stadium was so big that it contained a dormitory and several entire departments. One could almost imagine a student living there, studying there and going to the games there— and never needing to leave the building!

We know that most of you will not be attending a school that is this huge and where athletics are so dominating. But we live in a culture in which sports pervades everything. There are not many activities that have a whole section of the daily newspaper devoted to it. There are not many college activities in which the national championship team gets to visit the White House and have the President tell them how great they are. There are no other college activities that have created anything like ESPN (and its "family of networks") where games are played and replayed and discussed and analyzed by panels of experts (many of them former athletes) over and over again, until you realize that this is an alternative universe; people could (and maybe do) live here 24/7/365. So most college students are not removed from the world of athletics no matter which school they attend; and many students will be found on a Saturday afternoon watching "the game" on TV if not in person.

This could easily be considered the college experience's most exciting moment of the week: the gathering of the entire community, a time when the school finally unites in a body and with one shared purpose: *to win the game.* The pomp and ceremony are more powerful here than at any other time, even eclipsing commencement ceremonies, which draw a much smaller crowd.

The ease and innocence with which almost all members of the college community slip into "the game" mode is established in high school and even earlier grades and by American culture in general.[2] Sport has taken on a life of its own and created a community found in the sports pages and the TV networks and with them wall-to-wall games 24/7. Everyone can support these basic American values: *competitiveness* and *being number one.*

I remember my own excitement at age ten when our neighborhood team got our first game jerseys; we were the Orioles. This gave us identity, not only as Orioles but also in our opposition to every other team. Later, the spirit of competition continued for me in Cub Scouts and the team competition we encountered there. After that, we were fodder for the much better "Junior Bears" of the Chicago Park District. The Park District teams were well organized and coached. And they had uniforms! The best teams would play for a few minutes during the halftime of the professional Bears' games on Sunday afternoons.

---

2. According to the National Federation of State High School Associations, 1,032,682 high school students competed in eleven-player football during the 2012–2013 season. www.nfhs.org/.

My own sandlot team—no coach, no uniforms—played against these park-sponsored teams who always gave us a shellacking but enhanced our identity and sense of competitiveness. When we got to high school we were thoroughly ready to throw ourselves into the competitive athletic program of the public schools.

But let's get back to college and the "big game." The mood is different from what you experienced throughout the previous week of classes. There is an excitement and anticipation for the game. During the week, grudging compliance brought students to class. Now, people arrive early rather than just in time. It is a time for friends to socialize. It is the communal high point of the week.

Despite the presence of the entire college community, this is not a democracy; there is a definite *hierarchy*. The student body is in the stands, the important alumni and officers of the university are up in the box seats. (This hierarchical arrangement allows the availability of alcoholic beverages—usually prohibited in the lower seats—so that those in the upper seats can enjoy a drink or two as the game progresses.) The most important participants, of course, are the players and coaches. The former are the fabled heroes on whose strong shoulders, swift feet, sure hands, and gifted physical coordination rides the honor of the school. The latter are often the highest paid employees of the school. (Until recently, the basketball coach at the University of Connecticut was the *highest paid public employee* in the entire state!) And let's not forget the cheerleaders and the pep band. Everyone is identified in his or her place in the hierarchy with a uniform.

While coaches may not always be considered teachers, we shall see that they indeed are, for on their shoulders rides the effectiveness of many of the most dearly held values of the college experience. For the most valued coaches—the ones whose teams best embody the school's core values (to be *competitive* and to *win*)—the material rewards for their contribution can be stunning when compared to what other teachers or even leaders of the school earn.

Presidents or Coaches: Who Gets Paid More?[3]

School	President	Compensation 2011–2012	Coach	Compensation 2013
Auburn	Jay Gogue	$2,542,865	Gene Chizik	$3,577,500
Baylor	Kenneth Starr	$706,426	Art Briles	$2,232,807
Florida	Bernard Machen	$843,562	Will Muschamp	$2,474,500
Michigan	Mary Sue Coleman	$918,783	Brady Hoke	$3,046,120
Notre Dame	John Jenkins	$746,401	Brian Kelly	$2,424,301
Ohio State	E. Gordon Gee	$1,899,420	Urban Meyer	$4,300,000
Texas	Francisco Cigarroa	$815,833	Mack Brown	$5,353,750

Instead of salaries under yearly contract (like those received by faculty and other employees), coaches typically receive multi-year *"compensation packages."*[4] (Of course, most American colleges are not this "big time" in reality; but in spirit their lead is followed by other colleges and by students —and parents—across the country. So it is important to see the values at work in sports at the highest level because that is what sets the tone that the rest of us are expected to admire and embrace.)

While the "big game" is generally viewed as a sporting event, it is easy to see the elements of theater, politics, and even religion in the spectacle. The drama is clear: this is the topic of conversation and substance of news all week prior to the game. There are high stakes—a conference champion-ship, a traditional rivalry, or just pride—and gambling (a growing problem on college campuses). There are sidebars: will the star player recover from an injury in time for the game? Will the weather be good? What about that athlete-student suspended from the team? Will he be back? (Incidentally, what did he do that got him suspended?) Anticipation prior to the game is high. Intense feelings persist afterwards either as elation (we won!) or lamentation (we should have won). There is drama to die for.

3. *Almanac 2013–14*, 8, 10; http://usatoday30.usatoday.com/sports/graphics/datatables.

4. A salary package for one big-time football coach includes—in addition to the basic contract salary—$100,000 additional for winning the championship of his con-ference, $25,000 for end-of-year national ranking of tenth through sixth, or $50,000 for fourth or fifth, or $100,000 for third or second, or $450,000 for number one. Occasion-ally a coach will get an additional but relatively small amount if a certain percentage of his players graduate, but that is not typical, and it is not big bucks. Even getting fired has its benefits: according to the *CHE*, December 9, 2011, A6, in 2009 the Notre Dame foot-ball coach received a total compensation (or "separation agreement") of $7,284,548; that was the year that Notre Dame fired him.

And politics? There is the raising of the flag. How many classrooms have an American flag? And, what about the singing of the "Star Spangled Banner" (there are probably not many classes that open with the pledge of allegiance or the national anthem)? Isn't it clear that the powerful are the winners? The point is to dominate the opponent. That is a lesson that you will be taught repeatedly in secular life, in college, and especially on the athletic field (whether in person, watching the game on TV, or hearing about it later).

> WHO IS IMPORTANT? The largest schools with the biggest athletic programs spend up to twelve times more per athlete than they do on each non-athlete student. Schools in the Southeastern Conference spend an average of $176,429 on each athlete compared to the $13,229 spent on each non-athlete student.
>
> CHE (JANUARY 17, 2014), A15.

The religious fervor is there,[5] if only unconsciously, with the feeling of good (our team) versus evil (the other team) and the absolutely ritualized assembly of the uniformed participants.[6] There are schools where it is taken for granted that membership on the team carries the expectation that the players are committed Christians,[7] and there are schools hoping to evangelize through a winning football program.[8] The field itself can even produce a kind of religious nostalgia in the minds of old grads.[9]

---

5. Historically—virtually since Old Testament times—Jews and Christians have been dubious about the value of sports. Christians were generally the losers in the Roman gladiatorial events and the Emperor Theodosian discontinued the Olympics in 393/4 (after a run of over 1,168 years[!]). Then, after another millennium and a half, "muscular Christianity" emerged in the late 1800s with the conviction that athletics offered a great way to inculcate Christian belief, habits, and even virtues into young men. For an excellent but brief description and summary, see Mathisen, "From Muscular Christians to Jocks for Jesus."

6. The heroes, the goats, the legendary plays and players offer a kind of hagiography (compendium of "saints"). The devotion bestowed on the activities is seen by many critics as an alternative American religion. "Sports do exhibit many of the characteristics of established religious traditions . . . They exercise a power for shaping and engaging the world for millions of devoted fans . . . Sports constitute a form of popular religion." Price, "An American Apotheosis," 229.

7. Wolverton, "With God on Our Side."

8. Pennington, "A Football Crusade," 1.

9 Earl Broussard, "The Power of Place on Campus," CR, May 1, 2009, B12–B13, points out that the Latin religare, from which our word "religion" derives, means "to bind, connect." So we "often overlook the influential role that campus landscape can play . . . There are several distinct types of sacred spaces, among them ritual or ceremonial spaces . . . such as a football stadium, [that] showcase[s] an institution's culture."

But now it's game time!
Game on! Class is in session!

Is There a Problem?

If athletics is really the biggest college classroom, yes, there is a big problem. With all this investment of time, resources and enthusiasm, this "big game" is more than just a game. Think about it: biggest building on campus, largest crowd of the year, highest salaries, best known teachers (i.e., coaches), most interest and enthusiasm, and the most compelling factor in creating community spirit for most colleges. Athletics offer TV exposure, so monies changing hands for athletics is in the billions of dollars. Schools spend much more per athlete-student than they do per regular student. The budgets for athletics are the biggest (and so are the deficits) because the schools must believe that *this is the most important thing that colleges do.* (A budget is primarily a statement of values; the dollars are written in the budget to achieve the values held.) There is a message here about the central values embedded in and "taught" by the college experience: *competition* is of supreme importance; *hierarchy* is acceptable; *winning* is to be desired.

The "big game" is definitely a teaching occasion for all of these central values. The primary value taught is *competitiveness.* Not that this would be a new idea for students. Over one million boys will play high school football every Friday night each fall. Americans can watch live games virtually every day of the week, as well as get the radio, TV, print, and Internet analysis that are taken seriously and delivered in the context of one big happy (despite it being a fictitious) family of American sport enthusiasts. Today college students are nurtured in an atmosphere where competitiveness and competition are absolutely fundamental and universally taken for granted as a basic component of human-ness. Competitiveness is seen as God-given and its cultivation is almost universally deemed necessary for developing each person into a mature and marketable adult.

Even schools that exclude typical intercollegiate athletic competition are able to include institutionalized competitiveness in some form. For instance, one of the most conservative Christian colleges in America, where dating and most personal behavior is strictly controlled along (presumably) Christian lines loves sports: "Since Bob Jones [University] does not participate in intercollegiate sports . . . intramural teams . . . are enormously popular *and competitive.*"[10] Many parents who opt out of public education to

10. Riley, *God on the Quad,* 40; italics added.

home school their children still feel the need for honing the competitiveness accepted as crucial to Americans. Home schoolers, working at home alone on their academic work, organize for local games as well as for nationally recognized athletic tournaments![11]

In his famous collection of *Screwtape Letters*—letters of advice from a senior devil to his junior apprentice Wormwood—the Christian writer C. S. Lewis has Screwtape observe that his boss Satan's view of life is that one gains by competing with others and consuming them. "'To be' *means* to be in competition." Screwtape scorns "the Enemy" (God) for emphasizing love, which simply contradicts the notion of competition.[12]

At the regular monthly meeting of deans in a consortium of six church-related colleges, we were discussing this matter of assessment—measuring to see whether our students were actually learning the values that we publicly announced that we were teaching them. The dean from a school in the pacifist tradition[13] half-jokingly said that his school may have been afraid to test their graduates to see if they had acquired or improved in acquiring the primary and unique value the school tried to embody and teach: peace and peacemaking. He said, "Maybe we'd find out that our graduates were less peaceful and more aggressive."

It is remarkable that these values that the athletes, coaches and fans brag about—work ethic, teamwork, loyalty, competitiveness—are never tested for, to see if players are "getting it." Also, why do they never seriously ask whether there might be other ways to teach these values? Wouldn't there be other ways to ensure teamwork (community) and a work ethic (commitment)? The answer, of course, is an obvious "yes."

If competitiveness is so important, wouldn't there be other ways to teach it besides in the physically and economically costly arena of intercollegiate sports? What about some version of the one lonely example recommending competiveness in the Scripture, where Paul exhorts his Roman readers to "outdo one another in showing honor" (Rom 12:10b)? There could be any number of versions of this: Groups of technology majors could compete under the auspices of Habitat for Humanity. Which team could build more houses of the best quality? Or business majors could compete in advertising a fundraiser for AIDS research and be judged not only on the amount of money raised but also on the honesty and the informational

11. National championships in basketball, cross country, golf, soccer, track, and volleyball are held yearly for homeschoolers. See, for example, "National Christian Homeschool Basketball Championship," http://nchclive.com.

12. Lewis, *Screwtape*, 92.

13. The pacifist tradition includes Mennonites, Friends (Quakers), and the Church of the Brethren.

quality of their campaign. Or home economic majors could compete in designing a soup kitchen for the homeless and could be judged on the response of the clients but also on the nutritional and preventive health care benefits of their programs. These kinds of competitions would broaden participation of students and reduce both injury to the participants and costs to the college.

The fact is that competitiveness is so important that it sometimes seems to take over the college experience. Most college and university presidents probably lament that college athletics is more of a liability than an asset. One humorist suggested that the motto of one (originally church-related) school, which was *Eruditio et Religio* (Erudition and Religion), perhaps should be changed to *Eruditio et Basketballio* because of the publicized successes of its athletic program.[14] Misdeeds by athletes and coaches often make bigger headlines than the games their teams play. There are more rules governing athletics than control all other college activities combined. In order to win, schools will test the rules or break them. If too much of that happens, additional rules are made by governing bodies and the pressure to test or break the new rules begins all over again.

> *Several years ago an All-American basketball player at the University of North Carolina was being celebrated as the potential "player of the year" and was preparing for the "big game" with traditional rival Duke. The national newpaper USA TODAY gave him three times as many inches of reporting space on that day than it did to the murder of the student body at the same University of North Carolina.* USA TODAY Fri/Sat/Sun, March 7–9, 2008, 3A, 1C, 4C.

Colleges compete in many ways besides athletics. Colleges compete with one another for students, for faculty, for national rankings. They foster competition internally with intramural programs, grading of students, and teacher evaluations. Which is the best school? The best party school? The school with the most National Merit finalists? Which school has the most items in its library, the most graduates who have won the Congressional Medal of Honor or served on the Supreme Court? So when colleges behave competitively in so many areas, and when they reward competitiveness in almost every endeavor, yes, that is a problem. When colleges compete in any (or all) of these ways they are teaching students what is important, what to value: competition.

14. Harp, "The Palpable Word," 20.

Competitiveness is *not* a Christian virtue; it is not Christian in any way. That is a problem because Christians know that God did not create us to be competitive nor did God half-make us and leave us to our presumed competitiveness to finish the creation. This athletic and competitive aspect of college life has roots in the Greek education and philosophical tradition where we find the original Olympic Games and the glorification of physical competitiveness. The Olympic Games, the running and wrestling, were a highlight of Greek culture and closely affiliated with pagan religion.

The Judaeo-Christian tradition has only bad vibes for that (athletic) tradition. When the Romans took control of Palestine shortly before Jesus was born, religious Jews were scandalized by the activities of the Greco-Roman *gymnasium* (literally: a place to be naked). The earliest Christians' exposure to the Roman version of competitive sport was in the Coliseum, where gladiators competed (often to the death) with other gladiators, animals, and occasionally even Christians. Christians weren't very keen on the "competition" in arenas where they were sent to be victimized for the entertainment of the popular pagan masses.

The drive to be number one seems intensely American and certainly is a central part of the American experience and of the college experience.[15] In athletics, for example there are opportunities for many schools to become number one in many areas. Schools can be NCAA, NAIA, NJCAA, etc. Within each major category there might be sub-categories. Much of the emphasis on being number one focuses on activities exclusively American, limiting the playing field, so that the odds of being number one are more favorable (for example: rodeo and American football). And if your team is a loser this year, at least you can (1) wait until next year, (2) claim that your team worked hard enough (they have a good work ethic) to be considered number one anyway (this is what is called a moral victory), or (3) learn another important lesson: that most people are not number one and that you need to learn how to survive as a non-winner (i.e., loser). After all, only one team can be number one. All the rest are, well, losers. (That should *not* be the conclusion for anyone who takes Genesis 1:31 seriously.)

Of course, deep down, we all know that sports are not the most important thing in life. Coaches, players, and fans know it. When there is a real life crisis, the players and coaches and sports writers shift from their focus on the game to the business of "putting things into perspective," or recognizing

---

15. If we can't (individually or as a team) be number one, we can at least know who number one is. The Learfield Sports Directors' Cup is a listing of the top 25 colleges taking all sports into account (www.nacda.com). An "obscure Web site introduced by three friends in 2008" calculates the number one sports *nation* in the whole world (greatestsportingnation.com), according to the *NYT,* Sunday, October 30, 2011, SP 11.

that there are things of greater import. In cases of death or serious injury to a player, a momentary pause in the sport juggernaut occurs. But the pause is only momentary. Soon, the game goes on with some platitude like, "he [the injured or deceased] would have wanted us to go on."

If it is true that teaching secular values of *hierarchy* and *competitiveness* are important college goals, there is another curious problem: that colleges teach that it is okay to commit yourself to causes that are not ultimately significant. Commitment to the game becomes a way of saying that it is okay in the normal run of things to ignore that which is of ultimate significance in favor of commitment to what is "only a game." And yet the college community seems to commit much more to "the game" than to any other goal.

The only conclusion that can be drawn is that the real commitment of the college experience is to affirm some secular values that have no place in the Christian life. So a major value of college sport is that it encourages commitment to the penultimate, leaving the ultimate a matter for indifference. *Non-commitment* is the operative value. There is a problem if sport is a buffer against making serious decisions and commitments.

Finally, you have noticed the importance of one more value—*hierarchy*. We are all encouraged to think of a hierarchy, a pecking order, a "top ten" in virtually every aspect of the college experience. The world (of athletics) is arranged so that everyone can have a chance to be number one—or somehow be connected to number one. If you can't be the winning player or coach there is still a place in the hierarchy so that you can claim a connection with a number one as a manager, or cheerleader, or fan.

Throughout each college there is a glaringly clear hierarchy; it's not just in athletics. The board/regents/trustees are on top. Then comes the school president. After the president comes the provost and the dean, then full professors, then associate professors, then assistant professors, lecturers, adjuncts, teaching assistants, graduate students, seniors, juniors, sophomores, and finally the lowly freshmen. They are all followed by other employees who do the dirty work of keeping the whole machinery going. This is real hierarchy. It is a long way from the top to the bottom in the college hierarchy; sport is only one piece of it. Educational level—how many degrees you have—is a big separator between levels. This hierarchical reality is a college fact of life and it teaches the value of seeing all of life as split into levels. And college teaches that higher is better.

There are also hierarchies in the social side of college. In my case, the local equivalent of fraternities were the twenty "eating clubs" lined up along a street near the campus. Everyone knew which club was the number one club and which was the last one and what the order of the rest was (rich kids, scholars, jocks, etc.).

In order for this hierarchy not to be a problem, the Christian needs to understand that she is not higher or lower than others, or better or worse than others. In Scripture, to put it graphically, there are only two levels: God and creation, or God and humans, or God and the church. God's people, the kingdom of God, do not break down into a hierarchy of folks of differing worth, some better and some worse. Instead, the most biblical characterization of God's people is that of family—sisters and brothers who are equal; or parents in a loving relationship with children; or brides and grooms, loving one another in solid mutual commitment; or the body of Christ in which each member is unique and indispensable and all are vitally interconnected.

Enthusiasts of college athletic competition boast about other values that are taught or strengthened in sport: teamwork, loyalty, self-sacrifice, the "work ethic," honesty, fairness, and responsibility. But like so many assumptions about values, these claims have never been tested. Until recently.

Recently, there has been an effort to evaluate the effectiveness of college athletics in teaching the values assumed to be inculcated by sports. There was good news and bad news.[16] The good news was that athletes tested positively for the values of teamwork, loyalty, self-sacrifice, and the work ethic. The bad news was that they did not do well in honesty, fairness, and responsibility. Christians need to ask, "Does Jesus Christ offer a more helpful alternative?"

Christology: The Wall Breaker

The assignment in the Introduction to New Testament class was to come up with a Christology—an appropriate title for Jesus—that was both faithful to the Scripture (but not actually, literally found there) and meaningful to people today. One student found "A Man for Others" in his reading; another borrowed the title of a popular song: "Bridge over Troubled Waters." This was going well, I thought, until a student suggested "Coach." After lengthy discussion, I hope the class saw that the Jesus of the New Testament was not working people up to compete against and dominate others. Jesus was not a coach.

If we are so sure that competitiveness is a really Christian virtue, we ought to see some examples of it in Scripture. (We should also see some suggestion that God created people in different groups that were divinely ordained to compete with one another.) There are few references to athletics in the New Testament. The best argument to support a positive view of sport as Christian would be based on a positive reference to any game, sport,

16. Wolverton, "Morality Play."

or athletic contest. We do find seven references to contests—mostly foot races, which would have their source in the Greek and Roman competitions (which, we have pointed out, were hated by Jews, and later by Christians). The question is: When a biblical writer uses a sport reference, is that an endorsement of what happens in such contests? The answer? Not at all. (After all, references to *sin* cannot be interpreted as a biblical endorsement of *sin*.)

Note the following Scriptures and how references to the "race" or the "fight" are about Christians' self-control, perseverance, discipline, commitment, focus on the goal (of salvation); the biblical passages never refer to competitiveness or to beating an opponent or being number one:

- 1 Corinthians 9:24–26—Paul writes: "Do you not know that in a race the runners all compete, but only one receives the prize? Run in such a way that you may win it. Athletes exercise self-control in all things; they do it to receive a perishable wreath, but we an imperishable one. So I do not run aimlessly, nor do I box as though beating the air . . ."

- Galatians 2:2b—Paul had consulted with church leaders to evaluate his progress as an apostle and asked whether he had "run in vain."

- Galatians 5:7—Paul chastises Christians who had strayed from relying on faith to gaining salvation through works: "You were running well; who prevented you from obeying the truth?"

- Philippians 2:16—Paul hopes that "I can boast on the day of Christ that I did not run in vain or labor in vain."

- 1 Timothy 6:12—Paul exhorts the young minister Timothy to "Fight the good fight of the faith; take hold of the eternal life, to which you were called."

- 2 Timothy 4:7—Paul declares: "I have fought the good fight, I have finished the race, I have kept the faith."

- Hebrews 12:1—The author exhorts his readers: "Therefore since we are surrounded by so great a cloud of witnesses, let us also lay aside every weight and the sin that clings so closely, and let us run with perseverance the race that is set before us."

On only one occasion did Jesus ever get physical: he did throw the money-changers out of God's house (John 2:13-16), but he did not hurt anyone in the process.[17] Otherwise, he was usually pretty mild of manner. But we dare not view him as weak. In standing up against the whole system of his

---

17. Croy, "Messianic Whippersnapper."

day—political, military, religious and social—Jesus must be viewed as pretty tough. But he did not try to compete with or beat those who opposed him.

It is difficult to find a Jesus sympathetic to this competitive aspect of the college experience. We never encounter him trying to outdo or overcome others. We do find him seeking a deeper truth that will be more inclusive of others. We do find him trying to overcome that which separates people from God and/or each other. We do find him reaching out to the outcast, the foreigner, the stranger, the other. And we do find a Christology that expresses Jesus undermining the one basic premise of the competitive outlook—that there are competing forces.

It is found in Paul's letter to the Ephesians, 2:14-16. Paul recognized Jesus' ministry of reconciliation in bringing us to God and us to one another as one of breaking the "walls" that separate us. In this letter, Paul is specifically thinking of the Jewish law that separated Jews and Gentiles. Today, we are separated by other laws, by customs, language, politics, gender—you name it. Whatever it is, somebody will have used it as an excuse to separate someone from someone else. You can imagine Jesus going about knocking down walls that were constructed to separate A from B. After Jesus' work of demolition, you find yourself face to face with all of God's other children and under your feet the rubble of your best efforts at separating yourself from them. After all, Paul had observed that in Christ there (already) was no distinction between Jew and Gentile, slave and free, and even between male and female (Gal 3:28)!

There were a couple of instances where Jesus was questioned about being number one. When asked which of the 516 Jewish laws was the most important, Jesus claimed that there was a tie between loving God and loving your neighbor. When two of the disciples' mother asked Jesus if her boys could have the number one seats next to Jesus in the kingdom of God he answered that the number one ranking went to a servant ("slave" in Mattnew 20:27). That puts him in direct contradiction to the conventional wisdom of American culture, where greatness is associated with power and fame. Jesus the Teacher turns everything topsy-turvy. Jesus your Teacher shows you who you are to be and what God has chosen you for. It is to be someone loving, cooperative, and ultimately inclusive of all creation. You are not called to commit to something that is ultimately irrelevant and of only secondary importance (like winning the big game). Jesus was a servant, come to serve, to forgive, and his greatness was conferred on him by God, not gained in a contest.

What about Jesus as a winner because he overcame sin and death? Would naming him as the conqueror of death make him number one? Afraid not. Every description of the death of Jesus indicates that he was a sacrifice, a lamb (a Lamb of God Christology). Death did conquer him physically—he didn't fight it. It was God who vindicated Jesus, not Jesus himself.

As we have noted, there is only one Scripture verse in the whole Bible where competition is given any value. When Paul wrote to the Roman Christians he urged them to compete in showing honor (Rom 12:10b).

Application

I recently attended a meeting on the campus of a nationally famous Christian (or church-related) university. This is a school that has committed itself to be a great national research institution and to be Christian at the same time (whatever that might mean—as if an institution, like a grocery store, the post office, or an automobile factory, could be "Christian"). If that school succeeds, it will be an extraordinary achievement.[18] In the meantime, it faces the usual problem that schools face when they are saturated with secular American values. And this particular school has suffered notorious athletic scandals: athlete-students cheating; athlete-students on drugs; one athlete-student killing a fellow athlete-student; coaches cheating and lying; coaches being paid more than the university president.

The weekend I visited I had an interesting exposure to the college scene. It was a football weekend and as a part of the preparation for the big game there was to be a car bashing event at which participants, for a dollar a try, could pick up a sledge hammer and smash an old car. I could imagine how that sort of activity fit into a culture intent on consumption, expressions of power, and spectacle; I couldn't imagine how it fit a Christian community.

When it comes to competitiveness—so important for the typical American—we find that the only room for competitiveness in Christ is that of outdoing one another in showing honor (Rom 12:10b). One looks in vain for any approval of competition in the teaching of Jesus. The Christian subversion of competitiveness by the adoption of servanthood is truly countercultural but completely consistent with the "curriculum" Christ brings to your college experience. His emphasis on love, forgiveness, and reconciliation leaves no place logically or morally for competitiveness. In

---

18. It is extraordinarily difficult, if not impossible, for any "Christian," or "church-related," college to avoid secular influences. They are under all of the same pressures, rules, and regulations as secular schools, they hire faculty from the same graduate programs and recruit students from the same high schools, and are preparing graduates for the same jobs. The secular influences are much the same—particularly when it comes to the *hidden* or *implicit* curriculum.

this, Jesus' teaching is consistent with the portrayal of your destiny in the creation story, where it is clear that God made you to cooperate—not compete—with others.

Should you go to the "big game"? If so, how can you go *as a Christian?* What might a Christian model for behavior at an athletic contest be? Let's use all the critical thinking and analytical skills you need for college in applying your faith to the situation.

Since, as a Christian, you view the game itself and the final outcome as not of ultimate significance, you can ignore the final score and whether your team won or lost. Since, as a Christian, you are called upon to love your enemies, you can see the opposing players, team, and school as beloved; if God loves them you can have no reason not to love them. If you appreciate the game and the physical skills it involves and if you admire good execution in the play of the game, and if you appreciate God's creation in making people strong, fast, and agile—you can enjoy every good play—whether your player made it or the other team's player made it. If, as a Christian, you are committed to justice, you will appreciate and support the referees' calls, whether against the opponents or your own school.

What to do? Enjoy the display of skill by individuals and by the teams—*both* teams. Accept the referees' calls; take no interest in the win/loss columns; ignore the outrageous salaries paid to coaches. Think about being number one by outdoing everyone in honor—and love and good works.

The Gospels report several miracles in which Jesus heals the blind. Your Christian faith gives you "glasses" through which you too can look at the world and see clearly. In your college experience, those glasses of faith are so important. God has given them to you; there is a lot to see and sort out.

Thought and Discussion Questions

1. How important do you think competition is? On what do you base your thinking?

2. Can you think of activities (games, recreation, other) where cooperation rather than competition could be satisfying? Specify.

3. List some of the "walls" that Jesus needs to break down for us.

4. Dealing with loss: Name the resource(s) you rely on to deal with loss—like failing a class, breaking up with a friend, losing a loved one, suffering a serious illness, etc.

13

IT'S PARTY TIME!

The Social Side of College

"We may lose a game . . .
but we never lose a party."

—COLLEGE STUDENT[1]

"The kingdom of heaven may be compared to
a king who gave a wedding banquet . . ."

—MATTHEW 22:2

Scripture Focus

JOHN 2:2

Jesus and his disciples had also been invited to the wedding.

It is notable that Jesus' first miracle—turning water into wine—happened at a celebration, a party. The miraculous deed—turning water into wine (in case you missed it the first time)—ensured that the party could go on. Jesus' intention is for you to party at appropriate times. In his parables he describes a God who is most joyous when the lost are

1. Sperber, *Beer and Circus*, 153.

190

found (Luke 15:7, 10). He describes a God whose kingdom is like some-one throwing a party. He describes a God whose intention—at the end of time and in the culminating purpose of all there is—is to have a party: the messianic banquet (the banquet of Jesus, the messiah, the chosen one of God—Matt 8:11). Even during his life and when faced with the dif-ficulties of trying to get his message across to a resistant audience of Jew-ish authorities and Roman officials, Jesus seemed to have a pretty good time. In addition to just talking in parables about parties (into some of which people were forcibly dragged [Luke 14:15–24]), he seems to have been in some demand as a guest (by Pharisees [Luke 7:36, 14:1]) if for no other reason than to check him out. Much of the time he just hung out with his disciples. His final act was to celebrate with his disciples that which we join him in celebrating today—the Lord's Supper. In that final gathering—solemn and serious because he knew he would soon die—he promised to celebrate with them, and with us, in that messianic banquet at the end of time.

The nature of God is to want all in the kingdom to rejoice. It is not all work. We are to celebrate the good things of harvest, discovery, marriage, and certainly our time in college. In Jesus you have a teacher who knows what enjoyment is and is not averse to sharing it.

Prayer: Help this college experience be one of joy for me and for those whose lives I touch. Amen.

The College Experience: The Social Life

You have arrived at that part of the college experience about which you may have been warned: Watch out! Beware! Be careful! Avoid! Don't . . .

Let's just calm down for a bit and take a long, broad look. Many "how to be a Christian in college" books are quite insistent that your main re-sponsibility as a college student is to stay pure and be a witness to others (professors and fellow students). But that is *not* your main task. (Although it is a very good idea.) Your main *vocation* in college—your calling from God—is to be a student and to learn! Specifically, you are called to *love God with all your mind* (Matt 22:37//Mark 12:30//Luke 10:27). Let's be frank—at this stage in your life you don't know enough to be a missionary to college professors.

Do be committed to studying as hard as you can. That will be the best witness you could possibly be. Don't be guilt-tripped into worrying about being perfect and powerfully persuasive. Now, what about the time outside of the classroom?

When college graduates are asked to reflect on their college experiences, the thing that comes up most is the social life—the people, classmates, friends, roommates, dates, lab partners; some were different, hard to know or like; others were different, but became lifelong friends; a few wound up as best friends; one might have become a life-partner. (Yes, the likelihood of meeting your future life-partner in college is pretty high.)

A questionnaire was sent to members of a twentieth-year reunion class: *What was your most significant memory or the biggest thing that happened to you in school?* Almost every answer had to do with time spent with friends—cruising, hanging out, bull sessions. This is a typical response of those who have gone to college. What are the things that they found so memorable?

First, of course, are the people—the soulmates you never thought you'd meet; the really different people you never knew existed. Some Christians have expressed concerns about the *diversity* of people you would meet in college and the possibly negative influences they might have on you. The fact is that the mix of students in college is increasingly diverse; there are more and more *different* kinds of people in virtually every college setting. As a proportion of everyone in college, you will encounter fewer males, fewer Caucasians, fewer Christians, fewer American citizens, and proportionally more of everyone else.

There is nothing more interesting than people. And these fellow students are people who, like you, are seeking to sort out a lot of things like, *Who am I? What is so important that I might die for it? How can I know if I'm in love?* And so on. These fellow students will bring their questions, their different perspectives, their different answers. And you will struggle with them to "do college" and to sort out answers to the big questions. That is part of what makes the people you meet the best part of your college experience.

Then there is the freedom that you encounter. No one will be there to wake you up in time. No one will do your laundry or cook your breakfast. No one will keep track of your schedule, your eating, your friends, your TV watching, your studying, your checking account balance. You are *free!* This may not feel like a matter of your Christian faith. (But remember "Faith as Freedom" from chapter 1?) This may feel like the fellow I saw on TV who defined freedom as "being able to do whatever I want whenever I want to do it." Freedom is something that the college experience allows you—at least for awhile (until it's time for a test or when your checking account is overdrawn). But while it lasts, it is a gift that is a memorable part of that good feeling that graduates have about college.

And the activities. Colleges try to provide a lot of entertainment and other opportunities that allow you to express your particular interests. Those in charge know that college students need opportunities to break from the serious work of study. In this category you'll find everything from the archery club to Zen meditation groups, from organized athletics, music groups and service clubs to one-of-a-kind concerts. Participation is usually based on interest, not expertise. The point is to help students have a fun and relaxing break from studies. You can be fairly certain that your college will offer something that suits your interests. If it doesn't, colleges are usually quite open to allowing and even supporting students who want to try something new and different, like a wilderness rescue team or a field hockey club, or . . . whatever you want.

How you spend a lot of your "down" time will really be up to you since college-wide events and groups aren't always scheduled when you want or need a break. Again, there is a wide range of possibilities. *One of my most memorable (fun) college moments was hearing the band play the song I had written for the campus show. Another really memorable time, although not so much fun, was bucking the college administration and establishing a new social model on campus. In the first case I was following all the rules (of music); in the second, I was pushing to change the rules. Each offered personal opportunities for something out of the routine of classes and study.*

The college experience provides a wide range of possibilities for fun. Be ready to take advantage of all of them. If you take your college work seriously, you will get tired; your brain will get tired. Your body will get stiff from sitting in one position. You will need to move into something different. And there will be disappointments: failed tests, health problems, family disputes, tragedy in the world on a daily basis, and even deaths that will affect you. At times like these, something more than fun will be needed, so the party outlook needs to expand and deepen to include a full array of support that will provide pleasure, joy, happiness—even in the face of disappointment.

College is a time to try things you wouldn't otherwise have thought of trying and even to make mistakes, because it is a time to explore and experience many things. You can explore the possibilities offered by different kinds of people. You can take different classes and see if you really want to be a doctor, or would rather be a musician. You can find out that creative writing is not your thing and switch to psychology or math. College is a place to make *mistakes* that will *not* be disastrous. Those mistakes will not come back to haunt you. For example, if you find out that you don't want to be a teacher, how much better to find out in college and change to something else than to prepare to teach, get a job, move to another town, buy a house, go to your first teaching job and find out only then that you hate it?

But now it's party time! All work and no play make Jill a dull girl. Having fun is a part of life. Of course, sometimes it might seem like a bigger part of the college experience than some folks—like parents and college administrators—might like it to be. But still, after a seventy-hour week of reading, lectures, jobs, activities, labs, study and more study, you may well feel like you deserve some fun and relaxation. And you do.

It is probably in the social arena that you may be most likely to make mistakes and some of them could be devastating. So it is wise to be moderate, to be cautious, to be careful, and to be thoughtful as you face the interesting but challenging and dangerous opportunities related to drugs (alcohol, etc.), gambling, friends, and sex. By this time in your life you already know most of what the "no-no's" are and why they are bad.

Is There a Problem?

Speaking of making mistakes . . .

It was a Saturday night and we were having fun in the usual way boys do at an all-male school—brainlessly goofing off. It was the low point of the year and we really needed some fun. We had just returned to school after Christmas and were facing two weeks of final exams to finish off the fall semester. Any light at the end of the tunnel seemed distant.

Someone had the idea of taking our now dried up Christmas tree, setting it on fire, and throwing it from our room on the third floor of the dorm. It seemed like a great idea. We proceeded to get the tree, light it, and throw it out into the darkness of the night. What a sight!

We hadn't counted on someone in another dorm noticing, and concluding that there might be a fire, and calling the fire department. In addition to this being a false alarm, it was a Saturday night false alarm. That did not please the volunteer fire department. No wonder that they were soon followed by the police and we soon found ourselves in jail. By that time, of course, it wasn't so much fun. Our friends who were still free came to the rescue, posted bail, and we were soon back on campus. The next few weeks, however, were pretty much devoted to raising money for a lawyer, behaving ourselves, and thankfully getting off for good behavior.

We were fortunate. Our mistake was one of disregarding others and risking the possibility that we might hurt someone. We did not consider the effect of our behavior on others. Conclusion: I'll never do that again. And indeed, in

the years since I never have thrown a burning Christmas tree out of a window.
I'm not so sure that I have always been as careful to consider the impact of my
other actions on others. That is still a work in progress.

So we are in this Christian life together, always aware that "doing unto
others" and concern for others can be a quickie test of whether what we have
in mind doing is a good idea. And yes, there is a problem if the fun, social,
activity, co-curricular part of the college experience becomes an obstacle in
your path as you seek to grow in your Christian faith as a college student.
Let's look at some of the problem areas.

This is the part that you are not supposed to have to think so hard
about; this is the part that is usually the "don't's" and maybe a few "do's." You
know that you aren't supposed to drink (at least to excess) or have sex before
marriage. One reason that it may be hard to do what you are supposed to
or not do what you're not supposed to is that you don't always ask yourself
the right questions.

1. Who am I?

2. Just because I feel free to do this, is this what my freedom is for?

3. Who is Jesus?

4. What does Scripture have to say about this?

Christology: Lord of the Dance

The "who am I" and "freedom" questions are ones that Scripture answers.
According to the book of Genesis, God created humans in his own image
(*imago dei*) to be social beings: Adam *and* Eve. You are created in order that
you in turn should be creative. You do this most profoundly as a social being: neither Eve nor Adam by herself or himself can create children. Scripture always refers to God's people as social: the family, the tribe, the nation,
the church, the kingdom of God. That social reality in which you participate
and find fulfillment celebrates itself in gathering together—for meals, for
worship, for weddings, or just to shoot the breeze.

It is also the case that God created you with freedom. The main issue
with your freedom is whether or not you will use it to acknowledge God as
your creator and the one who knows best who you are and what you can
become. Since you are free, however, you are also free to reject God and
decide that you know best what is good for you.

So who are you? You are a copy of God, but in need of other creatures
in order to be as much like God as is possible for a created being. And you

are free to acknowledge God or to reject God, free to "do your own thing" or to have a little broader view and do God's things.

Now we come to Jesus. Believe it or not, he is still a part of your college experience in the co-curricular realm. And here is how. Jesus started his public ministry as the "life of the party" at the Cana wedding (John 2:1–12). He later spoke of himself as the bridegroom to suggest the level of joy his presence calls forth (Mark 2:19). In several parables he describes the kingdom of God—that happy state of affairs when God truly is sovereign—like a banquet, a wedding feast, or a party celebrating the return of a lost sheep, discovery of a lost coin, or the homecoming of a child considered lost forever (Luke 15).

An excellent Christology to behold the commitment of Jesus to sheer human happiness could well be the scriptural title Bridegroom (see Mark 2:19) or the one found in the 1967 hymn entitled "The Lord of the Dance." Jesus is not only living water and living bread, not only the resurrection and the life, but also the "life of the party." In broader terms, Jesus is the one who wants you to have a good time, to enjoy yourself, to enjoy others, to enjoy life.

In the Gospels, Jesus focuses on announcing the coming kingdom of God to everyone and trying his best to describe it to everyone who will listen in terms that would make sense to them. He was also helping people in many ways, but, because of that, wound up in big trouble with the authorities who cut his life short. Jesus was a "big picture" person as he announced the coming kingdom of God. He did not spell out details on the "how to's" of living in the kingdom. He was more focused on attracting people to the kingdom, getting them interested and excited about it.

The details of how to live among God's people—the kingdom, the church, the fellowship—begin to appear in the New Testament letters. They were written to Christians who were working hard at the details of living that life that Jesus had promised for those who recognized God as their creator and wanted to live in God's will. Those letters—more than a dozen of them—were written to people of faith (like you) who were living in secular environments (as you are) and were confronted every day with non-Christians who had their own, secular ways of living. The first Christians were really facing tough situations (as you may be). They were wondering *How should I act toward non-Christians? Are there foods I'm not supposed to eat? Can I drink wine? Should I take an oath not to marry or is marrying okay? Should I pay taxes? Can I do whatever I want since Jesus reconciled me to God and forgave my sins?*

Plus about a thousand other questions. But let's take a focused look at six of the problem areas that the first Christians faced. And they are the same ones you will face: picking friends, food, money, time management, drinking/partying, and dating/sex. Before delving into what the problems are on campuses and what Scripture urges Christians to do about them, there seems to be one thing that can help you to keep things in perspective and clarify your choices: understanding your freedom.

The freedom you have as a Christian comes from God. The kind of freedom the secular world desires—freedom from everything—does not come from God. It is only a poor substitute for the real thing. It is misused in the college experience. It is a perverted version of the freedom you have in Christ who "for freedom . . . has set us free" (Gal 5:1). The secular version is a freedom from whatever you thought was holding you down so that you could do something else that you wanted to do. Shorthand definition: a liberation from one constraint in order to accept slavery to another (bad) master. Jesus offers you a freedom from self, from sin, from societal pressure; the freedom he offers liberates you to be free *for* others. Jesus Christ frees you *from* every stifling confinement and influence so that you can be directed in the way you were created to live—for God and for others. You are freed to think "outside the lines" of popular culture, of secular culture. You are free to be moved by whatever the real needs of others might be and to be free from whatever might have prevented you from responding to those needs. Instead of perfect freedom (which is impossible), Jesus cautions you to choose your yoke carefully (Matt 11:28–30) and promises that the way to greatness is servanthood (Matt 20:26–27).

Picking Friends

As your college experience begins you will find yourself in a veritable whirlwind of activities and with a ton of new people surrounding you. Some are easy to sort out—faculty, administrators, other students' parents; they are probably not in the "pool" of potential friends. That pool of potential friends will include roommates, dorm mates, classmates, teammates, and workmates. Many of them will be confused by college and desperate to make new friends. Some will be shy; but don't blow them off. Others will be aggressively gregarious; don't necessarily believe their whole "pitch." Even if you proceed with care, you can make some mistakes (like picking as trusted confidants students who will not be helpful to you nor open to receive the good things you have to offer).

Do you remember Bob, the card player? He definitely used his freedom in a questionable way. He found his fun all day, every day, playing cards in his room with some friends. His folks finally found out the truth after two years!

He lived to tell about his fun, and eventually turned his college life around and today is a respected professional in his community. Note: We do not suggest that Bob was mainly responsible for this disaster nor do we blame it on his "friends"; we don't know; he probably wishes now that he had been more selective with his "friends" then; one of them might have suggested that they actually suspend the game and go to class! In Scripture, the Book of Proverbs is an excellent guide for sizing up and selecting friends. Trustworthy friends, who will have your best interests at heart, can be a lifelong treasure.

And then there are friends who are "different." One of the terrifying things to the authors of some survival manuals is the possibility of running into people at college who are *different*: people from other religions or other countries or other cultures; or people of other sexual orientations (lesbian, gay, bisexual, transgender).

Religious Diversity Among College Freshmen Increasing![2]

Faith Tradition	% in 2007	% in 2011
Roman Catholic	26.8	26.0
Protestant	43.2	39.9
Jewish	2.8	2.6
Buddhist	1.1	1.3
Muslim	.8	1.1
Hindu	.9	.8
Mormon	1.3	.3
Other	3.0	3.0
None	**19.4**	**24.5**

Such people may not be intent on leading you astray; they may just want to be themselves. For good or for ill, *diversity* is with us. Many colleges believe that it is one of the keys to providing you with a well-rounded education. So be ready for *diversity*; just think how others might think of you!

In the early church, deciding whether or not Christians should associate with non-Christians was an issue. Paul and the authors of other biblical letters were cautious about these associations; Jesus seemed not to mind associating with others—even others who seemed sinful or unclean. Today it is pretty hard to be just about anywhere without interacting with people whose faith is radically different from that which we have articulated in this

2. *CHE*, February 1, 2008, A23; *Almanac 2012–13*, 24.

guide. The best suggestion seems to be that you keep Christ at the center of your life and live fully and helpfully in this world.[3]

Food

Food? This sounds pretty benign. Food a problem? Could be. Your mom isn't at college to make the very best food for you, especially your favorites. Your mom isn't there to keep you from eating too much of the stuff that might make you sick, or add unnecessary pounds, or not be healthy for you.

There is something popularly called the "Freshman Fifteen," which refers to the fifteen pounds freshmen used to gain between Fall enrollment and Christmas break. That may no longer be the case as colleges are increasingly concerned about serving attractive and balanced meals, but . . . Those late night study sessions, or simply hanging out, have to be fuelled with pizza and pop and you're not doing anything to burn off calories except sitting there talking. Food is a necessity, but responsibility in using your freedom to eat whenever and however much you want is an important self-maintenance issue.

When we look at Scripture for the answer to a specific problem, we may not always be able to find just the right solution. The first Christians found themselves in conflict with the Jews over whether Jesus was *the* Messiah or not; the two groups—Jews and Christians—were running on parallel tracks in the early days of the church. One of the issues that divided them was their eating practices. These days, there are virtually no issues that connect what you eat with your religion, so when you look into Scripture for guidelines or rules for the college student to consult about the menu at school you look in vain.

Instead, you might be satisfied with this bit of "food for thought" from Paul's first letter to the Corinthian church; that was the church where the rich pigged out at home before coming to communion and many of the poor members had nothing much to eat. His suggestion to them was that whether they ate or drank, or did anything, to "do everything for the glory of God" (1 Cor 10:31).

---

3. "Love God and sin boldly" is the suggestion attributed to Martin Luther, who realized that it would be impossible to live in the world without sinning.

Money

Food can be a problem in terms of what and how much goes *in*. *Money* goes *out*; that can be a problem. College costs an enormous amount of money these days. You will probably wind up with a college loan to pay off—about 98 percent of today's students have loans. It might be a good idea to go over your total college bill (yes, for all four years) with someone who knows about lending and borrowing: your folks, a friend-of-the-family banker, your college financial aid officer. That is for the long-term issues.

For the short-term situation—like, where will you get the cash to pay for a movie and a burger this weekend—you will need immediate cash. Again your folks come to mind. Or perhaps you (plan to) have a part-time job. That can be a really good idea for a couple of reasons: first, the money can be *all yours* to spend as you like; second, if you are fortunate, your job might just be a great learning experience. *When my [future] wife was in college, she was a biology major and was thinking of medicine as a career. Her part-time job was an early morning shift as a nurses' aide at the local hospital. Perfect!*

And then there is the credit card problem. One really bad yet tempting thing you may confront is the availability of credit cards. Lenders (credit card companies) know that one day you will have lots more money than you have now. And they want to be "friends" and get you to partner with them: they will offer you credit. Oh yes, and then you will have to pay them back later with interest. Your interest will be high because as yet you probably are not a good credit risk.

We see a little more specificity about money in Scripture: remember the poor (Gal 2:10). As a college student, even one with a big debt ahead of you, you are still better off than most people in the world! Paul thought of himself "as poor, yet . . . possessing everything" (2 Cor 6:10). The author of Hebrews suggested: "Keep your lives free from the love of money, and be content with what you have" (Heb 13:5). The freer you are from "getting and spending," the freer you are give to the poor, to seek more satisfying pursuits, and attend to future bills. These attitudes are definitely countercultural; but as a Christian you know that your faith does not equal American culture.

Time

What is time? Now there is a great philosophical question that has tortured thinkers for ages. All you need to know is that it is not something you can control like food or money. It is just there—twenty-four hours of it every day. What you need to do—again, as one who is made free and freed by Christ from everything holding you back—is to use the gift of time in the most responsible way. Precisely because you are your own boss in college, it is easy to waste time rather than assign it to the necessary things for a college student: class, study, regular meals, work, play, and don't forget: sleep.

In the Old Testament book of Ecclesiastes we find the famous lines you may have heard read at funerals:

> there is a season, and a time for every matter under heaven:
> a time to be born, and a time to die . . .
> a time to weep, and a time to laugh;
> a time to mourn, and a time to dance . . .
> a time to embrace, and a time to refrain from embracing . . .
> a time to keep, and a time to throw away . . .
> a time to keep silence, and a time to speak . . . (Eccles 3:1–8)

Ecclesiastes is part of what is called "wisdom" literature—a biblical literature that is written not so much from God's inspiration as from humans' understanding of how the world works. The wisdom encapsulated in these few verses is that no one can spend all of her time doing just what she wants to do. Even though Ecclesiastes doesn't mention a "time to study," that is probably the first thing that you should put on your schedule.

Having to organize your time so that your studies, your personal time, and your job are all covered is a great discipline, and time management is something you can only learn by doing it. *I was teaching an introduction-to-college class of freshmen when I asked the students to fill out a daily schedule. By the time they had completed their schedules, each hour in the eighteen-hour daily schedule was filled, from early morning to late at night, with classes, work, meals, activities, favorite TV programs. Most of the freshmen had absolutely NO time left to do any studying. At least with this group we could start early on learning new disciplines.*

The standard expectation that your professors will have is that you will spend about two hours studying for every one hour that you spend in class. Your professors have this expectation because they know that you will learn better, you will benefit from their instruction, and contribute to the class a lot more if you have some clues about what is going to happen in class and what the collateral reading has offered. If you come into class with good questions, you will totally impress your instructor.

So make the most of the time (Col 4:5b, Eph 5:16a). You can do this by avoiding those who "are living in idleness" (2 Thess 3:6) and by taking seriously the observation that "now is the acceptable time" (2 Cor 6:2). If you fritter away your freedom and wait until later to study, to do an assignment, to start that paper, or to prepare for a test, that "later" may never come.

Drinking/Partying

Self-control, moderation, responsibility. These all come to mind when you think of the excessive partying that is one of the saddest hallmarks of the American college scene. There is a lot of data on campus drinking. Responsibility falls on American culture in general, college environment, partying, and . . . you.

Do you remember Liz, that "A" student, active in student government and cheerleading—the prototypical "all-around" student? She was a Christian from a deeply committed Christian family. As a student in one of my classes she distinguished herself, always prepared and ready to participate constructively in class discussions. She brought good feelings to everyone as "the perfect student." When she was found one Sunday morning of her junior year on the floor of her apartment dead from alcohol poisoning, we were all blown away with shock. There was some talk of blame—the roommate for not noticing what was happening, her date for the evening, the bar where the drinking began, the university, even Liz herself—but nothing came of it. An astonishing denial of responsibility marked the aftermath of Liz's tragic death. The dozens of employees and hundreds of students at the university gave the impression, as did the minister at the funeral, that death in a drunken stupor is "just one of those things" that happens in college. Amazingly, drinking, drunkenness, binging—all of that tends to be greeted with silent approval or sniggers in the college community.

Would you tell your parents that you actually spend your freedom/time doing this stuff? Hazing—initiation that willfully endangers someone physically or emotionally. (Illegal in most states.) Gambling—Waste of time and money that can become addictive. While a high percentage of college students (mostly male) do it, it is a gross abuse of Christ-given freedom. Pornography—Guys, if you want to have a good relationship with a female, don't do pornography. Women see it as demeaning as it makes them into sex object. Don't be among the 70 percent of eighteen- to thirty-four-year-olds male Internet porn users.
SAFEFAMILIES.ORG

The preceding about Liz is all true—except that her name wasn't Liz. It is true but, thankfully, rare. It is not "just one of those things" that happens in college. It happened because people misused their freedom. Party time starts on some campuses earlier than Saturday night. Probably Friday night. There are even some that have a pretty relaxed Thursday night ("thirsty Thursday") . . . or Wednesday. Or maybe your schedule is light on Mondays or Tuesdays so that you can party on Sunday and Monday. If there is too much of this kind of fun that would be a problem.

It goes without saying that Scripture frowns on drinking to excess and drunkenness; the problem with it is that it changes you from being you— you become a drunk. You do dumb things. It can be disgusting as well as dangerous. *Other than Liz, I have not known any college student who drank himself (or abused any drug) to death. However, I do remember that I had been informally "appointed"—since I did not drink—to be in charge of making sure that all of my fellow band members for our travelling school musical were to be in the orchestra pit and sober in time for the evening performance. That worked out well, but after the show . . . well, that was a different thing. I was no longer responsible, but I was not immune from the mess when one of the guys threw up in his bunk bed in the sleeping car of the train in which thirty of us had to sleep. Have you ever tried to clean vomit out of an upper berth of a Pullman sleeper car?*

Dating/Sex

You are likely to develop deep, meaningful, and long-lasting relationships in college. Why? Because you find yourself among others who share important things with you: interest in subjects, majors, activities; similar cultural characteristics; important time together. Or it can just be love; it doesn't always make sense, but it's fun, wonderful, and can last a lifetime.

But let's not get ahead of ourselves.

Socializing at college involves everything from being in class together to informal get-togethers in the dorm. It could mean that you are in activities together—clubs, theater, part-time jobs. It could mean that you have a friend who has a friend who . . . (*that's how I met my wife*).

You go to parties; you go on dates; you go to concerts; you go on activities' trips. You name it—in today's college atmosphere there are no limits to when, where, and how you date, party, or even get serious about another person. That is partly a result of the freedom students have and what college administrators allow. It is a fact that college students indulge or overindulge in social activities that may not be in their long-term best interests. (*Remember the Christmas tree incident?*)

Then there is sex. One thing leads to another—acquaintance, attraction, partying, time together, time alone together, feeling good, feeling really good about one another. All very normal and healthy. It is likely you will meet that special person that you wind up spending your life with. But again, let's not jump ahead. It is just as likely that the person you feel really drawn to is *not* that special person. So for a Christian the key feature of the whole "relationship" thing is your consideration of the other person—what is best for him/her? What is the larger context, the big picture and not just the moonlight and the romance? The combination of freedom (misunderstood) and sex (misused) can be toxic.

Scripture has a lot to say about sex; it usually says something like, "Don't" (outside of marriage). But don't make the mistake of thinking that the only objective of dating is marriage. It has much to do with discovering who you are and with growing up into a mature Christian adult. Seriously, when you unpack the meaning of Scriptures on sex, the message is that it is a gift of God and needs to be used properly by God's creatures so that we can continue to live in that *imago dei*, or image of God, after which we are modeled. Here is another Scriptural way to look at sex: the issue is one of self-identity. Who am I? Answer: The Christian is *imago dei*—made in God's image. God is free, yes, but also mostly concerned about others. God is creative, yes, but uses that creativity with care. When faced with big issues—like having sex—the Christian might want to think about who she or he is first, then fit the actions into the bigger picture of identity, relationships, and what is best for the other person.

Remember that you are a servant (slave) to that which you serve (1 Cor 6:12; 1 Pet 2:16). Pick your master(s) with utmost care. With regard to sex, we are called to honor Christ in our bodies (Phil 1:20); young men are cautioned to treat women like they would treat their mother or sister (1 Tim 5:2). There may be little need to tell women to be wary of sex—except to remind them—and make sure that the guys hear this news: that sex is not the same thing as love. All students—Christian or not—are looking for friendship, companionship and love. Unlike in popular culture (especially movies) where sex seems to come first in a relationship, for Christians—and anyone looking for a solid relationship—friendship, companionship, and love need to come first in order to provide a solid basis and context for sex.[4] So as an overloaded (with work) college student, you have a lot to do other than worry about sex.

Better than quoting a Scripture verse from here and a verse from there, Scripture has a couple of stories that explain sex from a Christian faith point

---

4. Like everything else, sex needs to be contextualized—put into the right (Christian) context.

of view. These stories are short, easy to remember, and quite astonishing in their power. Here is the first:

God created Adam and did so in such a way that Adam lacked completeness. The creation of Eve completed Adam. (And, of course, Adam completed Eve.) Since they are made in the image of God (*imago dei*), their ability to create is basic to who they are. But their most creative powers (i.e., to produce babies) can only be realized as a result of sexual intercourse. So sex is a basic part of who we are. (A philosopher might call sex an ontological dimension of our being; this is one word you can look up.) We are fundamentally sexual beings. Sex is not an add-on or a mistake that popped up later. We are sexual beings and God made us that way and saw that we are "very good" (Gen 1:31). More importantly, we are social beings made to live in constructive harmony with all other humans. That story is found in the very first chapter of the whole Bible. Talk about important!

And here is the second story about sex; it is found in Paul's letter to the Ephesians, chapter 5. Paul writes about Christians' interpersonal relationships. Christians are to "be subject to one another out of reverence for Christ" (Eph 5:21). The main frame of reference for all of your relationships is (your) reverence for Christ—taking Christ seriously. From there Paul jumps right to marriage, which is the context within which the Christian practices sex. In marriage, Christians are to be mainly concerned with the care of the other partner. In this narrative, sex is for marriage, marriage is for one another, the married couple is rooted in Christ, Christ is from God. The Christian can file "sex" under "marriage" and then file "marriage" under "Christ."

In both narratives, sex is good, but it is powerful, like an unstable element. Used carelessly it can produce anything from a bad headache to venereal disease, from a ruined relationship to an unwanted pregnancy. Used rightly it becomes one of the ways to be the person God created you to be.

Finally, Scripture can be pretty harsh about this business of being "carried away" by passion, by "the moment," by alcohol. Temptation is not an outside force but something we invent ourselves and are responsible for (Jas 1:14). It is no excuse (1 Cor 10:13). God has given us a spirit of "self-discipline" (2 Tim 1:7)—if we are willing to use it. No excuses.

The main issue in dealing with each of these behavioral challenges in college has to do with freedom. As we noted earlier, there are two kinds of freedom. There is freedom from and freedom for. The freedom from version is the typical definition that is popularly (but mistakenly) held. You may be looking to college as a place and a time with no parents and no rules. From that angle it looks like a world of great choices lying ahead. Freedom *from* sounds great, but the only great thing about it is that it is a great way to fail. Success in any pursuit can't be achieved through freedom, but only through discipline and following some rules—whether the rules of the road (for safe driving), rules of the game (for a tennis victory), rules of harmony (to perform a song), or the rules of your college (to succeed in class). So, *freedom for* is the real freedom.

Freedom for acknowledges that none of us is or can ever be completely free and unconstrained. It is a freedom that knows you are ultimately limited and controlled. The only real question is not so much the freedom as it is the identity of whom or what controls you. Are you limited or controlled by an addiction, a parent, a fear? Or are you controlled by God your creator? Reality check: none of us is perfectly free. Scripture reminds us that we are the slaves of the one we obey (Rom 6:16). Ironic but true, Peter assures us that "As servants of God, [you can] live as free people, yet do not use your freedom as a pretext for evil" (1 Pet 2:16). Being controlled by God offers the best kind of freedom.

Application

Some years ago, *Playboy* magazine ran a picture of Jesus entitled *The Laughing Jesus*. A lot of people were not pleased that a representation of Jesus would be pictured in a pin-up magazine that was based on a secular philosophy; and many didn't like it that he would be portrayed as laughing. But remember that Jesus was a real person who had friends, wanted to enjoy God's creation, and rejoiced at the good things of life. He made people happy and he told stories about the good times the kingdom of God would usher in. He is truly "the life" of the party.

Party time is a great part of the college experience. It is for relaxation, learning, growing, relating, becoming more fully human. So having a good time in college is part of enjoying the whole of the college experience. Here is your bumper sticker for that:

DISCIPLES PARTY WITH DISCIPLINE.

Enjoying the college experience within the framework provided by the Lord of the Dance will get you the best seat at the party.

Thought and Discussion Questions

1. What are the limits that should govern "having a good time" for a Christian? How do you find those limits? How does Christ Jesus figure in when you seek those limits?

2. Given the penchant for partying in college and given the opportunities Christians have for fun and relaxation in that environment, how does a Christian conduct herself in a way that will enable her to have the enjoyment to which she is entitled?

3. What is the difference between *fun, pleasure, joy, excitement, satisfaction*? Can you differentiate among those terms and can you name an experience that fits each one?

4. Give an example of freedom when it is a positive and contrast that with an example of freedom when it is a negative.

14

TIME OUT!

For the Rest of College

"A stitch in time saves nine."
—BENJAMIN FRANKLIN

"Be still and know that I am God."
—PSALM 46:10

Scripture Focus

MATTHEW 11:29

"Take my yoke upon you, and learn from me: for I am gentle and humble in heart, and you will find rest for your souls."

*I*t always seemed to me that no matter how good my teachers were, each one left me with a feeling that no matter how hard I worked I would never get to where I needed to be in class. There was so much to read, so much to research, so much to think about that I'd never get to rest. Staying up all night to read a book or finish a paper still didn't get everything done.

Yet here is an amazing promise from *the* Teacher, Jesus. He will give us rest; not just a nap, but deep, quieting, satisfying rest for our souls. Why would Jesus tell us to take his yoke?

What is a yoke anyway? In Jesus' day a yoke was that part of an animal harness that was placed over the shoulders of oxen to transfer the animals' power into useable form—to pull a load. Yokes were heavy. Why does Jesus invite us to take a yoke? Because the fact is that we are bound to be yoked to someone or something. Wouldn't it be preferable to have as our yoke something we know is worthy? The yoke Jesus holds out for us is that he invites us to be his pupils. He invites us to learn from him.

Here is a gift, an invitation. But it sounds like it could involve work on our part. Yes, there is an expectation that we learn. But you have already seen that the qualifications of Jesus as Teacher are special and different from those of any of the rest of your teachers. Here Jesus promises one more benefit—a unique benefit—of taking him as our teacher: we will find rest.

This startling paradox is typical of Jesus. We all know that any serious learning is a burden. Yet here it is a burden that, when borne, produces rest and peace in your heart. The yoke provides an instructive image. Only when oxen were yoked could they transfer or apply their power to the moving of the load to which they were attached. If we go to Jesus as our Teacher, we are promised learning that gives us both power and rest.

Prayer: Lord, thank you for offering me rest in body, mind, and soul. Amen.

The College Experience: Rest

If your college is typical, Sunday will not be considered a "day of rest." But at least there won't be any classes scheduled. So how do you rest up from the party, from the game, and from a week of classes and study? You may be indefatigable, with no apparent need for rest. You may just sleep in. Or you could use Sunday to catch up, write that paper, wash the car, work a part-time job, clean your room. With nothing planned there is not much to worry about. Or is there?

Is There a Problem?

The college experience has a way of making you feel that you are much too busy and that you don't even have time to do the bare minimum you need to accomplish, much less have time for other things that you would like to do. *Busy* is simply what you are as a college student. There is barely time to get assignments done. There is not enough time to get them done as well as you'd like. You may not like that feeling but you're not the only one who feels that way. Everyone is too busy. Everyone is running behind. Everyone is just wanting to get required classes "out of the way." Everyone is in a hurry to get to somewhere else.

Finally it's Sunday—a day of rest. This is God's gift to busy students. It is another gift, like the gift of freedom. And how will you use it? When Sunday rolls around, the secular culture of college tries to grab the day as an opportunity to work at something, even if it is only more partying or sports. Sunday is seen as the time to catch up: do laundry, check in at home, or just sleep until noon.

> Just a reminder about the implicit curriculum. That is what college teaches you by simply being the particular institution that it is. It teaches you things without your noticing that they are being taught. Or even noticing that you are learning them!

What is the *hidden* curriculum, the one hidden in Sunday, that elusive "day of rest"? By this time you could see that coming, couldn't you? Here it is: the college experience—the way it is set up in secular America—teaches you is that idleness is not good. It teaches that you should value a work ethic, being busy, busy-ness (sounds like "business" doesn't it?). Ironically, being busy or at least feeling busy in college is good preparation for life after college—busy is what most Americans are or will feel most of the rest of their lives. And it teaches you that if you aren't busy you're not good enough. Even if you are busy, you're not good enough. You have to get busier.

Even when relaxing we Americans relax energetically. You know that the typical American worker's vacation is two weeks. Did you also know that in other countries, typical vacations are two to three times longer than those in the US? When we vacation . . . boy, do we vacation! In order to "rest" we schedule activities that are supposed to enable us to rest, recuperate, rejuvenate, revitalize. Often those very activities tire us out even more. But to waste time is not valued. Rest is not something we do very well.

Perhaps the biggest "waste" of time that could have been used for work is—according to the secular world—time spent with God: in prayer, in worship, in silence. Typically Sunday morning is the time for Christians to gather as a community and celebrate in worship, communion, prayer, song, and other aspects of community life. Even that can be turned around, however, by churchgoers driven by secular values. In one survey, a man described his church attendance by saying that it was like going to a gas station where he "filled up his tank" in order to be ready for the next hectic week. He was able to make use of the Sabbath *rest* to get something important taken care of, namely revving up for the next work week. And what would happen if the church service didn't end on time?[1]

Yes, there is a problem if college teaches you that it is important to be busy and that you should not lose any opportunity for some gain—of pleasure, more study, overtime at work, acquiring new experiences or new acquaintances. The college years are typically years when it happens that many—though certainly not all—Christians drift away from the Christian community. This is not at all surprising considering that college—that gift of God fallen from its divine vocation—is secular and powered by values that really undermine Christian faith *and* that churches don't do a great job of keeping close to their college students to help them meet the college's secular challenges. Campus pastors work hard at filling the gap but can't reach everyone.

But even if Christian students who drift away from the Christian community to the secular life in college return to the church in later years they will have missed the richness of living the college experience *as Christians*. They may return to their churches without having noted, critiqued, and discarded the secular challenges that college typically offers to the essential features of a robust Christian faith. They may even think that many of those secular values that were part of college's implicit curriculum are Christian when they really are not.

What happens to college students? How has religious commitment fared on campus? The research studies that touch on the impact of the college experience on religiosity during the college years show "limited but consistent evidence of declines in students' traditional religious affiliations during their college years and in their general religious orientations . . . Religious beliefs became more individual and less doctrinaire, and tolerance for the religious views of others appeared to increase."[2] It seems that students are "constructing their own religious values quite apart from any of the traditional denominations."[3] Overall there is a generally liberalizing (secularizing) trend in students' religious outlook.[4] Beliefs are more eclectic and commitments are more personal and private. Students seeks their own way[5] of "piecing together their own spiritual homes."[6]

1. People might be late for lunch.
2. Pascaralla and Terenzini, *College Affects Students*, 284.
3. Ibid., 285.
4. Ibid., 284.
5. Chickering et al., *Encouraging Authenticity*, 68–69.
6. Ibid., 91.

So many are making up their faith—whatever it happens to be—as they go along. Students are using that freedom God gives to make up religion as they go along and leave the good stuff by the wayside. Interesting; we don't do that in any other realm, such as math, physics, medicine, or golf. So why would anyone take that risk when it comes to the faith commitment that would shape your life from here to eternity?

Students say they are religious or spiritual but not in recognizably traditional ways. This is a problem for Christians because the Christian faith is not something you make up as you go along. There is definite content and it is a shared content. It is not a solo performance.

The life of faith is not limited to certain external forms (for example, the form of baptism or the exact wording of the Lord's Prayer or the music used in worship). Nor is the life of faith to be measured by the extent to which students agree with propositions or "feel" inclined to one or another point of view. The life of faith is something lived out over the course of time and depends on its engagement with the Lord (and Teacher) Jesus Christ as one meets the challenges of everyday life and the hard days of major crises. To the extent that secularly motivated activity is valued to the exclusion of the exercise of the life of faith . . . yes, there is a problem.

Christians might want to use their free time to receive the rest promised by Christ in order to contemplate their faith journey.

Christology: The Good Shepherd

Americans don't value "wasting time." Time has to be used productively. That is a value that would—indeed, does—go well with the world of work for which colleges prepare students. Wasting time is not good . . . except. How about when you are watching your favorite TV program, or are on a date with that special person, or involved in a heavy game of cards, or just hanging out with friends? During such moments, you don't constantly look at your watch and worry about the passing of time. In fact, you value those moments and are sorry when they come to an end. We often find that one of the main benefits of such "wasted time" is that we are refreshed and rejuvenated and ready to get back to work. This is a kind of loitering.[7]

Someone—definitely not an American!—observed that worship was "wasting time with God." What he meant, of course, was that worship should

---

7. Castle, in "Pick Up," quotes French film director Jean Renoir: "the foundation of all civilization is loitering." Loitering is made up of unstructured hours in which thoughts, questions, and conversations range easily and at will, not necessarily expecting what may appear spontaneously with significant personal ramifications.

not be seen as "completing an assignment" or "fulfilling a responsibility" but rather as just being there, not in a hurry, not watching the clock or trying to finish up and get on with something else. Who is the Jesus who can give us rest without us feeling guilty about it? Jesus is the one who promises the "too good to be true" deal: study with him and get rest.

The roles Jesus plays for us cover a range from active (Wall Breaker, Artist) to passive (Bread of Life, Sacrifice). Jesus the Good Shepherd offers us a picture that is quiet and peaceful. We probably romanticize the Shepherd a lot but actually shepherds have to work hard at their jobs—being alert to wolves, bad weather, and dangerous terrain. But what are they doing? They are creating a zone of comfort in which their flock can eat and play and "work" (graze) and sleep without worry. That is what Jesus does for us.

What does Jesus the Teacher tell you? He tells you that worry and anxiety don't help. No matter what you do you cannot change most things. But instead of directing you to find peace and rest in yourself, he offers himself. He is your Shepherd, your peace (Eph 2:14), the one who gives you rest.

What About the Rest of the Story?

Jesus offers you the calm refreshment of promised peace. He offers freedom. He also offers much more. If you look at a second meaning of "rest" you will find an inventory of gifts—blessings that stretch from A to Z, *alpha* to *omega*. There is an entire treasury of Christian tradition that comes to you because of Jesus Christ. Two thousand years of believers who, in their Christian lives, experienced, preserved, and passed on a tradition rich in resources that you will find useful in the college experience and beyond.

Let's look at some of treasures that this Christian tradition offers to strengthen and enrich your faith. As with every other aspect of the college experience seen so far, this treasure house provides something better, more genuine and permanent, than what secular culture or secular education provides. Each of these topics is itself a rich treasury of resources that promises inspiration and information. Free for the taking, they connect you with the past and promise strength for the future; they connect you with Christian sisters and brothers across time and space. It is our prayer that you will be enriched by them and that you will be inspired by them always to expect continuing blessings from our Lord and Teacher, Jesus Christ.

A—*architecture*—Buildings: Places and Spaces.

Your college—if it is like almost all other colleges in America—probably has a campus—an attractive arrangement of buildings. Each school is different. That is one of the appealing things about colleges in America—they are so picturesque and uniquely beautiful. But there is a message there: the *implicit* message that reality is fractured and that there is no coherence or unity in life. The science building is over there; the humanities over here; education, history, and art are in three different buildings; computer science was a late-comer and had to be satisfied with two different locations; and so it goes. Integration, togetherness, harmony are not modeled for us by our campus architecture.

As Christians, while our main earthly support comes from the church community, we should not ignore the comfort that can come from the physical places where the church gathers. You have probably felt close to God in some particular location. Perhaps your home church; perhaps the campus chapel; perhaps some corner where your group can meet; or perhaps a lofty and spectacular cathedral that almost overpowers you. There are places that are meaningful and can offer hospitality when you need it.

Some campuses are blessed with such places: a labyrinth to help focus your thoughts; the Prayer Porch at Montreat College; or one of the several places showing on the map of spiritual sites at Boston College. Where is your favorite and most comfortable place to be, to have fellowship, to feel closer to God, to relax and be refreshed?

B—*baptism*—Initiation.

College is a place where initiations and harassment take place despite the dangers involved and the "official" posture of the college in opposition. It is so important to belong to a group that some students will undergo psychological and physical danger just to join a group.

You have joined the church (without hazing or harassment).

Let's try that again: you have accepted God's gracious invitation to acknowledge him as your creator and the one you want to be your parent and guide for your life. Although your actual baptism event is past history, it is worth pondering the nature of the foundation it laid for your current life as a Christian. In that baptism you died to the world, to sin, to this secular life, and entered into Christ's newness of life (Rom 6:4). That means that the life you now live is a totally new and different life from that which the secular world advocates and expects.

You have been initiated into a new life (better than any other) and into a new community (better, universal, eternal). All of these A to Z items are now yours, along with so many other blessings. Enjoy enjoying them.

C—*canon*

A canon is made up of the important texts up against which the truth, legitimacy, and importance of something can be evaluated. There is a canon— whether it concerns popular music, the best movies, the greatest novelists, or . . . whatever. "Canon" comes from the Greek word for *reed*, a plant that had a straight edge that could be used to draw a straight line or serve as a kind of "ruler" to determine straightness or rightness.

The Christian canon consists of those documents written by Christian believers and blessed by God that now form our Scripture. These writings were born in the crisis of Christian believers' struggles to survive and flourish in a cauldron of animosity, distrust, and persecution. They constitute the solid, objective center around which we can all gather to worship, study, comfort one another, and plan for a future that is good for everyone. This canon is super important for Christians.

Note: "canon" is not some kind of sacred howitzer Christians are given to use to blow away anyone who doesn't agree with them; it is not an explosive device we can use to seal an argument. It is simply that which we use to measure the closeness of our faith and actions to those of other Christians throughout time.

C—*church/community*

The community or group—or more likely groups—to which you belong are important for your well-being as a human being, since God created us to be social beings. But not all groups are equal or equally good for sustaining and enriching you as a human being. It is good to make a periodic review of the groups to which you belong.

You have come from a church where you are loved and supported; after college, you will participate in another church where you will continue to mature as a Christian and find many ways to praise God and be helpful to others. While in college, it is important for your own spiritual health that you have opportunities to share with others. It is important that you find a community of the faithful. It can be a regular church; it could be a campus center or campus ministry; it could be a parachurch (non-denominational) college ministry. The key thing is that you are not alone, but rather in community, part of the body of Christ even in college.

C—*creed*—What you stand for.

Everyone has at least one creed—something they believe in. Of course, it might only be that God doesn't exist or that life is not worth living or that aliens are in control of your mind. More likely, we have a number of positive beliefs as Americans ("freedom for all"), as scientists ("nature is orderly"), as Yankee fans ("we're number one"), or vegetarians ("meat isn't good for you").

In college you will be introduced to some powerful "creeds" that have enthusiastic defenders and long histories of success with wide audiences: Plato and Socrates and their belief in the perfection of knowledge; the Stoics and their belief in the inevitability of whatever happens; white supremacists and their racism; Marx's conviction that everything is explained by the material world, Christian Scientists and their conviction that illness and disease are not real. Are you ready to deal with these and many other powerful convictions?

Christians routinely articulate the content of their faith by using creeds that are almost as old as the New Testament itself; other useful creedal statements are of recent origin. They usually are comprehensive in the sense of summarizing the basics of the faith in a brief and memorable format. These statements help you express yourself and define who you are and identify you with other believers, regardless of their language, culture, level of education or even the era in which they lived! When you say a creed, you are confessing a faith shared by a universal community.

C—*confession*—What you are sorry for.

Confession of mistakes, shortcomings, or guilt is not frequent in secular society. For instance, politicians rarely admit a mistake; it's bad for a political career. Movie stars might confess a failure that publicizes a celebrity career. (Any publicity is good publicity!) But just confessing failure and shortcomings because you failed or came up short—that is not a regular American thing.

You know how true it is that even Christians can feel guilty about stuff they do or think or even fail to do. You also know that God is a gracious, forgiving God. God invites us to bring our guilt and sin to him and seek forgiveness. We can do that any time and any place. What a relief that is!

D—*devotions*—What a *devotee* does.

Fame calls forth some crazy stuff from an American public that can be totally taken with a celebrity one day and tosses them on the dust heap the next. When we go nuts for a politician, a movie star, or a sports icon, we want to be there for appearances, we buy T-shirts, get autographs, want to know about them—their favorite foods, how they party, who they are in love with. We are *devoted*.

Christians are devoted to God and to Jesus Christ. There are books, pamphlets, or just plain Bible reading that can help you to focus and organize your devotion—taking quiet time to focus on God, and thinking about what is going on in your life in the light of God's concerns and questions for and to you. This is an area of discipleship and Christian discipline over which you have total control. It is not like church (be there at 11:00) or saying the creed (use exact wording, please) or celebrating the Christian calendar (it can't be Christmas *and* Easter on the same day). Your devotions are *your* devotions—when, where, how you want. Enjoy them; they're about you and God.

E—*ethics*—Right behavior; morals.

There is right (good) behavior spelled out in virtually every aspect of life. Games have rules; businesses have codes of conduct; doctors have the Hippocratic Oath; married couples have that "'til death do us part" commitment. But then . . .

. . . A close call in the game exposes the need for a referee and for instant replay; businesses also hire lawyers in case they are sued for screwing up; doctors get sued too; marriages break up. Ethics is not just about the "do's" and "don'ts" of smoking, drinking, swearing. This is about the deeper questions of how tough and complex problems can be solved.

Christians may have the Ten Commandments, but they don't provide ready-made answers to really complicated problems. Even with Jesus' "revision" of the Commandments offered in the Beatitudes (Matt 5:3–12) not every problem is resolved easily. We frequently have to think very carefully about morality and think about how ethical and moral decisions ought to be made. This is not always easy. Sometimes Christians differ about how this ought to be done, and why there are differences, and what might be done about it. You may or may not have an issue that needs deciding right now. If you don't, that's okay; just remember that there are a lot of really smart Christians who think about morality and write books about how Christians should think about morality—about right and wrong.

If you do have an issue, find some smart and serious Christians, and find some of those books, and go online, and ask, and keep asking, and study the relevant parts of Scripture and . . . you will begin to get a clue on how to proceed. And remember that you can't get every decision right. God loves you no matter.

F—faith—Everyone believes in something. (See C—creed)

Always there; always a great resource. And to think, millions of Christians over time and in every place have shared this faith. That connects you to them. Some of them may even be at your college—still unknown to you. Maybe you will get to know them.

G—God—The most important thing.

God is always greater than you might have thought. One early Christian theologian (Anselm, 1033–1109) argued that God was "that which nothing greater can be conceived." Whatever you can think of that is really great, God is greater.

H—history—We each have our story; and we each love to tell our story.

We have a political history: the Declaration of Independence, the Revolution, the frontier, the Civil War, two World Wars, and a Depression; that is the background for the next chapter in your life that you will write.

Your family has its history and you want to know your family tree—are there any horse thieves among the ancestors? Any genuine heroes?

Christians have a history; it is "His-story"—God's story. It has good parts and bad parts. But it starts at the beginning and covers everything and comes right on down to today and includes you. You are a part of "His-story" as are millions who have gone before, who live around the world now, and those still to come in the future. You can feel great about being a part of such a story and about the fact that your own, personal story is a part of that wonderful, universal story that God is writing.

H—*hymns*—Music is universal; we all have our songs.

Singing is one way to express feelings that are hard to put into words and to express with your own voice things that poets have said so much better. Our hymns are a treasure chest of tunes and thoughts, expressions and emotions that help to tie us together and to remember and express things we carry in our hearts.

There are choruses and hymns that help me think about college:

List your favorites: _____

_____

I—*imago dei*—Identity: the perennial issue for college students: Who am I?

A lot of money is made in America by businesses that want to help you find or express your identity. Here's a quick way to save some cash:
  You are the image of God. Deal with it. Live up to it. (You're not God; you are made in the image of God.) Think about what God is like; start with one or two characteristics and see how they can be reflected in your life. This is pretty daunting stuff, but you are made in God's image.

J—*Jesus*—Just a reminder: keep Jesus at the center of your college experience.

K—*kingdom of God*—Xanadu, Somewhere Over the Rainbow, Never-Never Land, Erehwon.

Movies, politicians, artists do it; even little kids do it—dream of a perfect place. The truth is, in this world there is no such place. That's why the only way to get there is to dream or go to the movies.
  Using the picture of the kingdom of God, Jesus offers hints (with parables) in Scripture as a guide so that you can keep focused on the big picture of how your own particular major and vocation should be directed. And you can dream the *possible* dream that God has promised us.

L—*liturgy*—Rites for public worship.

This is what you might call the choreography or ceremonialism of Christian togetherness and worship. This is the who-does-what-when-where-and-how or the this-comes-first-and-then-we-do-that-next way of thinking of Sunday morning. Every church has this structure: it is obvious in a Catholic church and maybe not so obvious in a Baptist church (but it is there).

So every church has a liturgy or an organization for its communal gatherings. There are lots of reasons for that but the main one for you to understand is that it is just easier to have a routine. Why reinvent the wheel and have a completely different order of worship every time you gather? You don't need to brush your teeth differently every day. Worship can be both routine *and* genuine at the same time.

M—*mission*—Each of us is on a mission.

In the past, the wealthy, powerful, white cultures of Europe and North America used to send missionaries to help the poor people of the rest of the world. That is changing now. For one reason, there are growing numbers of Christians in other parts of the world, and the percentage of Christians in our part of the world is shrinking. And our definition of "poor" may be changing. It has become clear that our part of the world is not as self-sufficient and have-it-all/know-it-all as had been thought. Other peoples and cultures have brought much to America that we have needed. So you are invited to see yourself as part of an international, Christian mutual exchange project. You can learn from Christians elsewhere; and you can still contribute something to them that they lack and really need.

N—*names of Jesus*—These are really titles.

Like when you finish college you will have a title: AB, BA, BS, or something similar. You may acquire other titles: Dr., Rev., CEO, Sergeant, Superstar; notice that some are earned, and others attributed because of some characteristic of your own.

Jesus acquired a lot of titles; this is the whole business of Christology—the significance of Jesus. His titles ran all the way from A to (almost) Z: Author of Life, Bread of Life, Cornerstone . . . Son of David, Vine, Way. These are the Christological titles; we have looked carefully at how some of them are helpful in clarifying and meeting the challenges of college. But there are many more; and there is always the possibility that there will be

new ones. Have any ideas? Since Jesus is always with us there is the possibility that there will be new ones. What has Jesus done for or meant to you
lately? Can you see a new Christological title or name emerging from that
experience? It could be helpful for others to know about it.

I have a few of my own that have explained Jesus to me: *Glue* (the one
who makes everything hold together); *bridge over troubled waters* (a helper
in time of trouble); *life of the party* (one who brings joy into our lives). Have
you found any yet? Would you write them down here for the benefit of the
next reader? _____

Thanks.

O—Old Testament—Old stuff can be really important and helpful.

We have focused on the New Testament because that is where we find the
most information about Jesus and where we read of the early Christians'
struggles to understand their new faith and put it into action in tough situations. But don't forget the Old Testament. There are lots of ways in which it
can be helpful to you in your college experience. Here are just a few aspects
to consider: (a) prophecies form part of the "job description" applied to
Jesus in the New Testament and they can expand your Christological understanding; (b) the prophets are super-tough critics of the *status quo* and
offer a model for your critical attitude toward your college experience; (c)
the history of the chosen people is a sad but true depiction of human sin, inability to get along, and inability to live up to God's creation; (d) the Psalms
offer examples of how it's okay to complain to God; (e) and lots more.

P—prayer—You know that you can communicate with God any time and any place about anything.

That has got to be a really solid comfort and security. Feel free to do it any
time you want to. We know some key truths about prayer from Scripture:
It's okay to complain to God; and it's okay—probably a good idea—to pray
a lot (Luke 18:1–8).

Q—*questions*—Questions; it might seem that that's all there is to college.

I remember, however, that there are some questions you probably shouldn't ask. Like the time we were in Professor Ruby's class (his name wasn't Ruby; it was another precious stone, but should he read this . . .) and his trousers were unzipped. Of course nobody asked him about it. In general it is bad manners to ask embarrassing questions.

Unless you're a Christian. Just look at Scripture and the embarrassing questions that are asked.

- "Will you . . . let me alone until I swallow my spittle?" (Job 7:19)
- "Why do the wicked live on, reach old age, and grow mighty in power?" (Job 21:7)
- "Where then does wisdom come from?" (Job 28:20a)
- Pleasure . . . "What use is it?" (Eccles 2:2b)
- When James and John ask Jesus if they can sit next to him in the kingdom of God. (Mark 10:37)
- [to God], "Why do you forget our affliction and oppression?" (Ps 44:24b)
- Or when the desperate widow keeps asking for the judge to tend to her case (Luke 18:1–8)
- Or when Jesus, on the cross, cries out, "My God, my God, why have you forsaken me?" (Matt 27:46)

The Gospels record people questioning Jesus over and over and Paul writes to his fellow believers that he doesn't want them to be uninformed (2 Cor 1:8; 1 Thess 4:13).

So ask.

R—*resurrection*—This really is the game-changer.

The corrupt folks down at "city hall" want to be safe and comfortable. Getting Jesus out of the way should take care of it. They kill him in the kind of cold political calculus that plays out somewhere in the world every day.

God reversed that decision and everything for Christians has been reversed since. Resurrection of the dead. A real game-changer.

*S—sacraments—*These are actions "regarded as having a sacred character."[8]

The action (baptizing, eating bread, drinking wine) is an ordinary human activity, but since Jesus blessed these acts, we believe that they convey God's truth and comfort to us in special ways. Different churches have identified different numbers of sacraments, but you can be assured that God recognizes our need for his presence and comfort and can use many different means to communicate that to you. Sacraments are coming to a church near you right away.

*S—saints—*These are our heroes.

Actually you are a saint also. Paul defines "saints" as "those who are sanctified in Christ" (1 Cor 1:2). However, there are certain individuals who have led extraordinarily noteworthy lives and whom you might hold up as examples. They are worth studying and in some cases imitating. A Catholic friend once gave me a small medal with the image of St. Thomas Aquinas, the patron saint of scholars on it; not a bad companion on the way or example to emulate. (For girls and women, St. Catherine of Alexandria is the corresponding patron saint for scholars.) And there are others not recognized officially. At the top of my list is Dietrich Bonhoeffer, who resisted the horrors of Hitler's Nazi regime and served as pastor to other Christians imprisoned by the state while he continue to write as a scholar—until he was finally hanged for his faithful resistance to tyranny. Who might your "heroes/saints" be and what kind of inspiration do they offer that strengthens you in your vocation?

*T—theology—*The "logy" here is the clue: it is about working things out in an orderly, logical, consistent fashion.

This is the kind of thing to do when you are in a terrible mess with conflicting pressures (a paper due, a big date, no money on the credit card, and the car has no gas) or when you are trying to decide whether it is true love or just the "birds and the bees."

Theology is something we all do and in a lot of ways it is not as important as any of the other things on this list. Theology is about God (*theos*) but no matter how good a theology it is, it cannot save you, bring you closer

8. *WCDict,* 1261.

to God, or make you a better Christian. Theology is also about thinking in an organized way (*logos*) so in that sense it is about arranging *what you already believe about God* into an organized, systematic form. So while faith is the first order thing in your Christian life, theology can be second in importance. It can be helpful, however, in clearing your mind, seeing things clearly, working out confusions in your beliefs, and in general, thinking straight.

T—*Tradition*—Inherited practices.

Your college will have traditions that few or no other college has. Some may seem silly to outsiders—like *the tradition in my school where we waved our arm while singing the school song or the way the whole student body at my wife's school would walk from the football stadium to the "sport cemetery" to "bury" the losing team after a game*. Other traditions can be more uplifting. Colleges' commitment to service or to foreign study or to celebrate a religious or ethnic heritage are traditions that are part of the "value added" aspect of many educational experiences.

The Christian tradition operates similarly. While it is sad that Christendom has become fractured into many denominations, the ways in which different groups began and developed have enabled many fine traditions to flourish. Some traditions have emphasized the importance of fellowship, others that of scholarship, still others that of serving the needy. What has your tradition emphasized? What are particular traditions that have been important in your faith experience? It is likely that the larger church—that universal body of all believers—can benefit from having *your* traditions maintained for the good of all.

U—*Urbanus*—Who?

You are forgiven if you don't recognize this long-almost-forgotten "co-worker in Christ" mentioned by Paul in Romans 16:9a. Urbanus gets one half of a short verse in Scripture. Most of our fellow believers over the centuries get less mention than that. But it is important to remember that God loves each precious life that ever lived. And each one has something to contribute.

V—*vocation*—Calling; career; job.

My wife is an archaeologist. That means that she digs in the dirt to discover clues that—after careful study and analysis—reveal the way in which people lived long ago. If she hasn't been out "in the field" for a while she will say, "I hear the dirt calling me." She needs to get out and get digging. It is her calling. It is a powerful magnet.

Throughout this manual your focus has been on your vocation as a Christian and particularly as a Christian student. After college, your student vocation will give way to other vocations—work, perhaps marriage, other opportunities to which the God who called you to college will call you into other applications of your Christian vocation. You will hear God's call from others to "Come . . . and help us" as Paul heard it in a vision he had of a man from Macedonia (Greece) in Acts 16:9. For you it may be "Come and help" as a teacher, or as a nurse, or in any number of ways. God will always have a vocation for you.

W—*worship*—Worshipping anything other than God is idolatry; there is only one true God.

"Wasting time with God?" Yes, something like that. Spending time relating to God in many ways: thanksgiving, confession, singing, hearing the gospel, receiving the sacrament. Worship is what the Christian community does together; differences can be overcome in the sharing of the praise, confession, and reception of God's grace in sacraments.

X—*eXperience*

As a Christian, you probably have had heard of the positive experiences of others whose faith has sustained them in times of trouble; you yourself may have had such experiences. These are moments you can "take to the bank" and draw upon for encouragement and direction later in life. They are experiences that do not wear out; their number only increases as you grow in your Christian life and as you accumulate the stories of the experiences of others.

Y—year—Check your calendar: you have appointments, deadlines, dates; you are on the go.

You are familiar with the calendar year; it pretty much governs how you plan and spend your time. But there are some scary dates: like the anniversary of the death of a loved one, or the birthday of someone who is really hard to get a gift for. Then there is the college year, marked by enrollment, mid-terms, finals, repeat, repeat, and finally, hopefully, graduation. Then there is the fiscal year when the money has to be counted and everything needs to be accounted for.

And then there is the Christian year, which takes you through the story of God's creating you and reaching out to help you and placing you in a time that is *not* driven by the unsatisfying urgencies of the secular clock. It begins with Advent, the preparation for the coming/birth of Jesus Christ. The Christian calendar follows the life of Jesus up to his crucifixion (Good Friday) and resurrection on Easter. The forty days before Easter are set aside especially to focus on Jesus' suffering for us (Lent). The forty days after Easter lead up to Jesus' ascension to God and the gift of the Holy Spirit. While these are the main "dates" on the Christian calendar, attention to the Christian year can help you to focus your faith rather than be distracted by secular times and celebrations.

Z—Zacchaeus—This is the end. Of the alphabet, but not the end of the wonderful gifts God has in store for you.

Zacchaeus was a fellow who was despised by everyone because he was a tax collector (Luke 19:1–10). That was a job in which you worked for the hated Roman oppressors who had invaded and taken over the country of the Jews and, if that wasn't bad enough, made the Jews pay taxes to pay for the invading/occupying Roman army to hang around and run things. In other words, the tax collector ripped off all of his fellow Jews in order to make a living. And Zacchaeus worked on a commission basis: he collected as much as he could in order to pay what the Romans wanted and to have enough left over to cover his luxurious lifestyle. The guy was a creep. But Jesus invited himself to Zacchaeus' house. Zacchaeus had a complete makeover and committed himself to a whole new life.

Application

What is the point of closing our A to Z gift list with Zacchaeus? Just that it is always wise to be reminded that God acts in powerful and astonishing (and astonishingly good) ways. And the story never ends. These are some of the blessings that God, in Christ, makes available to you and all Christians. Even if you are up to your ears in the college experience, these gifts of God are near to you for your edification and strength.

College involves you in many different kinds of things, some challenging to your faith. The trick will be to keep things in balance. College is important because it is a terrific resource for you in living your faith to the fullest in God's world. At the same time you know that eventually you will be called to God to rest from your labors and be with the saints in heaven (Rev 14:13).

In the meantime, Jesus the Teacher will be your perfect resource—if not as Teacher, then in one of his many other Christological roles as Bread of Life, Resurrection . . . or in the words of that most practical of all disciples, Thomas, who, upon seeing the risen Jesus for the first time, blurted out: "My Lord and my God!" (John 20:28).

So in this moment, grab the rest you can so that tomorrow and tomorrow and tomorrow you can face the *rest* of the college experience with the resources of Jesus the Teacher close at hand.

Thought and Discussion Questions

1. List and discuss one or more ways to "rest." How do they help you be a good college student?

2. Discuss ways to balance the "rest" and worship parts of the Christian faith with the more active and demanding parts of life.

3. Several Christian resources are mentioned (A to Z), such as hymns and theological writings. Select one and discuss how it might be helpful in the Christian experience of college.

4. The Lord's Prayer (Matt 6:9–13): go through it slowly, phrase by phrase, and relate it to what you know of college, and what you have remembered from this manual, in ways that you believe will help you keep the faith and grow in faith.

Bibliography

Bonhoeffer, Dietrich. *Letters and Papers from Prison*. Enlarged ed. Edited by Eberhard Bethge. New York: Simon & Schuster, 1997.

Broussard. Earl. "The Power of Place on Campus." *CR* (May 1, 2009) B12–B13.

Buckley, Michael J., S.J. *The Catholic University as Promise and Project: Reflections in a Jesuit Idiom*. Washington, DC: Georgetown University Press, 1998.

Byrne, Patrick H. "Wholeness through Science, Justice, and Love." In *In Search of the Whole: Twelve Essays on Faith and Academic Life*, edited by John C. Haughey, 3–17. Washington, DC: Georgetown University Press, 2011.

Calvin, John. *Institutes of the Christian Religion*, vol. 1. Edited by John T. McNeill. Philadelphia: Westminster, 1960.

Castle, Terry. "Pick Up: Why kids need to separate from their parents." *CR* (May 11, 2012) B7.

Chickering, Arthur W., Jon C. Dalton, and Liesa Stamm. *Encouraging Authenticity and Spirituality in Higher Education*. San Francisco: Jossey-Bass, 2006.

Croy, N. Clayton. "The Messianic Whippersnapper: Did Jesus Use a Whip on People in the Temple (John 2:15)?" *JBL* 128/3 (Fall, 2009) 555–68.

Delio, Ilia. "Arriving at a Christocentric Universe." In *In Search of the Whole: Twelve Essays on Faith and Academic Life*, edited by John C. Haughey, 111–28. Washington, DC: Georgetown University Press, 2011.

Gibson, Nic, and Syler Thomas. *Game Plan: Practical Wisdom for the College Experience*. Brewster, MA: Paraclete, 2012.

Harp, Richard B. "The Palpable Word as Ground of *Koinonia*." In *Christianity and the Soul of the University: Faith as a Foundation for Intellectual Community*. edited by Douglas V. Henry and Michael D. Beaty, 19–36. Grand Rapids: Baker Academic, 2006.

Hassel, David J. *City of Wisdom: A Christian Vision of the American University*. Chicago: Loyola University Press, 1983.

Hawking, Stephen W. *A Brief History of Time: From the Big Bang to Black Holes*. New York: Bantam, 1998.

Institute of International Education. "Open Doors Report on International Educational Exchange." November 11, 2013. www.iie.org.

Lewis, C. S. *The Screwtape Letters*. New York: MacMillan, 1954.

Mathisen, James A. "From Muscular Christians to Jocks for Jesus." *The Christian Century* (January 1–8, 1992) 11–15.

McClendon, James Wm., Jr. *Systematic Theology: Ethics*. Nashville: Abingdon, 1986.

Moroney, Stephen. "How Sin Affects Scholarship: A New Model." *CSR* 28/3 (Spring, 1999) 432–51.

National Foundation on the Arts and Humanities Act of 1965. www.house.gov/ legcoun/Comps/NFAHA65.

Nye, Abby. *Fish out of Water: Surviving and Thriving as a Christian on a Secular Campus.* Green Forest, AR: New Leaf, 2005.

Parks, Sharon Daloz. *Big Questions, Worthy Dreams: Mentoring Young Adults in their Search for Meaning, Purpose, and Faith.* San Francisco: Jossey-Bass, 2000.

———. *The Critical Years: The Young Adult Search for a Faith to Live By.* San Francisco: Harper & Row, 1987.

Pascaralla, Ernest T., and Patrick T. Terenzini. *How College Affects Students.* San Francisco: Jossey-Bass, 2005.

Pennington, Bill. "In Virginia's Hills, a Football Crusade." *NYT SportsSunday* (November 11, 2012) 1, 10.

Pope John Paul II. *ex corde ecclesiae: Apostolic Constitution of the Supreme Pontiff John Paul II on Catholic Universities.* Washington, DC: United States Catholic Conference, 1966.

Price, Joseph L. "An American Apotheosis: Sports as Popular Religion." In *From Season to Season: Sports as American Religion,* 215–34. Macon, GA: Mercer University Press, 2001.

Reuben, Julie A. *The Making of the Modern University.* Chicago: University of Chicago, 1996.

Riley, Naomi Schaefer. *God on the Quad.* New York: St.Martin's, 2005.

Romano, Carlin. "When Death Breaches the Campus Walls." *CR* (February 23, 2001) B12.

Smith, Buffy. *Mentoring At-Risk Students through the Hidden Curriculum of Higher Education.* New York: Lexington, 2013.

Sperber, Murray. *Beer and Circus: How Big-Time College Sports Is Crippling Undergraduate Education.* New York: Henry Holt and Company, 2000.

Spradley, Joseph L. "Christological Influences on Science." *CSR* 31/1 (Fall 2001) 67–84.

Stebbins, J. Michael. "The 'Real World' of Business." In *In Search of the Whole: Twelve Essays on Faith and Academic Life,* edited by John C. Haughey, 85–96. Washington, DC: Georgetown University Press, 2011.

Summerfield, C. John. *The Decline of the Secular University.* Oxford: Oxford University Press, 2006.

Tobin, Gary A., and Aryeh K. Weinberg. *Profiles of the American University.* San Francisco: Institute for Jewish and Community Research, 2007.

Vanin, Cristina. "Attaining Harmony with the Earth." In *In Search of the Whole: Twelve Essays on Faith and Academic Life,* edited by John C. Haughey, 179–99. Washington, DC: Georgetown University Press, 2011.

Wheaton, David. *University of Destruction: Your Game Plan for Spiritual Victory on Campus.* Grand Rapids: Bethany House, 2005.

Willimon, William, and Thomas Naylor. *The Abandoned Generation: Rethinking Higher Education.* Grand Rapids: Eerdmans, 1995.

Wink, Walter. *Engaging the Powers: Discernment and Resistance in a World of Domination.* Minneapolis: Fortress, 1992.

———. *Naming the Powers: The Language of Power in the New Testament.* Philadelphia: Fortress, 1984.

———. *Unmasking the Powers: The Invisible Forces that Determine Human Existence.* Philadelphia: Fortress, 1986.

Wolverton, Brad. "Morality Play: A U. of Idaho professor says college athletes are ethically impaired, but can be taught to think differently." *CHE* (August 4, 2006) A33–A35.

———. "With God on our Side." *CHE* (November 29, 2013) A16–A20.

Young, Robert B. *No Neutral Ground: Standing By the Values We Prize in Higher Education.* San Francisco: Jossey-Bass, 1997.

Subject Index

Scripture Index

(Note: Page numbers in **boldface type** indicate
a direct quotation from the passage cited.)